Macbeth: Soliloquy P.18.

The Pitt Press Shakespeare

MACBETH

SHAKESPEARE

MACBETH

EDITED BY
A. W. VERITY

CAMBRIDGE
AT THE UNIVERSITY PRESS
1962

PUBLISHED BY
THE SYNDICS OF THE CAMBRIDGE UNIVERSITY PRESS

Bentley House, 200 Euston Road, London, N.W. 1
American Branch: 32 East 57th Street, New York 22, N.Y.
West African Office: P.O. Box 33, Ibadan, Nigeria

First Edition 1901
New Edition 1902
Reprinted 1904
1906
1908
1909
1911
1914
1917
1919
1922
1923
1925
1927
1930
1934
1939
1943
1945
1946
1947
1948
1949
1952
1954
1958
Reset 1962
(With additions and corrections
from time to time)

Printed in Great Britain at the University Press, Cambridge
(Brooke Crutchley, University Printer)

PREFACE

The edition of this play, published originally in the Pitt Press Shakespeare for Schools Series, having been considered too long and elaborate for school use, the present edition has been prepared which, it is believed, contains all that is practically wanted for the purpose. The earlier edition, which was designed primarily to meet the needs of candidates preparing for the higher examinations, will be issued immediately as a "Student's Edition".

I have the pleasure to repeat the acknowledgment of my great obligations to Dr Furness. It would be impossible to estimate what this volume owes to his incomparable Variorum edition of *Macbeth*. The letter "F" at the end of a paragraph means that the note is based entirely or mainly on materials quoted by Dr Furness from other editions, not that it represents necessarily his own views. Minor, unspecified obligations to him are, I hope, covered by this general acknowledgment here—an acknowledgment which I wish to be as full and emphatic as words can make it.

Apart from my general indebtedness to standard works, I must also mention the very considerable help I received from one of the readers of the University Press, who compiled the indexes and verified innumerable references and quotations.

A.W.V.

August 1902

CONTENTS

NOTE ON NEW EDITION (1962)

The whole book has been re-set in a more modern typographical style. Since many thousand copies of the earlier
impressions are in use, it has been thought best to retain the
system of marginal references unchanged, as far as possible,
so that the new and the old editions can be used together. It will
nevertheless be found that there is a slight discrepancy, of
not more than one or two lines, in respect of the marginal
numbering of some prose passages.

INTRODUCTION

I

DATES OF THE PUBLICATION AND COMPOSITION OF THE PLAY

Macbeth was first published, so far as we know, in 1623, in the first Folio[1] edition of Shakespeare's plays, where it is placed between *Julius Cæsar* and *Hamlet*. The play was evidently printed from a faulty—probably, in part, a dictated—copy of the original. As will be seen from the Notes to this edition, there are many difficulties of reading, and at least one notable confusion in the stage-directions (v. 8. 34).

The composition of *Macbeth* is commonly assigned to the period 1605–6. The evidence[2] bearing on the point is unusually full and interesting. It is as follows:

A sort of diary or note-book in ms., entitled *The Booke of Plaies and Notes thereof*, of an Elizabethan physician, Dr Simon Forman, shows that he was present at a performance of *Macbeth* on 20 April 1610. His account, therefore, furnishes a limit in the one direction.[3]

---

[1] The first collected edition of Shakespeare's plays, and the earliest authority for the text of many, e.g. *As You Like It*, *The Tempest*, *Julius Cæsar*; indeed, but for it they would be lost. It is often referred to by editors simply as "the Folio". The 2nd Folio (1632) was a reprint of the 1st, correcting some of its typographical errors, and introducing some conjectural changes which are often quite unnecessary. The later Folios have little value or interest, except that the edition of 1664 was the first to give *Pericles*. Where in the Notes to this edition of *Macbeth* the "1st Folio" alone is mentioned, it may be taken for granted that the others follow it.

[2] It is all given by other editors.

[3] See p. 243 of the Student's edition of *Macbeth* (Cambridge University Press).

On the other hand, internal evidence indicates very clearly that the play was not written earlier than 1603, the year of the accession of James I to the English throne. The Scottish subject and its treatment in one noticeable point;[1] the general Scottish colouring of the whole work; the specific allusion to James I's accession and the union of the two crowns (IV. I. 120, 121):

> And some I see
> That two-fold balls and treble sceptres carry;

the equally clear allusion to his exercise of the regal "healing benediction" or hereditary practice of "touching" for the "King's Evil" (IV. 3. 136–51); the prominence given to witchcraft:[2] these aspects and features of *Macbeth* associate it beyond dispute with the accession of Elizabeth's successor.

Hence, 'not earlier than 1603 and not later than 1610' is a formula which may be accepted with absolute confidence as regards the question of the date of *Macbeth*. But we can narrow the issue closer. The following words in Middleton's play, *The Puritan*, IV. I (published in 1607), have every appearance of an allusion to the introduction of

---

[1] I.e. the characterisation of Banquo, James's supposed ancestor.

[2] "The repeated references to witchcraft are similarly inspired" by a desire to do compliment to the King, "for it was a subject in which James had a peculiar interest. In 1589 the fleet in which he was bringing home his bride, Anne of Denmark, had been dispersed by a violent storm, and, in the belief that this was due to sorcery, he had taken vigorous proceedings against witches. In 1599 he had published his tract *Demonologie*, maintaining against sceptical attacks the reality of possession by evil spirits, and in 1604, the year after he came to the English throne, a new statute was passed against witchcraft. A play in which witches gave awful proof of their malign power would thus be peculiarly attractive to a monarch who believed himself to have been the victim of their baneful influence"— *Boas*.

Banquo's ghost in *Macbeth*: "instead of a jester we'll have a ghost in a white sheet sit at the upper end of the table".

Further, two passages in *Macbeth* itself point to 1606 as the year of its composition:

(1) The Porter's reference to the "equivocator" (II. 3. 8–11);

(2) his reference to the "farmer that hanged himself on the expectation of plenty".

That the passage about the "equivocator"[1] refers to the trial of the Jesuit Garnet in March 1606 is a view which may be said to have established itself. A reference of this kind (like that to James's accession) is only effective if the events referred to are fresh in men's minds. The passage would scarcely have been inserted had the trial not been of comparatively recent occurrence.

The passage about the "farmer"[2] connects itself naturally with the abundant harvest of 1606.

Moreover, three minor indications make the period 1605–6 probable, viz.:

(1) The incident, to which we shall return, at James's visit to Oxford in 1605;

(2) the insertion of the *Historie of Macbeth* in the new edition published in 1606 of Warner's rhymed chronicle *Albion's England*;

(3) "the investiture[3] of Sir James Murray on 7 April 1605 with the dignities of Scone forfeited by the Earl of Gowry for conspiracy against James".

The first of these incidents may have suggested the

---

[1] See p. 177. We may remember the probable allusion to the Gunpowder Plot in *King Lear*, I. 2. 122–4, written perhaps just before *Macbeth*.

[2] See the note on II. 3. 4, 5.

[3] F. S. Boas. Compare also Fleay's *Life of Shakespeare*, p. 239: "The applicability of the play to the Gowry conspiracy would be especially pleasing to James." For another indication of date, see p. 111.

subject of the whole play to Shakespeare, and the third the particular point of the bestowal of Cawdor's honours on Macbeth; while the addition made to *Albion's England* may have been due to the popularity of Shakespeare's tragedy.

II

THEORY OF A LATER DATE

Some have argued in favour of a much later date of composition. *Macbeth*, they say, was "a new play" when Dr Forman saw it: otherwise he would not have summarised its plot so elaborately. But the inference seems forced. A modern play-goer accustomed to make notes on the pieces he saw might surely mention and describe the revival in 1901 of some notable play which he had missed seeing on its first production in 1897. Dr Forman does not hint that *Macbeth* was a new piece. He simply says that he saw it, and describes what he saw. We cannot assume more than that it was new to him; nor need we be surprised that he had not seen it earlier (if he had not), when we remember the enormous number of fresh plays with which the Elizabethan stage was enriched.

Equally weak, to my mind, is the argument in favour of a late date based on the following allusion in Beaumont and Fletcher's *Knight of the Burning Pestle* (1611), v. 1:

> When thou art at thy table with thy friends,
> Merry in heart and fill'd with swelling wine,
> I'll come in midst of all thy pride and mirth,
> Invisible to all men but thyself,
> And whisper such a sad tale in thine ear,
> Shall make thee let the cup fall from thy hand,
> And stand as mute and pale as death itself.

The allusion to Banquo's ghost is patent, but it does not prove that in 1611 *Macbeth* was a new play: on the contrary, an equally fair inference, surely, is that is was *not* a new piece, which many of the audience might never have seen, but an old piece which had become so well known that an allusion to it would be recognised at once. And there is good reason, as we have observed, for thinking that Middleton had anticipated Beaumont and Fletcher in making the same allusion as far back as 1607.

Neither Forman's account, therefore, nor the passage just quoted, warrants our placing the composition of *Macbeth* so late as 1610, against all the evidence that makes for the earlier period 1605–6. And apart from that evidence the date 1610 is absolutely impossible from metrical considerations. To assign it to 1610 is to place it on the very threshold of the period of the "Romances" (the *Tempest* itself was probably written not later than 1610), after works which reveal in a much fuller degree than *Macbeth* the characteristics of Shakespeare's maturest blank verse. Thus *Macbeth* has only 2 "weak endings",[1] whereas *Antony and Cleopatra* has 28, *Coriolanus* 44, and *The Tempest* (a very short piece) 25. Again, of "light endings" *Macbeth* has 21, *Antony and Cleopatra* 71, *Coriolanus* 60, *The Tempest* 42. *Macbeth* has 339 "feminine endings", *The Tempest* 476. Again, apart from the scenes in which the supernatural element dominates, there is a considerable amount of rhyme in *Macbeth*, and its presence cannot be accounted for wholly by the extremely disputable theory of "interpolations". Briefly, then, we may say that the metrical characteristics are conclusive against the date 1610. Nor is the style of *Macbeth*, though elliptical and involved, quite that of Shakespeare's last period. In fact the theory of so late a date of composition as 1610 is untenable.

There is now practically a consensus of opinion that

[1] See pp. 188, 189 (note). The figures are Professor Ingram's. Of course, *Antony and Cleopatra* and *Coriolanus* are much longer than *Macbeth*; the former, indeed, is nearly double the length. Still, the metrical discrepancy, in the respects mentioned above, is great. It is most conspicuous when we compare *Macbeth* with *The Tempest*, which just exceeds it in the number of lines.

Macbeth belongs to the period 1605–6. Personally I am of those who, in view of the probable references in the Porter's speech, assign its composition to 1606, and its production to the latter part of that year. But that it was first "performed on the occasion of the festivities in celebration of King Christian IV of Denmark's visit to the English court in 1606 is a mere (and needless) conjecture" (Ward).

III

THE SOURCE OF THE PLAY

The source whence Shakespeare derived the story of *Macbeth* is Holinshed's *Chronicles*[1] *of Englande, Scotland, and Ireland*—the source of his English historical plays and of *King Lear*. How he used this source of information—sometimes, but not often, reproducing the words of the Chronicle,—may be inferred, to some extent, from the "Extracts" that are given in the Student's edition of *Macbeth* (Cambridge University Press).

The genesis of the Macbeth-story as given by Holinshed is interesting. The earliest extant versions are those contained in the Chronicles of John Fordun (who died about 1384) and his contemporary, Andrew Wynton (1350–1420), a Canon of St Andrew's. Fordun compiled *Chronica Gentis Scotorum*, a work continued in his *Gesta Annalia*. Wynton wrote in the Scottish vernacular, not in Latin, "a metrical chronicle of the history of Scotland, which he called 'The Oryginale', because it commenced with the beginning of the world".[2] These Chronicles were the starting-point of Scottish History. Unpublished, but known through MSS., they were copied and expanded

---

[1] A reference in *Richard II*, II. 4. 8 shows that Shakespeare used the second (1586–7) edition of Holinshed (to which many new passages were added). The omen of the withering of the bay-trees is not mentioned in the first edition (1577).

[2] *Dictionary of Biography*.

by Boece[1] in his *Historia Scotorum* (1527), who refers specially to Fordun as one of his authorities. Of Boece's *Historia* a translation into the vernacular was made by Bellenden, at the request of James IV of Scotland, and published in 1536. And Bellenden's work became in turn the source of Holinshed's Chronicle of Scotland, which, as Holinshed says, was "translated out of the Scottish" for him by a William Harrison. So the stages are Fordun's *Chronica* (containing in bk IV the history of Macbeth) and Wynton's *Oryginale*, Boece's *Historia*, Bellenden's version of the *Historia*, Holinshed's version of Bellenden. The picture of Macbeth in these successive narratives is consistent, as we should expect. It is an extremely unfavourable picture, untrue to history as recorded by more reliable authorities, which testify that, though a usurper, Macbeth was a good king (see again p. xviii).

There is a recent (and to my mind most fantastic) theory that Shakespeare consulted another Chronicle besides Holinshed's. It appears that a metrical rendering or adaptation of Bellenden's *History* was made by a certain "Master William Stewart", at the command of Margaret Tudor, Queen of Scotland, for her son James V. This metrical version of Bellenden differs often from the original (i.e. Bellenden) and consequently from Holinshed, who followed Bellenden; and an attempt has been made to show that there are in Shakespeare's *Macbeth* details which are also in Stewart's Chronicle but not in Holinshed. Stewart's Chronicle was unpublished: but (we are told) James VI (James I of England) "most certainly would have a copy" in MS., and quite possibly "lent it to the poet of his royal company of players to compare with Holinshed".

The theory is pure conjecture. There is not a shred of

[1] Hector Boece or Boethius (1465–1536), a Scotsman who studied at Paris, where his *Historia* was published, and afterwards was the first Principal of King's College in Aberdeen University.

evidence in favour of this supposition of a royal loan, except
(*a*) the fact that Shakespeare's company did receive considerable marks of grace from James,[1] and (*b*) the resemblance between *Macbeth* and Stewart's Chronicle in certain
details. But the details adduced are of the most trivial
character. To press resemblances so slender is to deny
Shakespeare the very elements of originality and mis-
represent him as the mere slave of "sources". Even if
Stewart's Chronicle had been published and were easily
accessible to Shakespeare, there would not, in my opinion,
be valid reason for assuming that he used it. Nor can I
see the smallest probability in the suggestion that he consulted Bellenden, whose narrative was available to Holinshed's Chronicles, and for English readers required to be
"translated out of the Scottish".

IV

THE MACBETH STORY IN ELIZABETHAN LITERATURE

Holinshed's Chronicle, then, is the one ascertained source
of Shakespeare's tragedy. But apparently Shakespeare was
not the first Elizabethan writer to handle the story of
Macbeth. Possibly it had been dramatised already. For a

---

[1] Soon after his accession he appointed them the "King's
Company" (the title they bore thenceforth instead of their old
name the "Lord Chamberlain's Company"), and granted them
permission to perform not only at the Globe Theatre but "in
the town-hall or moot-hall of any country-town"—a high
privilege. Further, by James's command, Shakespeare and
eight other actors of the company walked in the coronation-
procession from the Tower of London to Westminster,
15 March 1604, in scarlet cloaks which the royal generosity had
provided. And there were repeated court performances of
Shakespeare's plays by this Company (Lee, *Life of Shakespeare*).

It may be noted that from 1610 (the last year of Shakespeare's
life as an actor) the King's Company acted at the Blackfriars
Theatre as well as at the Globe.

"Ballad of Macdobeth" was entered on the Register of the Stationers' Company 27 August 1596; and the same entry records "the ballad entituled The Taming of a shrew". "If", says Collier, "*The Taming of a Shrew*, which we know to have been a play, were so recorded, it is not unlikely that the 'Ballad of Macdobeth' was of the same character."

Again, in the pamphlet *Kemp's Nine Days' Wonder* (1600) occur the words: "I met a proper vpright youth, onely for a little stooping in the shoulders, all hart to the heele, a penny Poet, whose first making was the miserable stolne story of Macdoel, or Macdobeth, or Macsomewhat, for I am sure a Mac it was, though I never had the maw[1] to see it."

Here the reference certainly appears to be to the "Ballad of Macdobeth", while the words "to *see* it" imply "that the piece had been publicly represented, and that it was not merely a printed 'ballad'. Kemp, as a highly popular actor, would most naturally refer to dramatic performances".[2]

There is ground, therefore, for supposing that the Macbeth-story had been handled in some literary form or other, whether a genuine ballad or a rough play like the old *King Leir and his Three Daughters* which preceded and partly inspired *King Lear*. The possibilities, indeed, of the story were obvious. Aptly had the Scots writer Buchanan in his *Rerum Scoticarum Historia* (1528) described the mysterious episodes of Macbeth's career as "*theatris... aptiora quam historiæ*".

Again, it is interesting to note that the attention of other unknown dramatists had been turned to the rich stores of Scottish history and legend. Thus[3] between July 1567 and March 1568 the Master of the Revels spent money on

---

[1] I.e. stomach, appetite.   [2] Collier. See Furness, p. 387.
[3] See *Athenæum*, 25 July 1896 ("Shakespeare's materials for *Macbeth*").

scenery for a "Tragedie of the King of Scottes". A play called "Malcolm King of Scottes" is mentioned in the diary of the theatrical manager Henslowe under the date 27 April 1602. The Gowry conspiracy, which presents an analogy to Cawdor's, is known to have been dramatised as early as December 1604.

Nor must we forget the incident, already glanced at, which associates King James's visit to Oxford in 1605 with the literary history of Shakespeare's play. On the King's arrival at the gate of St John's College a short scene or interlude was enacted. "Three young youths" (says a contemporary account), "in habit and attire like *Nymphes*, confronted him", and apostrophised the illustrious visitors in a florid Latin oration,[1] on behalf of England, Scotland and Ireland, comparing themselves with the Weird Sisters who had predicted to Banquo the regal honours of his line, and invoking a yet richer fulfilment of the prediction. This incident ("the conceipt whereof the King did very much applaude", as well he might, for the exceeding felicity of its flattering allusion to the Stuart's tradition of their ancestry) may have come to Shakespeare's knowledge and been the germ of *Macbeth*. On the other hand, it is not probable that this subject for the interlude would have been chosen, had Shakespeare already handled it.

---

[1] The verses are extant. They commence with the allusion to Banquo:

> Fatidicas olim fama est cecinisse sorores
> Imperium sine fine tuæ, rex inclyte, stirpis.
> Banquonem agnovit generosa Loquabria Thanum;
> Nec tibi, Banquo, tuis sed sceptra nepotibus illæ
> Immortalibus immortalia vaticinatæ:
> In saltum, ut lateas, dum Banquo recedis ab aula.
> Tres eadem pariter canimus tibi fata tuisque,
> Dum spectande tuis, e saltu accedis ad urbem;
> Teque salutamus.

V

SHAKESPEARE'S USE OF HOLINSHED

Let us now revert to the subject of *Macbeth's* relation to Holinshed's Chronicle. We have seen that Holinshed's narrative supplied the rude materials of the tragedy. "Nothing" (it has been said) "was wanting for the dramatic treatment of the subject except it psychological development." How did Shakespeare use these materials? The salient feature in his handling of them is the freedom he allowed himself. His deviations from history in his English and Roman historical plays are mainly changes of time and place, and do not often involve misrepresentation of fact[1] or character. But this criticism does not apply to *Macbeth*. "It is clear [rather] that Shakespeare, though he may have thought the story as historical as that of the Richards or Henries, no longer approached it as history." He approached it simply as the stuff out of which high tragedy might be wrought. Possibly the almost mythical remoteness of the dim, barbarous era to which the action belonged seemed to him to warrant whatever divergence from so-called history served his dramatic purpose. At any rate the divergences from his authority are very considerable. Those which affect the characterisation of the *dramatis personæ* may be summed up thus:

He whitens the character of Duncan, and blackens the character of Macbeth in a corresponding degree, for obvious purposes of contrast: he whitens the character of Banquo, for the same purpose, but also from a personal and complimentary motive; and he makes Lady Macbeth less odious because at least unselfish.

---

[1] A couple of minor deviations from Holinshed in historical or semi-historical matters may be dismissed at once with a bare reference to the Notes in which they are commented on; namely, the Note on I. 2. 61–3, and that on v. 8. 73. Each shows that alike at the outset and the close of the tragedy Shakespeare condensed two campaigns into one.

Holinshed's Duncan is a young and incapable king, too "soft and gentle of nature", and altogether dependent on Macbeth and Banquo; "a faint-hearted milkesop" (said his enemies), "more meet to gouerne a sort [= set] of idle moonks in some cloister, than to haue the rule of such valiant and hardie men of warre as the Scots were". His reign, we are told by historians, was as unfortunate as it was brief. Shakespeare's Duncan, a man of years (we are made to feel), is "every inch a king", a regal, illustrious figure; gracious, indeed, and "gentle", yet strong withal and capable; one whose merits extort from his slayer's own mouth the admission:

> this Duncan
> Hath borne his faculties so meek, hath been
> So clear in his great office, that his virtues
> Will plead like angels, trumpet-tongu'd, against
> The deep damnation of his taking-off;[1]

a ruler whose fate will waken universal grief throughout his realm.

The evident purpose of this departure from Holinshed's account is to deepen the pity of Duncan's end and the heinousness of a crime which lacks even the poor palliation of its victim's incompetence. "Vaulting ambition" is shown to be the usurper's sole motive, as himself recognises.

Holinshed's Macbeth is a just, a noble ruler, at least in the earlier and longer period of his usurpation. The Macbeth of the play proves himself from the outset of his reign a fear-stricken despot, with whom the instinct of self-preservation soon becomes a ruling passion for bloodshed.

In fact, all the good in Holinshed's picture of Macbeth as ruler is ignored and the evil intensified to the utmost. Yet Holinshed's picture itself did but scant justice to Macbeth, whom the more authentic of Scottish chronicles "paint as the greatest king that early Scotland had, respected by his enemies, honoured in the ancient Church, beloved of the Scottish people".

[1] See I. 7. 12–28 (a speech of the utmost significance).

Again, the Banquo of Holinshed's story is privy to the murder of Duncan. But the dramatic balance required that he should be made a foil to Macbeth in the face of similar "soliciting" by the powers of evil; nor could the traditional ancestor of the House of Stuart be held up to infamy in a play that was designed to pay special compliment to the first Stuart occupant of the English throne. So we get the Banquo of *Macbeth*.

On the other hand, Lady Macbeth is bettered. In the Chronicle she is fiercely self-seeking. "The woords of the three weird sisters greatlie incouraged him herevnto [i.e. the murder], but speciallie his wife lay sore vpon him to attempt the thing, as she that was verie ambitious, burning in vnquenchable desire to beare the name of a queene." Shakespeare has absolved his Lady Macbeth from this passion. She "unsexes" herself and renounces the influences of her better "nature", but she does it for Macbeth's sake alone; she exemplifies all the evils of uncontrolled ambition, but the ambition is not for self: rather, it costs her the most supreme sacrifice of self.

In all these points of characterisation, then, Shakespeare has broken boldly from his guide. But still bolder is the way he has grafted on to the Macbeth-story the circumstances of an older tragedy in Scottish history.

VI

THE DONWALD STORY

"Macbeth's career" (says Dr Herford),[1] "and to some extent his character, are modelled on those of another Scottish assassin, Donwald, whose treacherous murder of King Duff Holinshed had described in vivid detail some twenty pages before, while of Duncan's murder he recorded merely the bare fact. Donwald, an officer of the king, enjoying his absolute trust, entertained him in the castle of

[1] I am much indebted to his brief but most masterly introduction to the play in the "Eversley" *Shakespeare*.

Fores, of which he had charge. His wife incited him to use his opportunity, 'and shewed him the means whereby he might soonest accomplish it'. Donwald himself 'abhorred the act greatly in heart', but yields to his wife's urgency. Duff on retiring sends a present to his host; the grooms in the king's chamber, plied with meat and drink by his wife's care, sleep heavily, and fall victims, next morning, to Donwald's 'pious rage'. Fearful portents ensue: the sun is darkened; birds and beasts run counter to their common instincts. All these details Shakespeare has transferred to the story of Duncan, and they add greatly to its tragic force. Holinshed's Macbeth is only his victim's 'kinsman and his subject'; Shakespeare's violates a yet stronger instinct as 'his host', 'who should against his murderer shut the door, not bear the knife himself'. Holinshed's Macbeth plans and executes the murder with matter-of-fact promptitude, without a trace of hesitation or compunction; Shakespeare's Macbeth, like Donwald, has accesses of deep reluctance, in which his wife's resolute energy turns the scale. Holinshed's Lady Macbeth urges her husband 'to attempt the thing', but has no part in its execution. Thus the elements of the relation between Macbeth and Lady Macbeth, and of the hesitations and 'infirmity' which chiefly make him a tragic figure at all, are suggested by Holinshed's Donwald, not by his Macbeth. Much even of the political background of the murder belongs rather to the story of Duff. Holinshed's Macbeth acts with the complicity of 'his trusty friends',—Banquo among the rest,—and 'upon confidence of their promised aid'. Shakespeare's Macbeth, like Donwald, has no political confederates, can count upon no sympathy if his part in the 'deep damnation' of the king's 'taking off' is discovered, and precipitates discovery by over-acting his feigned grief.[1]

[1] "Stone's *Holinshed*, p. 26 f. It is interesting to note that Milton included both 'Macbeth' and 'Duff and Donwald' in his list of subjects for a tragedy. It is clear that he would have kept the two stories wholly distinct."

Even Donwald has the aid of trusty servants: Shakespeare
sends husband and wife unaided to their work amid the cry
of owls and the prayers of startled sleepers." And the very
fact that in respect of the actual execution of the ruthless
deed Shakespeare reverts from the Donwald-story to the
Macbeth-story and makes Macbeth slay the king with his
own hand is another illustration of the dramatist's conscious
and consistent purpose of not sparing him our utmost
execration.

One other point in the relation *Macbeth* bears to Holinshed—a point connected with the Macbeth-story, not the
Donwald-story—remains to be noticed. "Holinshed's
version" (says the same critic) "employs a formidable
apparatus of enchantment. Macbeth receives three warnings, on three occasions, from three distinct classes of
prophetically gifted beings." These are (1) the three
"weird sisters, that is (as ye would say) the goddesses of
destinie, or else some nymphs or feiries, indued with
knowledge of prophesie by their necromanticall science",
who met Macbeth on the fatal heath; (2) "certeine
wizzards, in whose words he put great confidence (for
that the prophesie had happened so right, which the three
faries or weird sisters had declared vnto him)", who warned
him to take heed of Macduff; and (3) "a certeine witch,
whome hee had in great trust", who duped him by her
"sweet bodements". These mysterious and malefic beings
are blended into the "weird-sister witches", for the evident
sake of concentration of dramatic effect.

VII

WHAT DO WE MEAN BY "SOURCES"?

Now, while it is proper always to recognise Shakespeare's
obligations where they exist, we must be very careful not to
over-estimate them. The word "source" or "original"
will mislead us unless we ask ourselves what constitutes

the greatness of his plays, and consider how little that greatness is due to any nominal sources: how such qualities as characterisation (ever the crown of the dramatist's art), humour and wit, poetry and pathos and tragic intensity, deft manipulation of plot and underplot and varied relief, are Shakespeare's own gift, never the inspiration of another. This is in truth a vital point, and on it Dr Furness has some valuable remarks, written indeed with reference to the tragedies, more particularly *King Lear*, but applicable (*mutatis mutandis*) to all Shakespeare's plays of which some "original" has been unearthed.

"What false impressions are conveyed in the phrases which we have to use to express the process whereby Shakespeare converted the stocks and stones of the old dramas and chronicles into living, breathing men and women! We say 'he drew his original' from this source, or he 'found his materials' in that source. But how much did he 'draw', or what did he 'find'? Granting that he drew from Holinshed, or whence you please, where did he find Lear's madness, or the pudder of the elements, or the inspired babblings of the Fool? Of whatsoever makes his tragedies sublime and heaven-high above all other human compositions,—of that we find never a trace.... When, after reading one of his tragedies, we turn to what we are pleased to call the 'original of his plot', I am reminded of those glittering gems, of which Heine speaks, that we see at night in lovely gardens, and think must have been left there by kings' children at play, but when we look for these jewels by day we see only wretched little worms which crawl painfully away, and which the foot forbears to crush only out of strange pity."

In this connection it may be noted that the two scenes of *Macbeth* which seem to exhaust the last possibilities of terror and pity—the banquet scene (III. 4) and the sleep-walking scene—have no counterpart in Shakespeare's "source", nor has the little less wonderful dagger-scene (II. 1).

VIII

TIME OF THE PLAY'S ACTION

The events of *Macbeth* are supposed to happen on nine days, separated by intervals; the arrangement being as follows:

Day 1. Act I, Sc. 1 to 3.
Day 2. Act I, Sc. 4 to 7.
Day 3. Act II, Sc. 1 to 4. *An interval*, say a couple of weeks.
Day 4. Act III, Sc. 1 to 5. [Act III, Sc. 6, an impossible time.]
Day 5. Act IV, Sc. 1.
Day 6. Act IV, Sc. 2. *An interval.* Ross's journey to England.
Day 7. Act IV, Sc. 3, Act V, Sc. 1. *An interval.* Malcolm's return to Scotland.
Day 8. Act V, Sc. 2 and 3.
Day 9. Act V, Sc. 4 to 8.

The historic period of the play is seventeen years—from 1040, the year of Duncan's death, to 1057, the year of Macbeth's. The dramatic time is less than a seventeenth part of the historic. One critic computes it at not more than two months, including intervals. This seems to me rather too short an estimate: could the political results of Macbeth's action as indicated in Acts IV and V have ripened so rapidly? Perhaps 'a few months' represents as close a conclusion as the evidence enables us to arrive at.

IX

SHAKESPEARE AND SCOTLAND

The Celtic atmosphere of *Macbeth* is well described in the following passage:[1]

"Thus, in *Macbeth* as in *Hamlet*, Shakspere sought his materials in the records of a semi-historic past. But, instead of Scandinavian saga, he now quarried in the richer mine of Celtic legend....During the fifteenth and

[1] F. S. Boas, *Shakspere and his Predecessors*, pp. 412, 413.

earlier sixteenth centuries the poets north of the Tweed,
from King James to Sir David Lyndesay, while showing a
sturdy patriotism in the spirit of their verse, had borrowed
its forms almost exclusively from Chaucer. Hitherto
England had received no equivalent,[1] but the balance was
more than redressed when the annals of 'Caledonia, stern
and wild' furnished Shakspere with the materials of one
of his mightiest creations. He may have visited Scotland
as a member of the company of which Laurence Fletcher,
one of the Lord Chamberlain's Servants, was the head,
and whose presence at Aberdeen is recorded in the register
of the Town Council for October 1601. But, however this
may be, he pierced, with an intuition that in an Elizabethan
Englishman was wellnigh miraculous, into the very heart
of Highland romance. The desolate storm-swept heaths,
where the evil powers of earth and sky may fittingly meet
and greet in hideous carnival; the lonely castles, where
passions of primeval intensity find their natural home, and
where, at dead of night, murder may stealthily move to its
design; the eerie atmosphere, where the hoarse croak of the
raven and the scream of the owl, the fatal bellman, foretell
the impending doom, and where the wraith of the victim
stalks to the head of the board in the assassin's banqueting-
hall—every detail is steeped in the peculiar genius of
Celtic Scotland. Hitherto this fertile poetic material had
found its chief expression in ballads of weird imaginative
power, but these, though of supreme excellence in their
kind, were only *Volkslieder*, and had no more than a local
circulation. But now Shakspere claimed for universal
purposes what had hitherto been the monoply of the clans.
His mighty art preserved all the mysticism and elemental
passion of the Highland story, while investing it with a
stupendous moral significance of which its Celtic origina-

---

[1] We have seen, however, that the English drama had begun
to owe something to the inspiration of Scottish history and its
romance.

tors had never dreamed. So Titanic is the theme as handled by the dramatist that, contrary to his usual practice, he does not complicate it with episodes, but develops it in its isolated grandeur. Thus *Macbeth* is of all the great tragedies the simplest in structure."

The question of Shakespeare's travels is one of the many fascinating problems of his little-known life. Was he one of "The English Comedians" who travelled and performed in Germany, and did he thus become acquainted with Ayrer's play *Die Schöne Sidea*, which preceded and in no small degree resembles *The Tempest*?[1] Did he acquire on Italian soil that knowledge of Italian life and local colour, and national characteristics, with which plays like *Romeo and Juliet*, *The Merchant of Venice*[2] and *Othello* are penetrated through and through? Each hypothesis has found advocates; and there are touches of description in the two Venetian plays which at least lend plausibility to the suggestion that he painted from the life, from personal observation. Yet the balance of probability is against his ever having been out of England, nor need we assume any other resources than his all-embracing sympathy and an imagination which enabled him to realise and harmonise into a vivid whole the miscellaneous information that might be derived from books and association with travellers.

As to the question naturally suggested by *Macbeth*, whether he ever set foot in Scotland, the most reliable of his biographers writes:[3]

"It has been repeatedly urged that Shakespeare's company visited Scotland, and that he went with it. In November 1599 English actors arrived in Scotland under the leadership of Lawrence Fletcher and one Martin, and were welcomed with enthusiasm by the king. Fletcher was a colleague of Shakespeare in 1603, but is not known to

---

[1] See Pitt Press ed., pp. xv, xvi.
[2] See Appendix to *The Merchant of Venice*, pp. 179–82.
[3] S. Lee.

have been one earlier. Shakespeare's company never included an actor named Martin. Fletcher repeated the visit in October 1601. There is nothing to indicate that any of his companions belonged to Shakespeare's company. In like manner, Shakespeare's accurate reference in 'Macbeth'[1] (1, 6. 1–10] to the 'nimble' but 'sweet' climate of Inverness, and the vivid impression he conveys of the aspects of wild Highland heaths, have been judged to be the certain fruits of a personal experience; but the passages in question, into which a more definite significance has possibly been read than Shakespeare intended, can be satisfactorily accounted for by his inevitable intercourse with Scotsmen in London and the theatres after James I's accession." With this conclusion we may rest satisfied.

X

MACBETH AND LADY MACBETH[2]

Macbeth has been termed the Tragedy of Ambition. All that a great work of art means and teaches can seldom, if ever, be crystallised in a phrase; nor is *Macbeth* an exception to the principle, though it is the least complex of Shakespeare's tragedies and is, indeed, marked by a sheer simplicity of theme, motive and treatment which consorts with the simple, unsophisticated period of the events. Still, "Tragedy of Ambition" seems a true and adequate description of the play, to this extent at least, that ambition is the main-spring of the action. Ambition alone calls into operation the forces that bring about the central deed and its train of fearful results. In Macbeth himself it is selfish ambition, the unqualified passion to possess what is not his, the conscious self-seeking that confesses itself to itself and dispenses with the hypocrisy of self-exculpation. In

---

[1] See the note on the lines.
[2] Many points in this section have been suggested by various essays.

Lady Macbeth it is selfless ambition, a more potent, a deadlier, incentive because born of love and misguided self-sacrifice. And in each the working of this passion, however different its origin, is the same, viz. the ruin of a nature not incapable of better things. For neither is "fiend-like": else they were not tragic figures at all; their fall would touch us with no sense of the "pity of it", their fate in all its terror of long-drawn torture and inglorious death would stir no sympathy.

The good side of Macbeth's chracter is brought into the greater prominence. The second scene represents him as the typical heroic warrior, "Bellona's bridegroom". In Duncan's eyes he is "a peerless kinsman". There must be great capacities of goodness in the man of whom these descriptions are spoken by those who should know him well. But these possibilities are annulled by inordinate ambition and signal weakness of will. With his ambition is joined an equally excessive imagination. On the positive side these two qualities, ambition and imagination, are the leading traits of his character. The one dominates in the earlier, the other in the latter part of the play; for the one instigates the crime which crowns his desires and leaves no further scope for ambition, and the other is the chief instrument by which Nemesis avenges the crime. On the negative side his character presents a weakness of moral courage in inverse proportion to his physical bravery, and a conscience that serves but to hamper his schemes by feeble, intermittent scruples, and to rob success of such satisfaction as the calculating, remorseless villainy of a Richard III enjoys.

The irony of life places Macbeth amid circumstances which seem designed to further the triumph of evil. He has meditated the crime before his first meeting with the Witches; and at that meeting he is already flushed with the pride of great achievement. Thus from his previous dreams of kingship and from his present consciousness of merit he is in a mental and moral condition specially susceptible to temptation. The temptation comes in the manner that would most appeal to him. Extreme imaginativeness makes him the easy prey of "supernatural soliciting". The effect of his first contact with this mysterious, external influence which harmonises so strangely with his inmost thoughts is profound. We see him "rapt" into one of those moods of abstraction and reverie in which, more than once in the play, he loses touch with the realities of the moment. Yet the influence of imagination soon works in the opposite direction to superstition. It paints with appalling vividness the consequences of his contemplated deed. Thus his whole "state of man" is shaken with the conflict of emotions and he would fain temporise in paralysed suspense. Events, however, are against him. Duncan's nomination of Malcolm compels a decision of some kind, and Duncan's coming furnishes the great opportunity.

The struggle in Macbeth's soul starts anew, and now his wife intervenes, with her terrible resources of evil influence. Still, imagination once more admonishes and holds him back, and conscience and prudence unite their voices in the warning. The victory over ambition and even his wife's influence seems gained: he will "proceed no further" in the "business", and halts on the brink. But Lady Macbeth is not to be diverted from the purpose which, suggested originally by him, has fascinated her. And now their very love becomes a curse to him: what should have been to his advantage is turned into an occasion of falling. For knowing his character, on its weak side at any rate, and knowing her power over him, she scruples not to use her knowledge and power to the full, playing on every motive of temptation and incitement which a swift brain and remorseless determination can suggest. Against such urgency, stronger than the "supernatural soliciting" itself, he cannot hold out. The iron will masters the irresolute will, sweeps aside scruples and fears, and bears him forward on its resistless current. The crime which originated in the promptings of ambition is consummated, and ambition as a dramatic motive of the tragedy is exhausted. Thenceforth imagination is the ruling motive. From the moment of Duncan's murder to Macbeth's latest breath imagination gives him no rest. At first, indeed, when the crisis calls for instant action, the instinct of absolute self-preservation asserts its sway. Macbeth shows much of his soldierly capacity for action, and plays his part well, save for the momentary impulse which makes him slay the grooms and thus rouse needless suspicion. But when the immediate peril is over and the time for reflection has come, then we see him self-tortured into a frenzy of unrest and wanton crime.

The turning-point of the plot may appear to be Banquo's murder, in that it precipitates Macbeth's downfall. Till that point events have played into his hands; he has won the crown, and the flight of Malcolm and Donalbain has left him in undisturbed possession. But now all goes against him. The similarity of the second murder converts to certainty men's suspicions as to the cause of the first, at the banquet scene he betrays himself irredeemably, and his thanes are driven to flight or measures of self-defence. Thus the murder of Banquo marks the decline of Macbeth's fortunes, it is the beginning of the end. But the end was inevitable, whatever the steps towards it. Everything that follows the murder of Duncan is the direct outcome of it. If Duncan lived so would Banquo. The first crime changed the whole course of Macbeth's career. It is the real dividing line, the essential turning-point, the parting in life's way. And the fact is expressed in his own words (ii. 3. 73–8).

"The Rubicon of crime" once crossed, the character-interest changes. Hitherto, as regards Macbeth, it has lain in study of the struggle within his soul. We have watched the unequal conflict between the good and the evil in him, the one supported by his scruples and fears, the other by his ambitious longings, by the intervention of "fate and metaphysical aid", and by his wife's incentives.

Now the contest gives place to a hideous consistency and singleness of purpose. "Things bad begun make strong themselves by ill" is his watchword and practice. For imagination, which once almost availed to withhold him from the deed, now works through his conscience and still more through fear, and goads him on to effect the removal of any in whom it sees a possible avenger of Duncan and claimant to the throne. The vessel of Macbeth's peace is poisoned and the poison corrodes his whole being. Not an instant's enjoyment has the successful accomplishment of villainy brought to him or her. Existence becomes a restless ecstasy of haunting fancies and alarms. He who could with difficulty bend himself up to the first terrible deed, and only did the second (II. 3. 89–101) in a fit of fury and panic, now becomes the deliberate contriver of murder, and soon passes to the third stage of blood-thirsty abandonment. Banquo, the more favoured of the Weird Sisters, is his chief dread and falls his speedy victim; but blood-steeped hallucination wreaks the ineffable avengement of that vision at the feast. Driven into deeper desperation, Macbeth must know the worst, by whatsoever means, and seeks inspiration of the Witches. Their prophecies instil a "security" that does but increase his reckless defiance of heaven and humanity. Logically his credulity should restrain him from the crimes that wring daily cries of agony from his bleeding land; they are wanton, causeless savagery in one who rests his trust on riddles that seem impossible of fulfilment against him. But Macbeth has passed far beyond the appeal of reason. Bloodshed has become a mania ("some say he's mad"), restless action the very condition of his being.

At length all the normal relations and interests of life have no reality in his eyes. An intolerable gloom settles down on him. He learns of his wife's death with absolute callousness, it merely evokes an outburst of weariness and contempt for existence itself. One thing alone he holds fast with blind desperation, his belief in the Witches'

supposed assurances of his safety. But at last the truth
which Banquo divined from the first is forced upon Macbeth and he sees these juggling fiends in their true light.
Naught now remains to him but the animal instinct that
clings to life:

> They have tied me to a stake; I cannot fly.
> But, bear-like, I must fight the course.

And this world-sated desperado had been "the brave
Macbeth", "Bellona's bridegroom", "the peerless kinsman"!

Lady Macbeth, the Clytemnestra of English tragedy, is
naturally drawn as a foil to Macbeth. She possesses "a
frightfully determined will", an iron stability of resolve.
It is to her what imagination is to Macbeth, the feature
that transcends and dominates all others in the character.
It is the secret of her influence over him and of her success
in winning him to consent. It enables her to carry her
share in the plot through, to remedy his errors, and come
to his rescue in the great crises of the action. But it proves
her ruin. It makes her impose upon herself and bear, for
a time, a strain beyond the ultimate endurance of the rest
of her powers. In fact, her imperious will, like his excess
of the imaginative faculty, disturbs the proper relation of
the forces of character. An abnormal element that knows
no restraint of conscience or common prudence, that
recks nothing of foresight or fear, it is the source of
abnormal effort, the reaction from which wrecks the whole
fabric. She has extreme self-reliance, unlike Macbeth,
who turns instinctively to her for co-operation, until his
sense of menacing retribution substitutes its fatal stimulus.
Intellectually, too, she is Macbeth's superior, as Portia is
the intellectual superior of Bassanio, and Rosalind of
Orlando. With what dexterity she meets Macbeth's
reluctance to go further in the work and assails his weak
points: how swiftly she perceives—too late—the effect of
the deed on Macbeth: what resource and alertness of brain

she manifests at the banquet-scene, where she tries first one method, and then another, and yet another of restoring his mental balance. But intellectual keenness does not compensate for the lack of imagination, and in the latter quality she is, surely, deficient. Gifted with true imaginative insight she could never have made her appalling miscalculation as to the moral results which their crime would produce in Macbeth, and in herself. She thinks that though he may shrink from the deed through fears or scruples, yet he will not wish it undone: that he will be able to reap joy of his sin. She never hints the least foreshadowing of the revolution which it really works in both. And this limitation of view argues inadequacy of penetrative imagination. It is significant, too, that the great outbursts of imaginative eloquence which signalise the play even among Shakespeare's works all come from Macbeth. And there are moments (e.g. in II. 2. 40) when his hectic fancy seems to transport him beyond her comprehension.

Of conscience she certainly manifests less than Macbeth. It has been held, indeed, that even the dire sleep-walking scene does not justify us in crediting her with true remorse: "from her lips, as from her husband's, no word of contrition for the past ever falls". Still, we should judge people less by what they say than by what we see them to be; and seeing Lady Macbeth wrecked in body and soul, we feel, I think, that of such an overthrow some working of conscience must be a potent cause. No doubt there are other causes. The recoil from the revolting effort; the physical horror of the scenes of that fatal night; the memory, uncontrolled in sleep by the normal will-power, of those appalling sights; the bitterness of isolation from Macbeth (for the separating power of partnership in guilt is one of the play's great lessons); the sheer sense of failure and frustrated hopes; the slow poison of brooding regret for which she lacks the man's antidote of action: all these have joined to make her this wraith-like figure of despair. Yet

deeper than all these, preying on her "nearest" of being, *must* be the *causa causans* of an outraged conscience.

The good in Lady Macbeth's character, what redeems her from unqualified detestation, is less on the surface than the good in Macbeth. But the better nature which her action belies is indicated by several traits. Thus she is wholly devoted to her husband. "Her whole ambition is for him and through him; of herself and of elevation for herself she never speaks. She lives only in him and in his greatness." The tenderness of his bearing witnesses her power of attraction and charm. She utters no word of reproach after his breakdown, but shows herself still solicitous for his welfare (III. 4. 141). It is indeed one of the regal notes of their relations that nothing of vulgar recrimination ever passes between them. They know that each has ruined the other, he her by his original suggestion of the crime and she him by her relentless instigation of it against his better judgment: but they separate in silence and "with averted eyes" move towards their several dooms unreproachful. And as she is shown us a loyal, though misguided and misguiding wife, so there are hints of maternal and filial tenderness in her nature (I. 7. 54–9, II. 2. 13, 14). Moreover, her invocation (rhetorical rather than imaginative) of the powers of darkness proves that she is no stranger to the gentler impulses of womanhood. A Goneril would not need to pray that she might be "unsexed", nor a Regan to petition for a richer measure of "direct cruelty". Neither of that hideous pair of Gorgons could apprehend or even comprehend the "compunctious visitings of nature". But Lady Macbeth knows that to execute her fell purpose she must be nerved by some unnatural access of ferocity.[1] And it seems as if her prayer were answered: the woman who can go into that chamber of death must be unsexed, for a space: but nature recurs, and while Macbeth

---

[1] "To make assurance doubly sure", she has recourse, also, to artificial means of stimulating her hardihood (II. 2. 1).

2

is brutalised by crime, her finer spirit is broken by the reaction from moral self-violence.

Lady Macbeth and Hamlet stand apart from the rest of Shakespeare's creations in the intensity and perplexity of the interest they arouse. Of all the women Shakespeare has drawn, none exercises so strange a fascination (not even the "serpent of old Nile") as this fragile,[1] indomitable northern Queen, who makes the great denial—denial of her sex—and greatly suffers,[2] even to the death.

XI

"OUR GREATEST POSSESSION"?

"I[3] regard *Macbeth*, upon the whole, as the greatest[4] treasure of our dramatic literature. We may look as Britons at Greek sculpture, and at Italian paintings, with a humble consciousness that our native art has never reached their perfection; but in the drama we can confront Æschylus himself with Shakespeare; and of all modern theatres, *ours* alone can compete with the Greek in the unborrowed nativeness and sublimity of its superstition. In the grandeur of tragedy *Macbeth* has no parallel, till we go back to the *Prometheus and the Furies* of the Attic stage. I could even produce, if it were not digressing too far from my subject, innumerable instances of striking similarity between the metaphorical mintage of Shakespeare's and of Æschylus's style,—a similarity, both in beauty and in the fault of excess, that unless the contrary had been proved, would lead me to suspect our great dramatist to have been a studious Greek scholar. But their resemblance arose

---

[1] "This little hand" (v. i. 50).

[2] To her, as to Richard III, *nemesis* comes in sleep.

[3] The poet Campbell (quoted in the "Temple" *Shakespeare*).

[4] I suppose that the judgment of modern criticism would be in favour of *Hamlet*, which expresses so much more of the introspection that characterises the modern spirit.

from the consanguinity of nature. In one respect, the tragedy of *Macbeth* always reminds me of Æschylus's poetry. It has scenes and conceptions absolutely too bold for representation. What stage could do justice to Æschylus, when the Titan Prometheus makes his appeal to the elements; and when the hammer is heard in the Scythian Desert that rivets his chains? Or when the Ghost of Clytemnestra rushes into Apollo's temple, and rouses the sleeping Furies? I wish to imagine these scenes: I should be sorry to see the acting of them attempted. In like manner, there are parts of *Macbeth* which I delight to read much more than to see in the theatre....Nevertheless, I feel no inconsistency in reverting from these remarks to my first assertion, that all in all, *Macbeth* is our greatest possession in dramatic poetry."

The main impressions left by the play stand out clearly in Gervinus's summary:

"This tragedy has ever been regarded and criticised with distinguishing preference among Shakespeare's works; our own Schiller reproduced it, Schlegel spoke of it with enthusiasm, Drake called it 'the greatest effort of our author's genius, and the most sublime and impressive drama which the world has ever beheld'. It has also obtained favour above the other plays of Shakespeare in lands peopled by other than the Teutonic race, either from its felt or perceived resemblance to ancient tragedy, or from its unity of design and the simple progress of its development, or from its distinct characterisation, in which the poet has employed less mystery than usual; most of all, indeed, from its pictorial charm and poetic colouring. If perhaps no other play of Shakespeare's can vie with *Hamlet* in philosophical insight into the nature and worth of the various powers at work in man, if none can compete with *Henry IV* in fresh delight in a vast and active career, if none can compare with *Othello* in profoundness of design and careful carrying out of the characters, if none with *Lear* in the power of contending passions, and none with *Cymbeline* in the importance of moral principles, *Macbeth*, in like manner, stands forth uniquely pre-eminent in the splendour of poetic and picturesque diction and in the living representation of persons, times, and places. Schlegel perceived the vigorous heroic age of the North depicted in it with powerful touches, the generations of an iron time, whose virtue is bravery. How grandly do the mighty forms rise, how naturally do they move in an heroic style! What a different aspect is presented by this tyrant Macbeth by the side of the heroes Macduff, Banquo, and Siward, compared to that of the crook-back Richard amid a crooked generation! Locally, we are transported into the Highlands of Scotland, where everything appears tinged with superstition, full of tangible intercommunion with the supernatural world and prognostics of the moral life by signs in the animate and inanimate kingdom; where, in conformity with this, men are credulous in belief and excitable in fancy; where they speak with strong expression, with highly poetical language, and with unusual imagery, such as strikes us even at the present day in popular orators of the Gaelic races.

"This mastery over the general representation of time and place is rivalled by the picture of single circumstances and situations. Reynolds justly admired that description of the martlet's resort to Macbeth's dwelling as a charming image of repose, following by way of contrast the lively picture of the fight. More justly still has praise been always lavished on the powerful representation of the horrible in that night-wandering of Lady Macbeth, in the banquet scene, and in the dismal creation of the weird sisters. And far above all this is the speaking truth of the scenes at the murder of Duncan, which produce a powerful effect even in the most imperfect representation. The fearful whispered conference, in the horrible dimness of which the pair arrange and complete their atrocious project; the heart-rending portraiture of Macbeth's state of mind at the deed itself; the uneasy half-waking condition of the sacrificed attendants, one of whom dreams on of the evening feast, the other, in paralysed consciousness, seems to anticipate the impending atrocity; lastly, the external terrors of the night, presenting a foreboding contrast to the tumult of merriment over the yawning graves; all this is so perfectly natural, and wrought to such powerful effect with so little art, that it would be difficult to find its equal in the poetry of any age."

MACBETH

DRAMATIS PERSONÆ

DUNCAN, King of Scotland.

MALCOLM
DONALBAIN } his sons.

MACBETH
BANQUO } generals of the King's army.

MACDUFF
LENNOX
ROSS
MENTEITH } noblemen of Scotland.
ANGUS
CAITHNESS

FLEANCE, son to Banquo.

SIWARD, Earl of Northumberland, general of the English forces.

Young SIWARD, his son.

SEYTON, an officer attending on Macbeth.

Boy, son to Macduff.

An English Doctor.

A Scotch Doctor.

A Sergeant.

A Porter.

An Old Man.

Lady MACBETH.

Lady MACDUFF.

Gentlewoman attending on Lady Macbeth.

Lords, Gentlemen, Officers, Soldiers, Murderers, Attendants, and Messengers.

Hecate.
Three Witches.
Apparitions.

SCENE—*Scotland; England.*

MACBETH

ACT I

Scene I. *A desert place*

Thunder and lightning. Enter three Witches

FIRST WITCH   When shall we three meet again
In thunder, lightning, or in rain?
SECOND WITCH   When the hurlyburly's done,
When the battle's lost and won.
THIRD WITCH   That will be ere the set of sun.   5
FIRST WITCH   Where the place?
SECOND WITCH   Upon the heath.
THIRD WITCH   There to meet with Macbeth.
FIRST WITCH   I come, Graymalkin!
SECOND WITCH   Paddock calls.
THIRD WITCH   Anon!   10
ALL   Fair is foul, and foul is fair:
Hover through the fog and filthy air.   [*Exeunt*

Scene II. *A camp near Forres*

Alarum within. Enter DUNCAN, MALCOLM, DONALBAIN,
LENNOX, *with* Attendants, *meeting a bleeding* Sergeant

DUNCAN   What bloody man is that? He can report,
As seemeth by his plight, of the revolt
The newest state.
MALCOLM   This is the sergeant,
Who, like a good and hardy soldier, fought
'Gainst my captivity. Hail, brave friend!   5

Say to the king the knowledge of the broil
As thou didst leave it.

SERGEANT   Doubtful it stood;
As two spent swimmers, that do cling together
And choke their art. The merciless Macdonwald—
Worthy to be a rebel, for to that   10
The multiplying villanies of nature
Do swarm upon him—from the western isles
Of kerns and gallowglasses is supplied;
And fortune, on his damned quarrel smiling,
Show'd like a rebel's whore: but all's too weak: 15
For brave Macbeth—well he deserves that name—
Disdaining fortune, with his brandish'd steel,
Which smoked with bloody execution,
Like valour's minion carv'd out his passage
Till he faced the slave;   20
Which ne'er shook hands, nor bade farewell to him,
Till he unseam'd him from the nave to the chaps,
And fix'd his head upon our battlements.

DUNCAN   O valiant cousin! worthy gentleman!

SERGEANT   As whence the sun 'gins his reflection   25
Shipwrecking storms and direful thunders break;
So from that spring, whence comfort seem'd to come,
Discomfort swells. Mark, king of Scotland, mark:
No sooner justice had, with valour arm'd,
Compell'd these skipping kerns to trust their heels,   30
But the Norweyan lord, surveying vantage,
With furbish'd arms and new supplies of men,
Began a fresh assault.

DUNCAN   Dismay'd not this
Our captains, Macbeth and Banquo?

SERGEANT   Yes;
As sparrows eagles, or the hare the lion.   35
If I say sooth, I must report they were
As cannons overcharg'd with double cracks; so they

(no cannon at this time)

Doubly redoubled strokes upon the foe:
Except they meant to bathe in reeking wounds,
Or memorize another Golgotha,   40
I cannot tell:—
But I am faint, my gashes cry for help.
DUNCAN   So well thy words become thee as thy
     wounds;
They smack of honour both. Go get him surgeons.
                         [*Exit Sergeant, attended*
Who comes here?
MALCOLM   The worthy thane of Ross.   45
LENNOX   What a haste looks through his eyes! So
     should he look
That seems to speak things strange.

Enter ROSS

ROSS   God save the king!
DUNCAN   Whence camest thou, worthy thane?
ROSS   From Fife, great king;
Where the Norweyan banners flout the sky
And fan our people cold. Norway himself,   50
With terrible numbers,
Assisted by that most disloyal traitor
The thane of Cawdor, began a dismal conflict;
Till that Bellona's bridegroom, lapp'd in proof,
Confronted him with self-comparisons,   55
Point against point rebellious, arm 'gainst arm,
Curbing his lavish spirit: and, to conclude,
The victory fell on us.
DUNCAN   Great happiness!
ROSS   That now
     Sweno, the Norways' king, craves composition; 60
Nor would we deign him burial of his men
Till he disbursed, at Saint Colme's inch,
Ten thousand dollars to our general use.

DUNCAN   No more that thane of Cawdor shall deceive
Our bosom interest: go pronounce his present death,   65
And with his former title greet Macbeth.
ROSS   I'll see it done.
DUNCAN   What he hath lost noble Macbeth hath won.

[*Exeunt*

SCENE III.   *A heath*

Thunder. Enter the three Witches

FIRST WITCH   Where hast thou been, sister?
SECOND WITCH   Killing swine.
THIRD WITCH   Sister, where thou?
FIRST WITCH   A sailor's wife had chestnuts in her lap,
And mounch'd, and mounch'd, and mounch'd:—
"Give me," quoth I: 5
"Aroint thee, witch!" the rump-fed ronyon cries.
Her husband's to Aleppo gone, master o' the Tiger:
But in a sieve I'll thither sail,
And, like a rat without a tail,
I'll do, I'll do, and I'll do.   10
SECOND WITCH   I'll give thee a wind.
FIRST WITCH   Thou art kind.
THIRD WITCH   And I another.
FIRST WITCH   I myself have all the other;
And the very ports they blow,   15
All the quarters that they know
I' the shipman's card.
I will drain him dry as hay:
Sleep shall neither night nor day
Hang upon his pent-house lid;   20
He shall live a man forbid:
Weary se'n-nights nine times nine
Shall he dwindle, peak and pine:

Though his bark cannot be lost,
Yet it shall be tempest-tost.　　　　　　　　　25
Look what I have.

SECOND WITCH　Show me, show me.

FIRST WITCH　Here I have a pilot's thumb,
Wreck'd as homeward he did come.　　*[Drum within*

THIRD WITCH　A drum, a drum!　　　　　　30
Macbeth doth come.

ALL　The weird sisters, hand in hand,
Posters of the sea and land,
Thus do go about, about:
Thrice to thine, and thrice to mine,　　　　35
And thrice again, to make up nine.
Peace! the charm's wound up.

Enter MACBETH *and* BANQUO

MACBETH　So foul and fair a day I have not seen.

BANQUO　How far is't call'd to Forres? What are these
So wither'd, and so wild in their attire,　　　40
That look not like the inhabitants o' the earth,
And yet are on't? Live you? or are you aught
That man may question? You seem to understand
　　me,
By each at once her choppy finger laying
Upon her skinny lips: you should be women,　　45
And yet your beards forbid me to interpret
That you are so.

MACBETH　　　　　Speak, if you can: what are you?

FIRST WITCH　All hail, Macbeth! hail to thee, thane of
Glamis!

SECOND WITCH　All hail, Macbeth! hail to thee, thane
of Cawdor!

THIRD WITCH　All hail, Macbeth, that shalt be king
hereafter!　　　　　　　　　　　　50

BANQUO　Good sir, why do you start; and seem to fear

Things that do sound so fair? I' the name of truth,
Are ye fantastical, or that indeed
Which outwardly ye show? My noble partner
You greet with present grace and great prediction   55
Of noble having and of royal hope,
That he seems rapt withal: to me you speak not:
If you can look into the seeds of time,
And say which grain will grow and which will not,
Speak then to me, who neither beg nor fear   60
Your favours nor your hate.

FIRST WITCH   Hail!

SECOND WITCH   Hail!

THIRD WITCH   Hail!

FIRST WITCH   Lesser than Macbeth, and greater.   65

SECOND WITCH   Not so happy, yet much happier.

THIRD WITCH   Thou shalt get kings, though thou be
    none:
So, all hail, Macbeth and Banquo!

FIRST WITCH   Banquo and Macbeth, all hail!

MACBETH   Stay, you imperfect speakers, tell me
    more: 70
By Sinel's death I know I am thane of Glamis;
But how of Cawdor? the thane of Cawdor lives,
A prosperous gentleman; and to be king
Stands not within the prospect of belief,
No more than to be Cawdor. Say from whence   75
You owe this strange intelligence? or why
Upon this blasted heath you stop our way
With such prophetic greeting? Speak, I charge you.
                              [*Witches vanish*

BANQUO   The earth hath bubbles, as the water has,
And these are of them: whither are they vanish'd?   80

MACBETH   Into the air; and what seem'd corporal
    melted
As breath into the wind. Would they had stay'd!

BANQUO   Were such things here as we do speak about?
  Or have we eaten on the insane root
  That takes the reason prisoner?   85
MACBETH   Your children shall be kings.
BANQUO   You shall be king.
MACBETH   And thane of Cawdor too: went it not so?
BANQUO   To the selfsame tune and words. Who's here?

Enter ROSS *and* ANGUS

ROSS   The king hath happily received, Macbeth,
  The news of thy success: and when he reads   90
  Thy personal venture in the rebels' fight,
  His wonders and his praises do contend
  Which should be thine or his: silenc'd with that,
  In viewing o'er the rest o' the selfsame day,
  He finds thee in the stout Norweyan ranks,   95
  Nothing afeard of what thyself didst make,
  Strange images of death. As thick as hail
  Came post with post; and every one did bear
  Thy praises in his kingdom's great defence,
  And pour'd them down before him.
ANGUS   We are sent   100
  To give thee from our royal master thanks;
  Only to herald thee into his sight,
  Not pay thee.
ROSS   And, for an earnest of a greater honour,
  He bade me, from him, call thee thane of Cawdor: 105
  In which addition, hail, most worthy thane!
  For it is thine.
BANQUO   [*Aside*] What, can the devil speak true?
MACBETH   The thane of Cawdor lives: why do you
    dress me
  In borrow'd robes?
ANGUS   Who was the thane lives yet;
  But under heavy judgment bears that life   110

Which he deserves to lose. Whether he was
    combined
With those of Norway, or did line the rebel
With hidden help and vantage, or that with both
He labour'd in his country's wreck, I know not;
But treasons capital, confess'd and proved,   115
Have overthrown him.

MACBETH   [*Aside*]   Glamis, and thane of Cawdor!
    The greatest is behind.—[*To Ross and Angus*]
        Thanks for your pains.—
[*To Banquo*] Do you not hope your children shall be
    kings,
When those that gave the thane of Cawdor to me
Promised no less to them?

BANQUO   That, trusted home,   120
    Might yet enkindle you unto the crown,
Besides the thane of Cawdor. But 'tis strange:
And oftentimes, to win us to our harm,
The instruments of darkness tell us truths,
Win us with honest trifles, to betray's   125
In deepest consequence.
Cousins, a word, I pray you.

MACBETH   [*Aside*]   Two truths are told,
    As happy prologues to the swelling act
Of the imperial theme.—I thank you, gentlemen.—
[*Aside*] This supernatural soliciting   130
Cannot be ill; cannot be good: if ill,
Why hath it given me earnest of success,
Commencing in a truth? I am thane of Cawdor:
If good, why do I yield to that suggestion
Whose horrid image doth unfix my hair,   135
And make my seated heart knock at my ribs,
Against the use of nature? Present fears
Are less than horrible imaginings:
My thought, whose murder yet is but fantastical,

Shakes so my single state of man that function   140
Is smother'd in surmise, and nothing is
But what is not.

BANQUO   Look, how our partner's rapt.

MACBETH   [*Aside*] If chance will have me king, why,
        chance may crown me,
Without my stir.

BANQUO   New honours come upon him,
Like our strange garments, cleave not to their mould   145
But with the aid of use.

MACBETH   [*Aside*]   Come what come may,
Time and the hour runs through the roughest day.

BANQUO   Worthy Macbeth, we stay upon your leisure.

MACBETH   Give me your favour: my dull brain was
        wrought
With things forgotten. Kind gentlemen, your pains   150
Are register'd where every day I turn
The leaf to read them. Let us toward the king.
[*To Banquo*] Think upon what hath chanced; and, at
        more time,
The interim having weigh'd it, let us speak
Our free hearts each to other.

BANQUO   Very gladly.   155

MACBETH   Till then, enough.—Come, friends.

                                            [*Exeunt*

SCENE IV. *Forres. The palace*

Flourish. Enter DUNCAN, MALCOLM, DONALBAIN,
        LENNOX, *and* Attendants

DUNCAN   Is execution done on Cawdor? Are not
Those in commission yet return'd?

MALCOLM   My liege,
They are not yet come back. But I have spoke

With one that saw him die: who did report

That very frankly he confess'd his treasons,   5

Implored your highness' pardon, and set forth

A deep repentance: nothing in his life

Became him like the leaving it; he died

As one that had been studied in his death,

To throw away the dearest thing he owed,   10

As 'twere a careless trifle.

DUNCAN   There's no art

To find the mind's construction in the face:

He was a gentleman on whom I built

An absolute trust.

Enter MACBETH, BANQUO, ROSS, *and* ANGUS

O worthiest cousin!

The sin of my ingratitude even now   15

Was heavy on me: thou art so far before,

That swiftest wing of recompense is slow

To overtake thee. Would thou hadst less deserved,

That the proportion both of thanks and payment

Might have been mine! only I have left to say,   20

More is thy due than more than all can pay.

MACBETH   The service and the loyalty I owe,

In doing it, pays itself. Your highness' part

Is to receive our duties; and our duties

Are to your throne and state children and servants;   25

Which do but what they should, by doing every

    thing

Safe toward your love and honour.

DUNCAN   Welcome hither:

I have begun to plant thee, and will labour

To make thee full of growing. Noble Banquo,

That hast no less deserved, nor must be known   30

No less to have done so; let me infold thee

And hold thee to my heart.

BANQUO   There if I grow,
  The harvest is your own.
DUNCAN   My plenteous joys,
  Wanton in fulness, seek to hide themselves
  In drops of sorrow. Sons, kinsmen, thanes,   35
  And you whose places are the nearest, know,
  We will establish our estate upon
  Our eldest, Malcolm, whom we name hereafter
  The Prince of Cumberland: which honour must
  Not unaccompanied invest him only,   40
  But signs of nobleness, like stars, shall shine
  On all deservers. From hence to Inverness,
  And bind us further to you.
MACBETH   The rest is labour, which is not used for you:
  I'll be myself the harbinger, and make joyful   45
  The hearing of my wife with your approach:
  So humbly take my leave.
DUNCAN   My worthy Cawdor!
MACBETH   [*Aside*] The Prince of Cumberland! that is
      a step,
  On which I must fall down, or else o'erleap,
  For in my way it lies. Stars, hide your fires;   50
  Let not light see my black and deep desires:
  The eye wink at the hand; yet let that be,
  Which the eye fears, when it is done, to see.   [*Exit*
DUNCAN   True, worthy Banquo; he is full so valiant,
  And in his commendations I am fed;   55
  It is a banquet to me. Let's after him,
  Whose care is gone before to bid us welcome:
  It is a peerless kinsman.   [*Flourish. Exeunt*

SCENE V. *Inverness.* MACBETH'S *castle*

Enter LADY MACBETH, *reading a letter*

LADY MACBETH   "They met me in the day of success; and
I have learned by the perfectest report, they have more
in them than mortal knowledge. When I burned in
desire to question them further, they made themselves
air, into which they vanished. Whiles I stood rapt in the   5
wonder of it, came missives from the king, who all-
hailed me 'Thane of Cawdor'; by which title, before,
these weird sisters saluted me, and referred me to the
coming on of time, with 'Hail, king that shalt be!' This
have I thought good to deliver thee, my dearest partner   10
of greatness, that thou mightst not lose the dues of
rejoicing, by being ignorant of what greatness is promised thee. Lay it to thy heart, and farewell."

Glamis thou art, and Cawdor; and shalt be
What thou art promised: yet do I fear thy nature;
It is too full o' the milk of human kindness   15
To catch the nearest way: thou wouldst be great;
Art not without ambition, but without
The illness should attend it: what thou wouldst highly,
That wouldst thou holily; wouldst not play false,
And yet wouldst wrongly win: thou'ldst have, great
   Glamis,   20
That which cries "Thus thou must do, if thou have it";
And that which rather thou dost fear to do
Than wishest should be undone. Hie thee hither,
That I may pour my spirits in thine ear,
And chastise with the valour of my tongue   25
All that impedes thee from the golden round,
Which fate and metaphysical aid doth seem
To have thee crown'd withal.

Enter a Messenger

What is your tidings?

MESSENGER   The king comes here to-night.

LADY MACBETH   Thou'rt mad to say it:
Is not thy master with him? who, were't so,   30
Would have inform'd for preparation.

MESSENGER   So please you, it is true: our thane is coming:
One of my fellows had the speed of him;
Who, almost dead for breath, had scarcely more
Than would make up his message.

LADY MACBETH   Give him tending; 35
He brings great news.   [*Exit Messenger*
                    The raven himself is hoarse
That croaks the fatal entrance of Duncan
Under my battlements. Come, you spirits
That tend on mortal thoughts, unsex me here,
And fill me, from the crown to the toe, top-full   40
Of direst cruelty! make thick my blood,
Stop up the access and passage to remorse,
That no compunctious visitings of nature
Shake my fell purpose, nor keep peace between
The effect and it! Come to my woman's breasts,   45
And take my milk for gall, you murdering ministers,
Wherever in your sightless substances
You wait on nature's mischief! Come, thick night,
And pall thee in the dunnest smoke of hell,
That my keen knife see not the wound it makes,   50
Nor heaven peep through the blanket of the dark,
To cry "Hold, hold!"

Enter MACBETH

Great Glamis! worthy Cawdor!
Greater than both, by the all-hail hereafter!
Thy letters have transported me beyond

This ignorant present, and I feel now   55
    The future in the instant.
MACBETH   My dearest love,
    Duncan comes here to-night.
LADY MACBETH   And when goes hence?
MACBETH   To-morrow, as he purposes.
LADY MACBETH   O, never
    Shall sun that morrow see!
    Your face, my thane, is as a book where men   60
    May read strange matters: to beguile the time,
    Look like the time; bear welcome in your eye,
    Your hand, your tongue: look like the innocent flower,
    But be the serpent under't. He that's coming
    Must be provided for: and you shall put   65
    This night's great business into my dispatch;
    Which shall to all our nights and days to come
    Give solely sovereign sway and masterdom.
MACBETH   We will speak further.
LADY MACBETH   Only look up clear;
    To alter favour ever is to fear: 70
    Leave all the rest to me.   [*Exeunt*

SCENE VI. *Before* MACBETH'S *castle*

Hautboys. Servants of MACBETH *attending, with torches.*
Enter DUNCAN, MALCOLM, DONALBAIN, BANQUO, LENNOX,
MACDUFF, ROSS, ANGUS, *and* Attendants

DUNCAN   This castle hath a pleasant seat; the air
    Nimbly and sweetly recommends itself
    Unto our gentle senses.
BANQUO   This guest of summer,
    The temple-haunting martlet, does approve,
    By his loved mansionry, that the heavens' breath   5

Smells wooingly here: no jutty, frieze,
Buttress, nor coign of vantage, but this bird
Hath made his pendent bed and procreant cradle:
Where they most breed and haunt, I have observed
The air is delicate.

Enter LADY MACBETH

DUNCAN   See, see, our honour'd hostess!   10
The love that follows us sometime is our trouble,
Which still we thank as love. Herein I teach you
How you shall bid God 'ild us for your pains,
And thank us for your trouble.
LADY MACBETH   All our service
In every point twice done, and then done double,   15
Were poor and single business to contend
Against those honours deep and broad wherewith
Your majesty loads our house: for those of old,
And the late dignities heap'd up to them,
We rest your hermits.
DUNCAN   Where's the thane of Cawdor?   20
We coursed him at the heels, and had a purpose
To be his purveyor: but he rides well;
And his great love, sharp as his spur, hath holp him
To his home before us. Fair and noble hostess,
We are your guest to-night.
LADY MACBETH   Your servants ever   25
Have theirs, themselves, and what is theirs, in compt,
To make their audit at your highness' pleasure,
Still to return your own.
DUNCAN   Give me your hand;
Conduct me to mine host: we love him highly,
And shall continue our graces towards him.   30
By your leave, hostess.   [*Exeunt*

Scene VII. macbeth's *castle*

Hautboys and torches. Enter a Sewer, *and divers* Servants
*with dishes and service, and pass over the stage. Then
enter* MACBETH

macbeth If it were done when 'tis done, then 'twere
   well
  It were done quickly: if the assassination
  Could trammel up the consequence, and catch,
  With his surcease, success; that but this blow
  Might be the be-all and the end-all here,   5
  But here, upon this bank and shoal of time,
  We'ld jump the life to come. But in these cases
  We still have judgment here; that we but teach
  Bloody instructions, which being taught return
  To plague the inventor: this even-handed justice   10
  Commends the ingredients of our poison'd chalice
  To our own lips. He's here in double trust:
  First, as I am his kinsman and his subject,
  Strong both against the deed; then, as his host,
  Who should against his murderer shut the door,   15
  Not bear the knife myself. Besides, this Duncan
  Hath borne his faculties so meek, hath been
  So clear in his great office, that his virtues
  Will plead like angels, trumpet-tongu'd, against
  The deep damnation of his taking-off;   20
  And pity, like a naked new-born babe,
  Striding the blast, or heaven's cherubin, horsed
  Upon the sightless couriers of the air,
  Shall blow the horrid deed in every eye,
  That tears shall drown the wind. I have no spur   25
  To prick the sides of my intent, but only
  Vaulting ambition, which o'erleaps itself
  And falls on the other.

Enter LADY MACBETH

How now! what news?

LADY MACBETH   He has almost supp'd: why have you
left the chamber?

MACBETH   Hath he ask'd for me?

LADY MACBETH   Know you not he has? 30

MACBETH   We will proceed no further in this business:
He hath honour'd me of late; and I have bought
Golden opinions from all sorts of people,
Which would be worn now in their newest gloss,
Not cast aside so soon.

LADY MACBETH   Was the hope drunk   35
Wherein you dress'd yourself? hath it slept since?
And wakes it now, to look so green and pale
At what it did so freely? From this time
Such I account thy love. Art thou afeard
To be the same in thine own act and valour   40
As thou art in desire? Wouldst thou have that
Which thou esteem'st the ornament of life,
And live a coward in thine own esteem,
Letting "I dare not" wait upon "I would,"
Like the poor cat i' the adage?

MACBETH   Prithee, peace: 45
I dare do all that may become a man;
Who dares do more is none.

LADY MACBETH   What beast was't then,
That made you break this enterprise to me?
When you durst do it, then you were a man;
And, to be more than what you were, you would   50
Be so much more the man. Nor time nor place
Did then adhere, and yet you would make both:
They have made themselves, and that their fitness now
Does unmake you. I have given suck, and know
How tender 'tis to love the babe that milks me: 55

    I would, while it was smiling in my face,
    Have pluck'd my nipple from his boneless gums,
    And dash'd the brains out, had I so sworn as you
    Have done to this.
MACBETH   If we should fail?
LADY MACBETH   We fail!
    But screw your courage to the sticking-place,   60
    And we'll not fail. When Duncan is asleep—
    Whereto the rather shall his day's hard journey
    Soundly invite him—his two chamberlains
    Will I with wine and wassail so convince,
    That memory, the warder of the brain,   65
    Shall be a fume, and the receipt of reason
    A limbeck only: when in swinish sleep
    Their drenched natures lie as in a death,
    What cannot you and I perform upon
    The unguarded Duncan? what not put upon   70
    His spongy officers, who shall bear the guilt
    Of our great quell?
MACBETH   Bring forth men-children only;
    For thy undaunted mettle should compose
    Nothing but males. Will it not be received,
    When we have mark'd with blood those sleepy two   75
    Of his own chamber, and used their very daggers,
    That they have done't?
LADY MACBETH   Who dares receive it other,
    As we shall make our griefs and clamour roar
    Upon his death?
MACBETH   I am settled, and bend up
    Each corporal agent to this terrible feat.   80
    Away, and mock the time with fairest show:
    False face must hide what the false heart doth know.
                        [*Exeunt*

ACT II

Scene I. *Inverness. Court of* MACBETH'S *castle*

Enter BANQUO, *and* FLEANCE *bearing a torch before him*

BANQUO   How goes the night, boy?
FLEANCE   The moon is down; I have not heard the clock.
BANQUO   And she goes down at twelve.
FLEANCE   I take't, 'tis later, sir.
BANQUO   Hold, take my sword. There's husbandry in
   heaven,
  Their candles are all out. Take thee that too.   5
  A heavy summons lies like lead upon me,
  And yet I would not sleep. Merciful powers,
  Restrain in me the cursed thoughts that nature
  Gives way to in repose! Give me my sword.
  Who's there?   10

Enter MACBETH, *and a* Servant *with a torch*

MACBETH   A friend.
BANQUO   What, sir, not yet at rest? The king's a-bed:
  He hath been in unusual pleasure, and
  Sent forth great largess to your offices:
  This diamond he greets your wife withal,   15
  By the name of most kind hostess; and shut up
  In measureless content.
MACBETH   Being unprepared,
  Our will became the servant to defect;
  Which else should free have wrought.
BANQUO   All's well.
  I dreamt last night of the three weird sisters: 20
  To you they have show'd some truth.

MACBETH   I think not of them:
 Yet, when we can entreat an hour to serve,
 We would spend it in some words upon that business,
 If you would grant the time.
BANQUO   At your kind'st leisure.
MACBETH   If you shall cleave to my consent, when 'tis,   25
 It shall make honour for you.
BANQUO   So I lose none
 In seeking to augment it, but still keep
 My bosom franchised and allegiance clear,
 I shall be counsell'd.
MACBETH   Good repose the while!
BANQUO   Thanks, sir: the like to you!   30
     [Exeunt Banquo and Fleance
MACBETH   Go bid thy mistress, when my drink is ready,
 She strike upon the bell. Get thee to bed. [Exit Servant
 Is this a dagger which I see before me,
 The handle toward my hand? Come, let me clutch thee:
 I have thee not, and yet I see thee still.   35
 Art thou not, fatal vision, sensible
 To feeling as to sight? or art thou but
 A dagger of the mind, a false creation,
 Proceeding from the heat-oppressed brain?
 I see thee yet, in form as palpable   40
 As this which now I draw.
 Thou marshall'st me the way that I was going;
 And such an instrument I was to use.
 Mine eyes are made the fools o' the other senses,
 Or else worth all the rest: I see thee still;   45
 And on thy blade and dudgeon gouts of blood,
 Which was not so before. There's no such thing:
 It is the bloody business which informs
 Thus to mine eyes. Now o'er the one half-world
 Nature seems dead, and wicked dreams abuse   50
 The curtain'd sleep; witchcraft celebrates

Pale Hecate's offerings; and wither'd murder,
Alarum'd by his sentinel, the wolf,
Whose howl's his watch, thus with his stealthy pace,
With Tarquin's ravishing strides, towards his design   55
Moves like a ghost. Thou sure and firm-set earth,
Hear not my steps, which way they walk, for fear
Thy very stones prate of my whereabout,
And take the present horror from the time,
Which now suits with it. Whiles I threat, he lives: 60
Words to the heat of deeds too cold breath gives.

                       [A bell rings

I go, and it is done; the bell invites me.
Hear it not, Duncan; for it is a knell
That summons thee to heaven or to hell.   *[Exit*

SCENE II. *The same*

Enter LADY MACBETH

LADY MACBETH   That which hath made them drunk
   hath made me bold;
  What hath quench'd them hath given me fire. Hark!
   Peace!
  It was the owl that shriek'd, the fatal bellman,
  Which gives the stern'st good-night. He is about it:
  The doors are open; and the surfeited grooms   5
  Do mock their charge with snores: I have drugg'd their
   possets,
  That death and nature do contend about them,
  Whether they live or die.
MACBETH   [*Within*] Who's there? what, ho!
LADY MACBETH   Alack, I am afraid they have awaked,   10
  And 'tis not done: the attempt and not the deed
  Confounds us. Hark! I laid their daggers ready;

He could not miss 'em. Had he not resembled
My father as he slept, I had done't.

Enter MACBETH

                                  My husband!

MACBETH I have done the deed. Didst thou not hear
    a noise?   15

LADY MACBETH I heard the owl scream and the crickets
    cry.

    Did not you speak?

MACBETH   When?

LADY MACBETH   Now.

MACBETH   As I descended?

LADY MACBETH Ay.

MACBETH Hark!

    Who lies i' the second chamber?

LADY MACBETH   Donalbain.   20

MACBETH This is a sorry sight. [*Looking on his hands*

LADY MACBETH A foolish thought, to say a sorry sight.

MACBETH There's one did laugh in's sleep, and one
    cried "Murder!"

    That they did wake each other: I stood and heard them:
    But they did say their prayers, and address'd them 25
    Again to sleep.

LADY MACBETH There are two lodg'd together.

MACBETH One cried "God bless us!" and "Amen!"
    the other;

    As they had seen me with these hangman's hands.
    Listening their fear, I could not say "Amen!"
    When they did say "God bless us!"

LADY MACBETH   Consider it not so deeply. 30

MACBETH But wherefore could not I pronounce
    "Amen"?

    I had most need of blessing, and "Amen"
    Stuck in my throat.

LADY MACBETH   These deeds must not be thought
   After these ways; so, it will make us mad.

MACBETH   Methought I heard a voice cry "Sleep no
   more!   35
   Macbeth does murder sleep,"—the innocent sleep,
   Sleep that knits up the ravell'd sleave of care,
   The death of each day's life, sore labour's bath,
   Balm of hurt minds, great nature's second course,
   Chief nourisher in life's feast,—

LADY MACBETH   What do you mean?   40

MACBETH   Still it cried "Sleep no more!" to all the
   house:
   "Glamis hath murder'd sleep, and therefore Cawdor
   Shall sleep no more: Macbeth shall sleep no more!"

LADY MACBETH   Who was it that thus cried? Why,
   worthy thane,
   You do unbend your noble strength, to think   45
   So brainsickly of things. Go get some water,
   And wash this filthy witness from your hand.
   Why did you bring these daggers from the place?
   They must lie there: go carry them, and smear
   The sleepy grooms with blood.

MACBETH   I'll go no more: 50
   I am afraid to think what I have done;
   Look on't again I dare not.

LADY MACBETH   Infirm of purpose!
   Give me the daggers: the sleeping and the dead
   Are but as pictures: 'tis the eye of childhood
   That fears a painted devil. If he do bleed,   55
   I'll gild the faces of the grooms withal,
   For it must seem their guilt. [*Exit. Knocking within*

MACBETH   Whence is that knocking?
   How is't with me, when every noise appals me?
   What hands are here? ha! they pluck out mine eyes!
   Will all great Neptune's ocean wash this blood   60

Clean from my hand? No; this my hand will rather
The multitudinous seas incarnadine,
Making the green one red.

Re-enter LADY MACBETH

LADY MACBETH   My hands are of your colour; but I
      shame
   To wear a heart so white. [*Knocking within*] I hear a
      knocking   65
   At the south entry: retire we to our chamber:
   A little water clears us of this deed:
   How easy is it, then! Your constancy
   Hath left you unattended. [*Knocking within*] Hark!
      more knocking:
   Get on your nightgown, lest occasion call us,   70
   And show us to be watchers: be not lost
   So poorly in your thoughts.
MACBETH   To know my deed, 'twere best not know
      myself.   [*Knocking within*
   Wake Duncan with thy knocking! I would thou
      couldst!   [*Exeunt*

SCENE III

Enter a Porter. *Knocking within*

PORTER   Here's a knocking indeed! If a man were
   porter of hell-gate, he should have old turning the key.
   [*Knocking within*] Knock, knock, knock! Who's there,
   i' the name of Beelzebub? Here's a farmer that hanged
   himself on the expectation of plenty: come in time; 5
   have napkins enow about you; here you'll sweat for't.

[*Knocking within*] Knock, knock! Who's there, in the
other devil's name? Faith, here's an equivocator that
could swear in both the scales against either scale; who
committed treason enough for God's sake, yet could 10
not equivocate to heaven: O, come in, equivocator.
[*Knocking within*] Knock, knock, knock! Who's there?
Faith, here's an English tailor come hither, for
stealing out of a French hose: come in, tailor; here you
may roast your goose. [*Knocking within*] Knock, 15
knock; never at quiet! What are you? But this place is
too cold for hell. I'll devil-porter it no further: I had
thought to have let in some of all professions, that go
the primrose way to the everlasting bonfire. [*Knocking
within*] Anon, anon! I pray you, remember the porter. 20
                              [*Opens the gate*

Enter MACDUFF *and* LENNOX

MACDUFF   Was it so late, friend, ere you went to bed,
  That you do lie so late?
PORTER   Faith, sir, we were carousing till the second cock.
MACDUFF   Is thy master stirring?
  Our knocking has awaked him; here he comes.   25

Re-enter MACBETH

LENNOX   Good morrow, noble sir.
MACBETH   Good morrow, both.
MACDUFF   Is the king stirring, worthy thane?
MACBETH   Not yet.
MACDUFF   He did command me to call timely on him:
  I have almost slipp'd the hour.
MACBETH   I'll bring you to him.
MACDUFF   I know this is a joyful trouble to you;   30
  But yet 'tis one.
MACBETH   The labour we delight in physics pain.
  This is the door.

3

MACDUFF   I'll make so bold to call,
For 'tis my limited service.   [*Exit*
LENNOX   Goes the king hence to-day?
MACBETH   He does: he did appoint so. 35
LENNOX   The night has been unruly: where we lay,
Our chimneys were blown down; and, as they say,
Lamentings heard i' th' air; strange screams of death;
And prophesying, with accents terrible,
Of dire combustion and confused events   40
New hatch'd to the woful time: the obscure bird
Clamour'd the livelong night: some say, the earth
Was feverous and did shake.
MACBETH   'Twas a rough night.
LENNOX   My young remembrance cannot parallel
A fellow to it.   45

Re-enter MACDUFF

MACDUFF   O horror, horror, horror! Tongue nor heart
Cannot conceive nor name thee!
MACBETH, LENNOX   What's the matter?
MACDUFF   Confusion now hath made his masterpiece!
Most sacrilegious murder hath broke ope
The Lord's anointed temple, and stole thence   50
The life o' the building!
MACBETH   What is't you say? the life?
LENNOX   Mean you his majesty?
MACDUFF   Approach the chamber, and destroy your sight
With a new Gorgon: do not bid me speak;
See, and then speak yourselves.
            [*Exeunt Macbeth and Lennox*
            Awake, awake!   55
Ring the alarum-bell. Murder and treason!
Banquo and Donalbain! Malcolm! awake!
Shake off this downy sleep, death's counterfeit,
And look on death itself! up, up, and see

The great doom's image! Malcolm! Banquo!　　60
As from your graves rise up, and walk like sprites,
To countenance this horror! Ring the bell.

[Alarum-bell rings

Re-enter LADY MACBETH

LADY MACBETH　What's the business,
That such a hideous trumpet calls to parley
The sleepers of the house? speak, speak!
MACDUFF　　　　　　　　　　　O gentle lady, 65
'Tis not for you to hear what I can speak:
The repetition, in a woman's ear,
Would murder as it fell.

Enter BANQUO

　　　　　　　　　O Banquo, Banquo,
Our royal master's murder'd!
LADY MACBETH　　　　　　　Woe, alas!
What, in our house?
BANQUO　　　　　　Too cruel any where.　　70
Dear Duff, I prithee, contradict thyself,
And say it is not so.

Re-enter MACBETH *and* LENNOX

MACBETH　Had I but died an hour before this chance,
I had lived a blessed time; for, from this instant,
There's nothing serious in mortality:　　75
All is but toys: renown and grace is dead;
The wine of life is drawn, and the mere lees
Is left this vault to brag of.

Enter MALCOLM *and* DONALBAIN

DONALBAIN　What is amiss?

MACBETH   You are, and do not know't:
The spring, the head, the fountain of your blood   80
Is stopp'd; the very source of it is stopp'd.

MACDUFF   Your royal father's murder'd.

MALCOLM   O, by whom?

LENNOX   Those of his chamber, as it seem'd, had
   done't:
Their hands and faces were all badg'd with blood;
So were their daggers, which unwiped we found   85
Upon their pillows:
They stared, and were distracted; no man's life
Was to be trusted with them.

MACBETH   O, yet I do repent me of my fury,
That I did kill them.

MACDUFF   Wherefore did you so?   90

MACBETH   Who can be wise, amazed, temperate and
   furious,
Loyal and neutral, in a moment? No man:
The expedition of my violent love
Outrun the pauser, reason. Here lay Duncan,
His silver skin laced with his golden blood;   95
And his gash'd stabs look'd like a breach in nature
For ruin's wasteful entrance: there, the murderers,
Steep'd in the colours of their trade, their daggers
Unmannerly breech'd with gore: who could refrain,
That had a heart to love, and in that heart   100
Courage to make's love known?

LADY MACBETH   Help me hence, ho!

MACDUFF   Look to the lady.

MALCOLM   [Aside to Donalbain] Why do we hold our
   tongues,
That most may claim this argument for ours?

DONALBAIN   [Aside to Malcolm] What should be spoken
   here, where our fate,
Hid in an auger-hole, may rush, and seize us?   105

Let's away;
Our tears are not yet brew'd.
MALCOLM   [*Aside to Donalbain*] Nor our strong sorrow
Upon the foot of motion.
BANQUO   Look to the lady:
                          [*Lady Macbeth is carried out*
And when we have our naked frailties hid,
That suffer in exposure, let us meet,   110
And question this most bloody piece of work,
To know it further. Fears and scruples shake us:
In the great hand of God I stand, and thence
Against the undivulg'd pretence I fight
Of treasonous malice.
MACDUFF   And so do I.
ALL   So all.   115
MACBETH   Let's briefly put on manly readiness,
And meet i' the hall together.
ALL   Well contented.
              [*Exeunt all except Malcolm and Donalbain*
MALCOLM   What will you do? Let's not consort with
    them:
To show an unfelt sorrow is an office
Which the false man does easy. I'll to England.   120
DONALBAIN   To Ireland I; our separated fortune
Shall keep us both the safer: where we are,
There's daggers in men's smiles: the near in blood,
The nearer bloody.
MALCOLM   This murderous shaft that's shot
Hath not yet lighted, and our safest way   125
Is to avoid the aim. Therefore, to horse;
And let us not be dainty of leave-taking,
But shift away: there's warrant in that theft
Which steals itself, when there's no mercy left.
                                        [*Exeunt*

SCENE IV.   *Outside* MACBETH'S *castle*

Enter ROSS *and an* Old Man

OLD MAN   Threescore and ten I can remember well:
    Within the volume of which time I have seen
    Hours dreadful and things strange; but this sore night
    Hath trifled former knowings.
ROSS   Ah, good father,
    Thou seest, the heavens, as troubled with man's act,   5
    Threaten his bloody stage: by the clock 'tis day,
    And yet dark night strangles the travelling lamp:
    Is't night's predominance, or the day's shame,
    That darkness does the face of earth entomb,
    When living light should kiss it?
OLD MAN   'Tis unnatural,   10
    Even like the deed that's done. On Tuesday last,
    A falcon, towering in her pride of place,
    Was by a mousing owl hawk'd at and kill'd.
ROSS   And Duncan's horses—a thing most strange and
    certain—
    Beauteous and swift, the minions of their race,   15
    Turn'd wild in nature, broke their stalls, flung out,
    Contending 'gainst obedience, as they would make
    War with mankind.
OLD MAN   'Tis said they eat each other.
ROSS   They did so, to the amazement of mine eyes,
    That look'd upon't. Here comes the good Macduff.   20

Enter MACDUFF

    How goes the world, sir, now?
MACDUFF   Why, see you not?
ROSS   Is't known who did this more than bloody deed?
MACDUFF   Those that Macbeth hath slain.

ROSS　　　　　　　　　　　Alas, the day!
　What good could they pretend?

MACDUFF　　　　　　　They were suborn'd:
　Malcolm and Donalbain, the king's two sons,　　25
　Are stol'n away and fled; which puts upon them
　Suspicion of the deed.

ROSS　　　　　　　'Gainst nature still:
　Thriftless ambition, that wilt ravin up
　Thine own life's means! Then 'tis most like
　The sovereignty will fall upon Macbeth.　　　30

MACDUFF　He is already named, and gone to Scone
　To be invested.

ROSS　　　　　Where is Duncan's body?

MACDUFF　Carried to Colme-kill,
　The sacred storehouse of his predecessors,
　And guardian of their bones.

ROSS　　　　　　　　　Will you to Scone?　35

MACDUFF　No, cousin, I'll to Fife.

ROSS　　　　　　　　Well, I will thither.

MACDUFF　Well, may you see things well done there:
　adieu!
　Lest our old robes sit easier than our new!

ROSS　Farewell, father.

OLD MAN　God's benison go with you, and with those　40
　That would make good of bad, and friends of foes!

　　　　　　　　　　　　　　　[*Exeunt*

ACT III

Scene I. *Forres. The palace*

Enter BANQUO

BANQUO Thou hast it now: king, Cawdor, Glamis, all,
As the weird women promised, and, I fear,
Thou play'dst most foully for't: yet it was said
It should not stand in thy posterity,
But that myself should be the root and father   5
Of many kings. If there come truth from them—
As upon thee, Macbeth, their speeches shine—
Why, by the verities on thee made good,
May they not be my oracles as well,
And set me up in hope? But hush; no more.   10

Sennet sounded. Enter MACBETH, *as king;* LADY MACBETH,
as queen; LENNOX, ROSS, Lords, Ladies, *and* Attendants

MACBETH Here's our chief guest.
LADY MACBETH   If he had been forgotten,
It had been as a gap in our great feast,
And all-thing unbecoming.
MACBETH To-night we hold a solemn supper, sir,
And I'll request your presence.
BANQUO   Let your highness   15
Command upon me; to the which my duties
Are with a most indissoluble tie
For ever knit.
MACBETH Ride you this afternoon?
BANQUO Ay, my good lord.   20
MACBETH We should have else desired your good advice,
Which still hath been both grave and prosperous,

In this day's council; but we'll take to-morrow.
Is't far you ride?

BANQUO As far, my lord, as will fill up the time   25
'Twixt this and supper: go not my horse the better,
I must become a borrower of the night
For a dark hour or twain.

MACBETH   Fail not our feast.

BANQUO My lord, I will not.

MACBETH We hear, our bloody cousins are bestow'd   30
In England and in Ireland, not confessing
Their cruel parricide, filling their hearers
With strange invention: but of that to-morrow,
When therewithal we shall have cause of state
Craving us jointly. Hie you to horse: adieu,   35
Till you return at night. Goes Fleance with you?

BANQUO Ay, my good lord: our time does call upon's.

MACBETH I wish your horses swift and sure of foot;
And so I do commend you to their backs.
Farewell.   [Exit Banquo 40
Let every man be master of his time,
Till seven at night; to make society
The sweeter welcome, we will keep ourself
Till supper-time alone: while then, God be with you!
        [Exeunt all except Macbeth and an Attendant
Sirrah, a word with you: attend those men   45
Our pleasure?

ATTENDANT They are, my lord, without the palace-gate.

MACBETH Bring them before us.   [Exit Attendant
                    To be thus is nothing;
But to be safely thus. Our fears in Banquo
Stick deep; and in his royalty of nature   50
Reigns that which would be fear'd: 'tis much he dares:
And, to that dauntless temper of his mind,
He hath a wisdom that doth guide his valour
To act in safety. There is none but he

Whose being I do fear: and under him   55
My Genius is rebuked; as, it is said,
Mark Antony's was by Cæsar. He chid the sisters,
When first they put the name of king upon me,
And bade them speak to him; then prophet-like
They hail'd him father to a line of kings: 60
Upon my head they placed a fruitless crown,
And put a barren sceptre in my gripe,
Thence to be wrench'd with an unlineal hand,
No son of mine succeeding. If't be so,
For Banquo's issue have I filed my mind;   65
For them the gracious Duncan have I murder'd;
Put rancours in the vessel of my peace
Only for them, and mine eternal jewel
Given to the common enemy of man,
To make them kings, the seed of Banquo kings!   70
Rather than so, come, fate, into the list,
And champion me to the utterance! Who's there?

Re-enter Attendant, *with two* Murderers

Now go to the door, and stay there till we call.
                              [*Exit Attendant*
Was it not yesterday we spoke together?
FIRST MURDERER   It was, so please your highness.
MACBETH   Well then, now 75
Have you consider'd of my speeches? Know
That it was he in the times past which held you
So under fortune; which you thought had been
Our innocent self: this I made good to you
In our last conference, pass'd in probation with you, 80
How you were borne in hand, how cross'd, the
    instruments,
Who wrought with them, and all things else that might
To half a soul and tò a notion crazed
Say "Thus did Banquo."

FIRST MURDERER   You made it known to us.

MACBETH   I did so; and went further, which is now   85
    Our point of second meeting. Do you find
    Your patience so predominant in your nature,
    That you can let this go? Are you so gospell'd
    To pray for this good man and for his issue,
    Whose heavy hand hath bow'd you to the grave,   90
    And beggar'd yours for ever?

FIRST MURDERER   We are men, my liege.

MACBETH   Ay, in the catalogue ye go for men;
    As hounds and greyhounds, mongrels, spaniels,
      curs,
    Shoughs, water-rugs, and demi-wolves are clept
    All by the name of dogs: the valued file   95
    Distinguishes the swift, the slow, the subtle,
    The housekeeper, the hunter, every one
    According to the gift which bounteous nature
    Hath in him closed, whereby he does receive
    Particular addition, from the bill   100
    That writes them all alike: and so of men.
    Now, if you have a station in the file,
    Not i' the worst rank of manhood, say't;
    And I will put that business in your bosoms,
    Whose execution takes your enemy off,   105
    Grapples you to the heart and love of us,
    Who wear our health but sickly in his life,
    Which in his death were perfect.

SECOND MURDERER   I am one, my liege,
    Whom the vile blows and buffets of the world
    Have so incens'd that I am reckless what   110
    I do to spite the world.

FIRST MURDERER   And I another
    So weary with disasters, tugg'd with fortune,
    That I would set my life on any chance,
    To mend it or be rid on't.

MACBETH   Both of you
  Know Banquo was your enemy.

BOTH MURDERERS   True, my lord.   115

MACBETH   So is he mine, and in such bloody distance
  That every minute of his being thrusts
  Against my near'st of life; and though I could
  With barefaced power sweep him from my sight,
  And bid my will avouch it, yet I must not,   120
  For certain friends that are both his and mine,
  Whose loves I may not drop, but wail his fall
  Who I myself struck down: and thence it is
  That I to your assistance do make love,
  Masking the business from the common eye   125
  For sundry weighty reasons.

SECOND MURDERER   We shall, my lord,
  Perform what you command us.

FIRST MURDERER   Though our lives—

MACBETH   Your spirits shine through you. Within this
    hour at most,
  I will advise you where to plant yourselves,
  Acquaint you with the perfect spy o' the time,   130
  The moment on't; for't must be done to-night,
  And something from the palace; always thought
  That I require a clearness: and with him—
  To leave no rubs nor botches in the work—
  Fleance his son, that keeps him company,   135
  Whose absence is no less material to me
  Than is his father's, must embrace the fate
  Of that dark hour. Resolve yourselves apart:
  I'll come to you anon.

BOTH MURDERERS   We are resolved, my lord.

MACBETH   I'll call upon you straight: abide within.   140
                      [*Exeunt Murderers*
  It is concluded: Banquo, thy soul's flight,
  If it find heaven, must find it out to-night.   [*Exit*

Scene II. *The palace*

Enter LADY MACBETH *and a* Servant

LADY MACBETH　Is Banquo gone from court?

SERVANT　Ay, madam, but returns again to-night.

LADY MACBETH　Say to the king, I would attend his leisure
For a few words.

SERVANT　　　　　Madam, I will.　　　　　[*Exit*

LADY MACBETH　　　　　Naught's had, all's spent, 5
Where our desire is got without content:
'Tis safer to be that which we destroy,
Than by destruction dwell in doubtful joy.

Enter MACBETH

How now, my lord! why do you keep alone,
Of sorriest fancies your companions making;
Using those thoughts which should indeed have died 10
With them they think on? Things without all remedy
Should be without regard: what's done is done.

MACBETH　We have scotch'd the snake, not kill'd it:
She'll close and be herself, whilst our poor malice
Remains in danger of her former tooth. 15
But let the frame of things disjoint, both the worlds suffer,
Ere we will eat our meal in fear, and sleep
In the affliction of these terrible dreams
That shake us nightly: better be with the dead,
Whom we, to gain our peace, have sent to peace, 20
Than on the torture of the mind to lie
In restless ecstasy. Duncan is in his grave;
After life's fitful fever he sleeps well;
Treason has done his worst: nor steel, nor poison,

Malice domestic, foreign levy, nothing,   25
Can touch him further.

LADY MACBETH   Come on;
Gentle my lord, sleek o'er your rugged looks;
Be bright and jovial among your guests to-night.

MACBETH   So shall I, love; and so, I pray, be you:
Let your remembrance apply to Banquo;   30
Present him eminence, both with eye and tongue:
Unsafe the while that we
Must lave our honours in these flattering streams,
And make our faces vizards to our hearts,
Disguising what they are.

LADY MACBETH   You must leave this.   35

MACBETH   O, full of scorpions is my mind, dear wife!
Thou know'st that Banquo and his Fleance live.

LADY MACBETH   But in them nature's copy's not eterne.

MACBETH   There's comfort yet; they are assailable;
Then be thou jocund: ere the bat hath flown   40
His cloister'd flight, ere to black Hecate's summons
The shard-borne beetle with his drowsy hums
Hath rung night's yawning peal, there shall be done
A deed of dreadful note.

LADY MACBETH   What's to be done?

MACBETH   Be innocent of the knowledge, dearest chuck, 45
Till thou applaud the deed. Come, seeling night,
Scarf up the tender eye of pitiful day;
And with thy bloody and invisible hand
Cancel and tear to pieces that great bond
Which keeps me pale! Light thickens, and the crow 50
Makes wing to the rooky wood:
Good things of day begin to droop and drowse,
Whiles night's black agents to their preys do rouse.
Thou marvell'st at my words: but hold thee still;
Things bad begun make strong themselves by ill: 55
So, prithee, go with me.   [Exeunt

SCENE III. *A park near the palace*

Enter three Murderers

FIRST MURDERER　　But who did bid thee join with us?
THIRD MURDERER　　　　　　　　　　Macbeth.
SECOND MURDERER　　He needs not our mistrust; since he
　　delivers
　　Our offices, and what we have to do,
　　To the direction just.
FIRST MURDERER　　　　　Then stand with us.
　　The west yet glimmers with some streaks of day:　　5
　　Now spurs the lated traveller apace
　　To gain the timely inn; and near approaches
　　The subject of our watch.
THIRD MURDERER　　　　　Hark! I hear horses.
BANQUO　[*Within*] Give us a light there, ho!
SECOND MURDERER　　　　　　　Then 'tis he: the rest
　　That are within the note of expectation　　　　10
　　Already are i' the court.
FIRST MURDERER　　　　　His horses go about.
THIRD MURDERER　　Almost a mile: but he does usually,
　　So all men do, from hence to the palace-gate
　　Make it their walk.
SECOND MURDERER　　A light, a light!
THIRD MURDERER　　　　　　　　　　'Tis he.
FIRST MURDERER　　Stand to't.　　　　　　　　15

Enter BANQUO, *and* FLEANCE *with a torch*

BANQUO　It will be rain to-night.
FIRST MURDERER　　　　　　　Let it come down.
　　　　　　　　　　　　[*They assault Banquo*
BANQUO　O, treachery! Fly, good Fleance, fly, fly, fly!
　　Thou mayst revenge. O slave! [*Dies. Fleance escapes*

THIRD MURDERER   Who did strike out the light?
FIRST MURDERER   Was't not the way?
THIRD MURDERER   There's but one down; the son is fled.
SECOND MURDERER   We have lost 20
   Best half of our affair.
FIRST MURDERER   Well, let's away, and say how much is
   done.   [*Exeunt*

SCENE IV.   *The same. Hall in the palace*

A banquet prepared. Enter MACBETH, LADY MACBETH,
   ROSS, LENNOX, Lords, *and* Attendants

MACBETH   You know your own degrees, sit down: at first
   And last the hearty welcome.
LORDS   Thanks to your majesty.
MACBETH   Ourself will mingle with society,
   And play the humble host.
   Our hostess keeps her state, but in best time   5
   We will require her welcome.
LADY MACBETH   Pronounce it for me, sir, to all our
   friends:
   For my heart speaks they are welcome.
MACBETH   See, they encounter thee with their hearts'
   thanks.
   Both sides are even: here I'll sit i' the midst: 10

Enter first Murderer *to the door*

   Be large in mirth; anon we'll drink a measure
   The table round. [*Approaching the door*] There's blood
   upon thy face.
MURDERER   'Tis Banquo's then.
MACBETH   'Tis better thee without than he within.
   Is he dispatch'd?   15

MURDERER   My lord, his throat is cut; that I did for him.

MACBETH   Thou art the best o' the cut-throats: yet he's good
     That did the like for Fleance: if thou didst it,
     Thou art the nonpareil.

MURDERER   Most royal sir,
     Fleance is scaped.   20

MACBETH   Then comes my fit again: I had else been perfect;
     Whole as the marble, founded as the rock,
     As broad and general as the casing air:
     But now I am cabin'd, cribb'd, confined, bound in
     To saucy doubts and fears. But Banquo's safe?   25

MURDERER   Ay, my good lord: safe in a ditch he bides,
     With twenty trenched gashes on his head;
     The least a death to nature.

MACBETH   Thanks for that:
     There the grown serpent lies; the worm that's fled
     Hath nature that in time will venom breed,   30
     No teeth for the present. Get thee gone: to-morrow
     We'll hear, ourselves, again.   [*Exit Murderer*

LADY MACBETH   My royal lord,
     You do not give the cheer: the feast is sold
     That is not often vouch'd, while 'tis a-making,
     'Tis given with welcome: to feed were best at home;   35
     From thence the sauce to meat is ceremony;
     Meeting were bare without it.

MACBETH   Sweet remembrancer!
     Now, good digestion wait on appetite,
     And health on both!

LENNOX   May't please your highness sit.
          [*The Ghost of Banquo enters, and sits in
                              Macbeth's place*

MACBETH   Here had we now our country's honour roof'd,   40
     Were the graced person of our Banquo present;

Who may I rather challenge for unkindness
Than pity for mischance!

ROSS   His absence, sir,
Lays blame upon his promise. Please't your highness
To grace us with your royal company.   45

MACBETH   The table's full.

LENNOX   Here is a place reserv'd, sir.

MACBETH   Where?

LENNOX   Here, my good lord. What is't that moves
your highness?

MACBETH   Which of you have done this?

LORDS   What, my good lord?

MACBETH   Thou canst not say I did it: never shake   50
Thy gory locks at me.

ROSS   Gentlemen, rise; his highness is not well.

LADY MACBETH   Sit, worthy friends: my lord is often
thus,
And hath been from his youth: pray you, keep seat;
The fit is momentary; upon a thought   55
He will again be well: if much you note him,
You shall offend him, and extend his passion:
Feed, and regard him not. Are you a man?

MACBETH   Ay, and a bold one, that dare look on that
Which might appal the devil.

LADY MACBETH   O proper stuff!   60
This is the very painting of your fear:
This is the air-drawn dagger which, you said,
Led you to Duncan. O, these flaws and starts,
Impostors to true fear, would well become
A woman's story at a winter's fire,   65
Authorized by her grandam. Shame itself!
Why do you make such faces? When all's done,
You look but on a stool.

MACBETH   Prithee, see there! behold! look! lo! how
say you?

Why, what care I? If thou canst nod, speak too.   70
If charnel-houses and our graves must send
Those that we bury back, our monuments
Shall be the maws of kites.   *[Ghost disappears*

LADY MACBETH   What, quite unmann'd in folly?

MACBETH   If I stand here, I saw him.

LADY MACBETH   Fie, for shame!

MACBETH   Blood hath been shed ere now, i' the olden
    time,   75
Ere humane statute purged the gentle weal;
Ay, and since too, murders have been perform'd
Too terrible for the ear: the time has been,
That, when the brains were out, the man would die,
And there an end; but now they rise again,   80
With twenty mortal murders on their crowns,
And push us from our stools: this is more strange
Than such a murder is.

LADY MACBETH   My worthy lord,
Your noble friends do lack you.

MACBETH   I do forget:
Do not muse at me, my most worthy friends;   85
I have a strange infirmity, which is nothing
To those that know me. Come, love and health to
    all;
Then I'll sit down. Give me some wine, fill full.
I drink to the general joy o' the whole table,
And to our dear friend Banquo, whom we miss;   90
Would he were here! to all, and him, we thirst,
And all to all.

LORDS   Our duties, and the pledge.

Re-enter Ghost

MACBETH   Avaunt! and quit my sight! let the earth
    hide thee!

Thy bones are marrowless, thy blood is cold;
Thou hast no speculation in those eyes   95
Which thou dost glare with!

LADY MACBETH   Think of this, good peers,
But as a thing of custom: 'tis no other;
Only it spoils the pleasure of the time.

MACBETH   What man dare, I dare:
Approach thou like the rugged Russian bear,   100
The arm'd rhinoceros, or the Hyrcan tiger;
Take any shape but that, and my firm nerves
Shall never tremble: or be alive again,
And dare me to the desert with thy sword;
If trembling I inhabit then, protest me   105
The baby of a girl. Hence, horrible shadow!
Unreal mockery, hence!   [*Ghost disappears*
                    Why, so; being gone,
I am a man again. Pray you, sit still.

LADY MACBETH   You have displaced the mirth, broke
    the good meeting,
With most admired disorder.

MACBETH   Can such things be,   110
And overcome us like a summer's cloud,
Without our special wonder? You make me strange
Even to the disposition that I owe,
When now I think you can behold such sights,
And keep the natural ruby of your cheeks,   115
When mine is blanch'd with fear.

ROSS   What sights, my lord?

LADY MACBETH   I pray you, speak not; he grows worse
    and worse;
Question enrages him: at once, good night:
Stand not upon the order of your going,
But go at once.

LENNOX   Good night; and better health   120
Attend his majesty!

LADY MACBETH   A kind good night to all!
          [*Exeunt all except Macbeth and Lady Macbeth*
MACBETH   It will have blood; they say blood will have
     blood:
  Stones have been known to move and trees to speak:
  Augures and understood relations have
  By magot-pies and choughs and rooks brought forth 125
  The secret'st man of blood. What is the night?
LADY MACBETH   Almost at odds with morning, which is
     which.
MACBETH   How say'st thou, that Macduff denies his
     person
  At our great bidding?
LADY MACBETH   Did you send to him, sir?
MACBETH   I hear it by the way; but I will send: 130
  There's not a one of them but in his house
  I keep a servant fee'd. I will to-morrow—
  And betimes I will—to the weird sisters:
  More shall they speak; for now I am bent to know,
  By the worst means, the worst. For mine own good, 135
  All causes shall give way: I am in blood
  Stepp'd in so far that, should I wade no more,
  Returning were as tedious as go o'er:
  Strange things I have in head, that will to hand;
  Which must be acted ere they may be scann'd.   140
LADY MACBETH   You lack the season of all natures, sleep.
MACBETH   Come, we'll to sleep. My strange and self-
     abuse
  Is the initiate fear that wants hard use:
  We are yet but young in deed.   [*Exeunt*

SCENE V. *A heath*

Thunder. Enter the three Witches, *meeting* HECATE

FIRST WITCH   Why, how now, Hecate! you look angerly.

HECATE   Have I not reason, beldams as you are,
Saucy and overbold? How did you dare
To trade and traffic with Macbeth
In riddles and affairs of death;   5
And I, the mistress of your charms,
The close contriver of all harms,
Was never call'd to bear my part,
Or show the glory of our art?
And, which is worse, all you have done   10
Hath been but for a wayward son,
Spiteful and wrathful; who, as others do,
Loves for his own ends, not for you.
But make amends now: get you gone,
And at the pit of Acheron   15
Meet me i' the morning: thither he
Will come to know his destiny:
Your vessels and your spells provide,
Your charms and every thing beside.
I am for the air; this night I'll spend   20
Unto a dismal and a fatal end:
Great business must be wrought ere noon:
Upon the corner of the moon
There hangs a vaporous drop profound;
I'll catch it ere it come to ground: 25
And that, distill'd by magic sleights,
Shall raise such artificial sprites
As by the strength of their illusion
Shall draw him on to his confusion:
He shall spurn fate, scorn death, and bear   30
His hopes 'bove wisdom, grace and fear:

And you all know security
Is mortals' chiefest enemy.
[*Music and a song within*, "Come away, come away," &c.
　Hark! I am call'd; my little spirit, see,
　Sits in a foggy cloud, and stays for me.　　　[*Exit* 35
FIRST WITCH　Come, let's make haste; she'll soon be
　　back again.　　　　　　　　　　　　　[*Exeunt*

SCENE VI.　*Forres. The palace*

Enter LENNOX *and another* Lord

LENNOX　My former speeches have but hit your thoughts,
　Which can interpret further: only, I say,
　Things have been strangely borne. The gracious
　　Duncan
　Was pitied of Macbeth: marry, he was dead:
　And the right-valiant Banquo walk'd too late;　　5
　Whom, you may say, if't please you, Fleance kill'd,
　For Fleance fled: men must not walk too late.
　Who cannot want the thought, how monstrous
　It was for Malcolm and for Donalbain
　To kill their gracious father? damned fact!　　10
　How it did grieve Macbeth! did he not straight
　In pious rage the two delinquents tear,
　That were the slaves of drink and thralls of sleep?
　Was not that nobly done? Ay, and wisely too;
　For 'twould have anger'd any heart alive　　15
　To hear the men deny't. So that, I say,
　He has borne all things well: and I do think
　That, had he Duncan's sons under his key—
　As, an't please heaven, he shall not—they should find
　What 'twere to kill a father; so should Fleance.　　20
　But, peace! for from broad words, and 'cause he fail'd

His presence at the tyrant's feast, I hear
Macduff lives in disgrace: sir, can you tell
Where he bestows himself?

LORD   The son of Duncan,
From whom this tyrant holds the due of birth,   25
Lives in the English court, and is received
Of the most pious Edward with such grace
That the malevolence of fortune nothing
Takes from his high respect: thither Macduff
Is gone to pray the holy king, upon his aid   30
To wake Northumberland and warlike Siward:
That, by the help of these—with Him above
To ratify the work—we may again
Give to our tables meat, sleep to our nights,
Free from our feasts and banquets bloody knives,   35
Do faithful homage, and receive free honours;
All which we pine for now: and this report
Hath so exasperate the king that he
Prepares for some attempt of war.

LENNOX   Sent he to Macduff?

LORD   He did: and with an absolute "Sir, not I,"   40
The cloudy messenger turns me his back,
And hums, as who should say, "You'll rue the time
That clogs me with this answer."

LENNOX   And that well might
Advise him to a caution, to hold what distance
His wisdom can provide. Some holy angel   45
Fly to the court of England and unfold
His message ere he come; that a swift blessing
May soon return to this our suffering country
Under a hand accursed!

LORD   I'll send my prayers with him.
                                        [Exeunt

ACT IV

Scene I. *A cavern. In the middle, a boiling caldron*

Thunder. Enter the three Witches

FIRST WITCH　Thrice the brinded cat hath mew'd.
SECOND WITCH　Thrice and once the hedge-pig whined.
THIRD WITCH　Harpier cries "'tis time, 'tis time."
FIRST WITCH　Round about the caldron go;
　In the poison'd entrails throw.　　　　　　5
　Toad, that under cold stone
　Days and nights hast thirty-one
　Swelter'd venom sleeping got,
　Boil thou first i' the charmed pot.
ALL　Double, double toil and trouble;　　　10
　Fire burn and caldron bubble.
SECOND WITCH　Fillet of a fenny snake,
　In the caldron boil and bake;
　Eye of newt and toe of frog,
　Wool of bat and tongue of dog,　　　　　15
　Adder's fork and blind-worm's sting,
　Lizard's leg and howlet's wing,
　For a charm of powerful trouble,
　Like a hell-broth boil and bubble.
ALL　Double, double toil and trouble;　　　20
　Fire burn and caldron bubble.
THIRD WITCH　Scale of dragon, tooth of wolf,
　Witches' mummy, maw and gulf
　Of the ravin'd salt-sea shark,
　Root of hemlock digg'd i' the dark,　　　25
　Liver of blaspheming Jew,
　Gall of goat, and slips of yew

Sliver'd in the moon's eclipse,
Nose of Turk, and Tartar's lips,
Finger of birth-strangled babe   30
Ditch-deliver'd by a drab,
Make the gruel thick and slab:
Add thereto a tiger's chaudron,
For the ingredients of our caldron.
ALL   Double, double toil and trouble;   35
Fire burn and caldron bubble.
SECOND WITCH   Cool it with a baboon's blood,
Then the charm is firm and good.

Enter HECATE

HECATE   O, well done! I commend your pains;
And every one shall share i' the gains: 40
And now about the caldron sing,
Like elves and fairies in a ring,
Enchanting all that you put in.
                    [*Music and song*, "Black spirits," &c.
                              [*Hecate retires*
SECOND WITCH   By the pricking of my thumbs,
Something wicked this way comes: 45
                    Open, locks,
                    Whoever knocks!

Enter MACBETH

MACBETH   How now, you secret, black, and midnight
    hags!
What is't you do?
ALL   A deed without a name.
MACBETH   I conjure you, by that which you profess, 50
Howe'er you come to know it, answer me:
Though you untie the winds and let them fight
Against the churches; though the yesty waves
Confound and swallow navigation up;

Though bladed corn be lodged and trees blown down; 55
Though castles topple on their warders' heads;
Though palaces and pyramids do slope
Their heads to their foundations; though the treasure
Of nature's germens tumble all together,
Even till destruction sicken; answer me   60
To what I ask you.

FIRST WITCH   Speak.
SECOND WITCH   Demand.
THIRD WITCH   We'll answer.
FIRST WITCH   Say, if thou'dst rather hear it from our
    mouths,
Or from our masters?
MACBETH   Call 'em, let me see 'em.
FIRST WITCH   Pour in sow's blood, that hath eaten
Her nine farrow; grease that's sweaten   65
From the murderer's gibbet throw
Into the flame.
ALL   Come, high or low;
Thyself and office deftly show!

Thunder. First Apparition: *an armed Head*

MACBETH   Tell me, thou unknown power,—
FIRST WITCH   He knows thy thought:
Hear his speech, but say thou naught.   70
FIRST APPARITION   Macbeth! Macbeth! Macbeth! be-
    ware Macduff:
Beware the thane of Fife. Dismiss me: enough.
                                        [*Descends*
MACBETH   Whate'er thou art, for thy good caution,
    thanks;
Thou hast harp'd my fear aright: but one word more,—
FIRST WITCH   He will not be commanded: here's another, 75
More potent than the first.

Thunder.   Second Apparition: *a bloody Child*

SECOND APPARITION   Macbeth! Macbeth! Macbeth!
MACBETH   Had I three ears, I'ld hear thee.
SECOND APPARITION   Be bloody, bold, and resolute;
    laugh to scorn
  The power of man, for none of woman born   80
  Shall harm Macbeth.   [*Descends*
MACBETH   Then live, Macduff: what need I fear of thee?
  But yet I'll make assurance double sure,
  And take a bond of fate: thou shalt not live;
  That I may tell pale-hearted fear it lies,   85
  And sleep in spite of thunder.

Thunder. Third Apparition: *a Child crowned, with a
tree in his hand*

                What is this,
  That rises like the issue of a king,
  And wears upon his baby-brow the round
  And top of sovereignty?
ALL   Listen, but speak not to't.
THIRD APPARITION   Be lion-mettled, proud; and take
    no care   90
  Who chafes, who frets, or where conspirers are:
  Macbeth shall never vanquish'd be until
  Great Birnam wood to high Dunsinane hill
  Shall come against him.   [*Descends*
MACBETH   That will never be:
  Who can impress the forest, bid the tree   95
  Unfix his earth-bound root? Sweet bodements! good!
  Rebellion's head, rise never till the wood
  Of Birnam rise, and our high-placed Macbeth
  Shall live the lease of nature, pay his breath
  To time and mortal custom. Yet my heart   100

Throbs to know one thing: tell me, if your art
Can tell so much: shall Banquo's issue ever
Reign in this kingdom?

ALL   Seek to know no more.

MACBETH   I will be satisfied: deny me this,
And an eternal curse fall on you! Let me know.   105
Why sinks that caldron? and what noise is this?

[*Hautboys*

FIRST WITCH   Show!

SECOND WITCH   Show!

THIRD WITCH   Show!

ALL   Show his eyes, and grieve his heart;   110
Come like shadows, so depart!

A show of Eight Kings, *the last with a glass in his hand;*
BANQUO's Ghost *following*

MACBETH   Thou art too like the spirit of Banquo; down!
Thy crown does sear mine eyeballs: and thy hair,
Thou other gold-bound brow, is like the first:
A third is like the former. Filthy hags!   115
Why do you show me this? A fourth? Start, eyes!
What, will the line stretch out to the crack of doom?
Another yet? A seventh? I'll see no more:
And yet the eighth appears, who bears a glass
Which shows me many more; and some I see   120
That twofold balls and treble sceptres carry:
Horrible sight! Now I see 'tis true;
For the blood-bolter'd Banquo smiles upon me,
And points at them for his. What, is this so?

FIRST WITCH   Ay, sir, all this is so: but why   125
Stands Macbeth thus amazedly?
Come, sisters, cheer we up his sprites,
And show the best of our delights:
I'll charm the air to give a sound,
While you perform your antic round;   130

That this great king may kindly say
Our duties did his welcome pay.
[*Music. The Witches dance, and then vanish, with Hecate*
MACBETH   Where are they? Gone? Let this pernicious
    hour
Stand aye accursed in the calendar!
Come in, without there!

Enter LENNOX

LENNOX   What's your grace's will?   135
MACBETH   Saw you the weird sisters?
LENNOX   No, my lord.
MACBETH   Came they not by you?
LENNOX   No, indeed, my lord.
MACBETH   Infected be the air whereon they ride,
And damn'd all those that trust them! I did hear
The galloping of horse: who was't came by?   140
LENNOX   'Tis two or three, my lord, that bring you word
Macduff is fled to England.
MACBETH   Fled to England!
LENNOX   Ay, my good lord.
MACBETH   Time, thou anticipatest my dread exploits:
The flighty purpose never is o'ertook   145
Unless the deed go with it: from this moment
The very firstlings of my heart shall be
The firstlings of my hand. And even now,
To crown my thoughts with acts, be it thought and
    done:
The castle of Macduff I will surprise;   150
Seize upon Fife; give to the edge o' the sword
His wife, his babes, and all unfortunate souls
That trace him in his line. No boasting like a fool;
This deed I'll do before this purpose cool:
But no more sights!—Where are these gentlemen?   155
Come, bring me where they are.   [*Exeunt*

SCENE II. *Fife.* MACDUFF'S *castle*

Enter LADY MACDUFF, *her* Son, *and* ROSS

LADY MACDUFF   What had he done, to make him fly the
   land?
ROSS   You must have patience, madam.
LADY MACDUFF   He had none:
   His flight was madness: when our actions do not,
   Our fears do make us traitors.
ROSS   You know not
   Whether it was his wisdom or his fear.   5
LADY MACDUFF   Wisdom! to leave his wife, to leave his
   babes,
   His mansion and his titles in a place
   From whence himself does fly? He loves us not;
   He wants the natural touch: for the poor wren,
   The most diminutive of birds, will fight,   10
   Her young ones in her nest, against the owl.
   All is the fear, and nothing is the love;
   As little is the wisdom, where the flight
   So runs against all reason.
ROSS   My dearest coz,
   I pray you, school yourself: but for your husband,   15
   He's noble, wise, judicious, and best knows
   The fits o' the season. I dare not speak much further:
   But cruel are the times, when we are traitors,
   And do not know ourselves; when we hold rumour
   From what we fear, yet know not what we fear,   20
   But float upon a wild and violent sea
   Each way and move. I take my leave of you:
   Shall not be long but I'll be here again:
   Things at the worst will cease, or else climb upward
   To what they were before. My pretty cousin,   25
   Blessing upon you!

LADY MACDUFF Father'd he is, and yet he's fatherless.

ROSS I am so much a fool, should I stay longer,
  It would be my disgrace and your discomfort:
  I take my leave at once.   [*Exit*

LADY MACDUFF   Sirrah, your father's dead: 30
  And what will you do now? How will you live?

SON As birds do, mother.

LADY MACDUFF   What, with worms and flies?

SON With what I get, I mean; and so do they.

LADY MACDUFF Poor bird! thou'ldst never fear the net
    nor lime,
  The pitfall nor the gin.   35

SON Why should I, mother? Poor birds they are not
    set for.
  My father is not dead, for all your saying.

LADY MACDUFF Yes, he is dead: how wilt thou do for
    a father?

SON Nay, how will you do for a husband?

LADY MACDUFF Why, I can buy me twenty at any market. 40

SON Then you'll buy 'em to sell again.

LADY MACDUFF Thou speak'st with all thy wit, and yet,
    i' faith,
  With wit enough for thee.

SON Was my father a traitor, mother?

LADY MACDUFF Ay, that he was.   45

SON What is a traitor?

LADY MACDUFF Why, one that swears and lies.

SON And be all traitors that do so?

LADY MACDUFF Every one that does so is a traitor, and
    must be hanged.   50

SON And must they all be hanged that swear and lie?

LADY MACDUFF Every one.

SON Who must hang them?

LADY MACDUFF Why, the honest men.

SON Then the liars and swearers are fools; for there 55

are liars and swearers enow to beat the honest men, and
hang up them.

LADY MACDUFF　Now, God help thee, poor monkey! But
how wilt thou do for a father?

SON　If he were dead, you'ld weep for him: if you 60
would not, it were a good sign that I should quickly
have a new father.

LADY MACDUFF　Poor prattler, how thou talk'st!

Enter a Messenger

MESSENGER　Bless you, fair dame! I am not to you
known,
Though in your state of honour I am perfect. 65
I doubt some danger does approach you nearly:
If you will take a homely man's advice,
Be not found here; hence, with your little ones.
To fright you thus, methinks, I am too savage;
To do worse to you were fell cruelty, 70
Which is too nigh your person. Heaven preserve you!
I dare abide no longer. [Exit

LADY MACDUFF　　　　　　Whither should I fly?
I have done no harm. But I remember now
I am in this earthly world; where to do harm
Is often laudable, to do good sometime 75
Accounted dangerous folly: why then, alas,
Do I put up that womanly defence,
To say I have done no harm?

Enter Murderers

　　　　　　　　　　　What are these faces?

FIRST MURDERER　Where is your husband?

LADY MACDUFF　I hope, in no place so unsanctified 80
Where such as thou mayst find him.

FIRST MURDERER　　　　　　He's a traitor.

SON　Thou liest, thou shag-ear'd villain!

FIRST MURDERER   What, you egg!
                                        [*Stabbing him*

   Young fry of treachery!
SON   He has kill'd me, mother:
   Run away, I pray you!   [*Dies*
                    [*Exit Lady Macduff, crying* "Murder!" *and*
                              pursued by the Murderers

SCENE III. *England. Before the* King's *palace*

Enter MALCOLM *and* MACDUFF

MALCOLM   Let us seek out some desolate shade, and there
   Weep our sad bosoms empty.
MACDUFF   Let us rather
   Hold fast the mortal sword, and like good men
   Bestride our down-fall'n birthdom: each new morn
   New widows howl, new orphans cry, new sorrows   5
   Strike heaven on the face, that it resounds
   As if it felt with Scotland and yell'd out
   Like syllable of dolour.
MALCOLM   What I believe, I'll wail;
   What know, believe; and what I can redress,
   As I shall find the time to friend, I will.   10
   What you have spoke, it may be so perchance.
   This tyrant, whose sole name blisters our tongues,
   Was once thought honest: you have loved him well;
   He hath not touch'd you yet. I am young; but some-
      thing
   You may deserve of him through me, and wisdom   15
   To offer up a weak, poor, innocent lamb
   To appease an angry god.
MACDUFF   I am not treacherous.
MALCOLM   But Macbeth is.
   A good and virtuous nature may recoil

In an imperial charge. But I shall crave your pardon; 20
That which you are, my thoughts cannot transpose:
Angels are bright still, though the brightest fell:
Though all things foul would wear the brows of grace,
Yet grace must still look so.

MACDUFF   I have lost my hopes.

MALCOLM   Perchance even there where I did find my
     doubts.   25
Why in that rawness left you wife and child,
Those precious motives, those strong knots of love,
Without leave-taking? I pray you,
Let not my jealousies be your dishonours,
But mine own safeties: you may be rightly just,   30
Whatever I shall think.

MACDUFF   Bleed, bleed, poor country!
Great tyranny, lay thou thy basis sure,
For goodness dare not check thee! wear thou thy
     wrongs,
The title is affeer'd! Fare thee well, lord:
I would not be the villain that thou think'st   35
For the whole space that's in the tyrant's grasp,
And the rich East to boot.

MALCOLM   Be not offended:
I speak not as in absolute fear of you.
I think our country sinks beneath the yoke;
It weeps, it bleeds, and each new day a gash   40
Is added to her wounds: I think, withal,
There would be hands uplifted in my right;
And here from gracious England have I offer
Of goodly thousands: but, for all this,
When I shall tread upon the tyrant's head,   45
Or wear it on my sword, yet my poor country
Shall have more vices than it had before,
More suffer and more sundry ways than ever,
By him that shall succeed.

MACDUFF   What should he be?

MALCOLM   It is myself I mean: in whom I know   50
  All the particulars of vice so grafted
  That, when they shall be open'd, black Macbeth
  Will seem as pure as snow, and the poor state
  Esteem him as a lamb, being compared
  With my confineless harms.

MACDUFF   Not in the legions   55
  Of horrid hell can come a devil more damn'd
  In evils to top Macbeth.

MALCOLM   I grant him bloody,
  Luxurious, avaricious, false, deceitful,
  Sudden, malicious, smacking of every sin
  That has a name: but there's no bottom, none,   60
  In my voluptuousness: and my desire
  All continent impediments would o'erbear,
  That did oppose my will: better Macbeth
  Than such a one to reign.

MACDUFF   Boundless intemperance
  In nature is a tyranny; it hath been   65
  The untimely emptying of the happy throne,
  And fall of many kings. But fear not yet
  To take upon you what is yours: you may
  Convey your pleasures in a spacious plenty,
  And yet seem cold, the time you may so hoodwink.   70

MALCOLM   With this, there grows
  In my most ill-composed affection such
  A stanchless avarice that, were I king,
  I should cut off the nobles for their lands;
  Desire his jewels and this other's house: 75
  And my more-having would be as a sauce
  To make me hunger more; that I should forge
  Quarrels unjust against the good and loyal,
  Destroying them for wealth.

MACDUFF   This avarice

Sticks deeper, grows with more pernicious root　　80
Than summer-seeming lust, and it hath been
The sword of our slain kings: yet do not fear;
Scotland hath foisons to fill up your will
Of your mere own: all these are portable,
With other graces weigh'd.　　85

MALCOLM　　But I have none: the king-becoming graces,
As justice, verity, temperance, stableness,
Bounty, perseverance, mercy, lowliness,
Devotion, patience, courage, fortitude,
I have no relish of them; but abound　　90
In the division of each several crime,
Acting it many ways. Nay, had I power, I should
Pour the sweet milk of concord into hell,
Uproar the universal peace, confound
All unity on earth.

MACDUFF　　　　　　O Scotland, Scotland!　　95

MALCOLM　　If such a one be fit to govern, speak:
I am as I have spoken.

MACDUFF　　　　　　　Fit to govern!
No, not to live. O nation miserable,
With an untitled tyrant bloody-scepter'd,
When shalt thou see thy wholesome days again,　　100
Since that the truest issue of thy throne
By his own interdiction stands accursed,
And does blaspheme his breed? Thy royal father
Was a most sainted king: the queen that bore thee,
Oftener upon her knees than on her feet,　　105
Died every day she lived. Fare thee well!
These evils thou repeat'st upon thyself
Have banish'd me from Scotland. O my breast,
Thy hope ends here!

MALCOLM　　　　　　Macduff, this noble passion,
Child of integrity, hath from my soul　　110
Wiped the black scruples, reconciled my thoughts

To thy good truth and honour. Devilish Macbeth
By many of these trains hath sought to win me
Into his power, and modest wisdom plucks me
From over-credulous haste: but God above   115
Deal between thee and me! for even now
I put myself to thy direction, and
Unspeak mine own detraction, here abjure
The taints and blames I laid upon myself,
For strangers to my nature. I am yet   120
Unknown to love, I never was forsworn,
Scarcely have coveted what was mine own,
At no time broke my faith, would not betray
The devil to his fellow, and delight
No less in truth than life: my first false speaking   125
Was this upon myself: what I am truly,
Is thine and my poor country's to command:
Whither indeed, before thy here-approach,
Old Siward, with ten thousand warlike men,
Already at a point, was setting forth.   130
Now we'll together; and the chance of goodness
Be like our warranted quarrel! Why are you silent?
MACDUFF   Such welcome and unwelcome things at once
'Tis hard to reconcile.

Enter a Doctor

MALCOLM   Well; more anon. Comes the king forth, I 135
     pray you?
DOCTOR   Ay, sir; there are a crew of wretched souls
That stay his cure: their malady convinces
The great assay of art: but at his touch—
Such sanctity hath heaven given his hand—
They presently amend.
MALCOLM   I thank you, doctor.   140

[*Exit Doctor*

MACDUFF   What's the disease he means?

MALCOLM   'Tis call'd the evil:
A most miraculous work in this good king;
Which often, since my here-remain in England,
I have seen him do. How he solicits heaven,
Himself best knows: but strangely-visited people,   145
All swoln and ulcerous, pitiful to the eye,
The mere despair of surgery, he cures;
Hanging a golden stamp about their necks,
Put on with holy prayers: and 'tis spoken,
To the succeeding royalty he leaves   150
The healing benediction. With this strange virtue,
He hath a heavenly gift of prophecy,
And sundry blessings hang about his throne,
That speak him full of grace.

MACDUFF   See, who comes here?

MALCOLM   My countryman; but yet I know him not.   155

Enter ROSS

MACDUFF   My ever-gentle cousin, welcome hither.

MALCOLM   I know him now: good God, betimes remove
The means that makes us strangers!

ROSS   Sir, amen.

MACDUFF   Stands Scotland where it did?

ROSS   Alas, poor country,
Almost afraid to know itself! It cannot   160
Be call'd our mother, but our grave: where nothing,
But who knows nothing, is once seen to smile;
Where sighs and groans and shrieks that rent the air
Are made, not mark'd; where violent sorrow seems
A modern ecstasy: the dead man's knell   165
Is there scarce ask'd for who; and good men's lives
Expire before the flowers in their caps,
Dying or ere they sicken.

MACDUFF   O, relation
  Too nice, and yet too true!
MALCOLM   What's the newest grief?
ROSS   That of an hour's age doth hiss the speaker;   170
  Each minute teems a new one.
MACDUFF   How does my wife?
ROSS   Why, well.
MACDUFF   And all my children?
ROSS   Well, too.
MACDUFF   The tyrant has not batter'd at their peace?
ROSS   No; they were well at peace when I did leave 'em.
MACDUFF   Be not a niggard of your speech: how goes't? 175
ROSS   When I came hither to transport the tidings,
  Which I have heavily borne, there ran a rumour
  Of many worthy fellows that were out;
  Which was to my belief witness'd the rather,
  For that I saw the tyrant's power a-foot: 180
  Now is the time of help; your eye in Scotland
  Would create soldiers, make our women fight,
  To doff their dire distresses.
MALCOLM   Be't their comfort
  We are coming thither: gracious England hath
  Lent us good Siward and ten thousand men;   185
  An older and a better soldier none
  That Christendom gives out.
ROSS   Would I could answer
  This comfort with the like! But I have words
  That would be howl'd out in the desert air,
  Where hearing should not latch them.
MACDUFF   What concern they? 190
  The general cause? or is it a fee-grief
  Due to some single breast?
ROSS   No mind that's honest
  But in it shares some woe; though the main part
  Pertains to you alone.

MACDUFF   If it be mine,
  Keep it not from me, quickly let me have it.   195
ROSS Let not your ears despise my tongue for ever,
  Which shall possess them with the heaviest sound
  That ever yet they heard.
MACDUFF   Hum! I guess at it.
ROSS Your castle is surprised; your wife and babes
  Savagely slaughter'd; to relate the manner,   200
  Were, on the quarry of these murder'd deer,
  To add the death of you.
MALCOLM   Merciful heaven!
  What, man! ne'er pull your hat upon your brows;
  Give sorrow words: the grief that does not speak
  Whispers the o'er-fraught heart and bids it break.   205
MACDUFF My children too?
ROSS   Wife, children, servants, all
  That could be found.
MACDUFF   And I must be from thence!
  My wife kill'd too?
ROSS   I have said.
MALCOLM   Be comforted:
  Let's make us medicines of our great revenge,
  To cure this deadly grief.   210
MACDUFF He has no children. All my pretty ones?
  Did you say all? O hell-kite! All?
  What, all my pretty chickens and their dam
  At one fell swoop?
MALCOLM Dispute it like a man.
MACDUFF   I shall do so;   215
  But I must also feel it as a man:
  I cannot but remember such things were,
  That were most precious to me. Did heaven look
    on,
  And would not take their part? Sinful Macduff,
  They were all struck for thee! naught that I am,   220

Not for their own demerits, but for mine,
Fell slaughter on their souls. Heaven rest them now!
MALCOLM   Be this the whetstone of your sword: let grief
Convert to anger; blunt not the heart, enrage it.
MACDUFF   O, I could play the woman with mine eyes,   225
And braggart with my tongue! But, gentle heavens,
Cut short all intermission; front to front
Bring thou this fiend of Scotland and myself;
Within my sword's length set him; if he scape,
Heaven forgive him too!
MALCOLM   This tune goes manly.   230
Come, go we to the king; our power is ready;
Our lack is nothing but our leave: Macbeth
Is ripe for shaking, and the powers above
Put on their instruments. Receive what cheer you may:
The night is long that never finds the day.   235
                                        [Exeunt

ACT V

SCENE I. *Dunsinane. Ante-room in the castle*

Enter a Doctor of Physic *and a* Waiting-Gentlewoman

DOCTOR　I have two nights watched with you, but can perceive no truth in your report. When was it she last walked?

GENTLEWOMAN　Since his majesty went into the field, I have seen her rise from her bed, throw her nightgown 5 upon her, unlock her closet, take forth paper, fold it, write upon't, read it, afterwards seal it, and again return to bed; yet all this while in a most fast sleep.

DOCTOR　A great perturbation in nature, to receive at once the benefit of sleep, and do the effects of watching! 10 In this slumbery agitation, besides her walking and other actual performances, what, at any time, have you heard her say?

GENTLEWOMAN　That, sir, which I will not report after her.

DOCTOR　You may to me; and 'tis most meet you 15 should.

GENTLEWOMAN　Neither to you nor any one; having no witness to confirm my speech. Lo you, here she comes!

Enter LADY MACBETH, *with a taper*

This is her very guise; and, upon my life, fast asleep. Observe her; stand close.　　　　　　　　　　　　20

DOCTOR　How came she by that light?

GENTLEWOMAN　Why, it stood by her: she has light by her continually; 'tis her command.

DOCTOR   You see, her eyes are open.

GENTLEWOMAN   Ay, but their sense is shut.   25

DOCTOR   What is it she does now? Look, how she
rubs her hands.

GENTLEWOMAN   It is an accustomed action with her, to
seem thus washing her hands: I have known her
continue in this a quarter of an hour.   30

LADY MACBETH   Yet, here's a spot.

DOCTOR   Hark! she speaks: I will set down what comes
from her, to satisfy my remembrance the more strongly.

LADY MACBETH   Out, damned spot! out, I say!—One,
two; why, then 'tis time to do't.—Hell is murky!—Fie, 35
my lord, fie! a soldier, and afeard? What need we fear
who knows it, when none can call our power to
account?—Yet who would have thought the old man
to have had so much blood in him?

DOCTOR   Do you mark that?   40

LADY MACBETH   The thane of Fife had a wife: where
is she now?—What, will these hands ne'er be clean?—
No more o' that, my lord, no more o' that: you mar all
with this starting.

DOCTOR   Go to, go to; you have known what you 45
should not.

GENTLEWOMAN   She has spoke what she should not, I
am sure of that: heaven knows what she has known.

LADY MACBETH   Here's the smell of the blood still: all
the perfumes of Arabia will not sweeten this little hand. 50
Oh, oh, oh!

DOCTOR   What a sigh is there! The heart is sorely
charged.

GENTLEWOMAN   I would not have such a heart in my
bosom for the dignity of the whole body.   55

DOCTOR   Well, well, well,—

GENTLEWOMAN   Pray God it be, sir.

DOCTOR   This disease is beyond my practice: yet I

have known those which have walked in their sleep who
have died holily in their beds. 60

LADY MACBETH Wash your hands, put on your nightgown; look not so pale:—I tell you yet again, Banquo's
buried; he cannot come out on's grave.

DOCTOR Even so?

LADY MACBETH To bed, to bed; there's knocking at 65
the gate: come, come, come, come, give me your hand:
what's done cannot be undone: to bed, to bed, to bed.

[*Exit*

DOCTOR Will she go now to bed?

GENTLEWOMAN Directly.

DOCTOR Foul whisperings are abroad: unnatural deeds 70
Do breed unnatural troubles: infected minds
To their deaf pillows will discharge their secrets:
More needs she the divine than the physician.
God, God forgive us all! Look after her;
Remove from her the means of all annoyance, 75
And still keep eyes upon her: so, good night:
My mind she has mated, and amazed my sight:
I think, but dare not speak.

GENTLEWOMAN Good night, good doctor.

[*Exeunt*

SCENE II. *The country near Dunsinane*

Enter, with drum and colours, MENTEITH, CAITHNESS,
ANGUS, LENNOX, *and* Soldiers

MENTEITH The English power is near, led on by
  Malcolm,
His uncle Siward and the good Macduff:
Revenges burn in them; for their dear causes
Would to the bleeding and the grim alarm
Excite the mortified man.

ANGUS   Near Birnam wood   5
   Shall we well meet them; that way are they coming.
CAITHNESS   Who knows if Donalbain be with his brother?
LENNOX   For certain, sir, he is not: I have a file
   Of all the gentry: there is Siward's son,
   And many unrough youths that even now   10
   Protest their first of manhood.
MENTEITH   What does the tyrant?
CAITHNESS   Great Dunsinane he strongly fortifies:
   Some say he's mad; others, that lesser hate him,
   Do call it valiant fury: but, for certain,
   He cannot buckle his distemper'd cause   15
   Within the belt of rule.
ANGUS   Now does he feel
   His secret murders sticking on his hands;
   Now minutely revolts upbraid his faith-breach;
   Those he commands move only in command,
   Nothing in love: now does he feel his title   20
   Hang loose about him, like a giant's robe
   Upon a dwarfish thief.
MENTEITH   Who then shall blame
   His pester'd senses to recoil and start
   When all that is within him does condemn
   Itself for being there?
CAITHNESS   Well, march we on,   25
   To give obedience where 'tis truly owed:
   Meet we the medicine of the sickly weal,
   And with him pour we in our country's purge
   Each drop of us.
LENNOX   Or so much as it needs,
   To dew the sovereign flower and drown the weeds.   30
   Make we our march towards Birnam.
                           [Exeunt, marching

SCENE III. *Dunsinane. A room in the castle*

Enter MACBETH, Doctor, *and* Attendants

MACBETH   Bring me no more reports; let them fly all:
  Till Birnam wood remove to Dunsinane,
  I cannot taint with fear. What's the boy Malcolm?
  Was he not born of woman? The spirits that know
  All mortal consequences have pronounced me thus,   5
  "Fear not, Macbeth; no man that's born of woman
  Shall e'er have power upon thee." Then fly, false thanes,
  And mingle with the English epicures:
  The mind I sway by and the heart I bear
  Shall never sag with doubt nor shake with fear.   10

Enter a Servant

  The devil damn thee black, thou cream-faced loon!
  Where gott'st thou that goose look?
SERVANT   There is ten thousand—
MACBETH   Geese, villain?
SERVANT   Soldiers, sir.
MACBETH   Go, prick thy face, and over-red thy fear,
  Thou lily-liver'd boy. What soldiers, patch?   15
  Death of thy soul! those linen cheeks of thine
  Are counsellors to fear. What soldiers, whey-face?
SERVANT   The English force, so please you.
MACBETH   Take thy face hence.   [*Exit Servant*
                    Seyton!—I am sick at heart,
  When I behold!—Seyton, I say!—This push   20
  Will cheer me ever, or disseat me now.
  I have lived long enough: my way of life
  Is fall'n into the sear, the yellow leaf;
  And that which should accompany old age,
  As honour, love, obedience, troops of friends,   25

I must not look to have; but, in their stead,
Curses, not loud but deep, mouth-honour, breath,
Which the poor heart would fain deny, and dare not.
Seyton!

Enter SEYTON

SEYTON   What is your gracious pleasure?
MACBETH   What news more? 30
SEYTON   All is confirm'd, my lord, which was reported.
MACBETH   I'll fight, till from my bones my flesh be
     hack'd.
     Give me my armour.
SEYTON   'Tis not needed yet.
MACBETH   I'll put it on.
     Send out moe horses, skirr the country round;   35
     Hang those that talk of fear. Give me mine armour.
     How does your patient, doctor?
DOCTOR   Not so sick, my lord,
     As she is troubled with thick-coming fancies
     That keep her from her rest.
MACBETH   Cure her of that:

     Canst thou not minister to a mind diseased,   40
     Pluck from the memory a rooted sorrow,
     Raze out the written troubles of the brain,
     And with some sweet oblivious antidote
     Cleanse the stuff'd bosom of that perilous stuff
     Which weighs upon the heart?
DOCTOR   Therein the patient   45
     Must minister to himself.
MACBETH   Throw physic to the dogs, I'll none of it.
     Come, put mine armour on; give me my staff:
     Seyton, send out. Doctor, the thanes fly from me.
     Come, sir, dispatch. If thou couldst, doctor, find   50
     My land's disease,
     And purge it to a sound and pristine health,

I would applaud thee to the very echo,
That should applaud again.—Pull't off, I say.—
What rhubarb, senna, or what purgative drug,   55
Would scour these English hence? Hear'st thou of
   them?

DOCTOR Ay, my good lord; your royal preparation
   Makes us hear something.

MACBETH   Bring it after me.
I will not be afraid of death and bane,
Till Birnam forest come to Dunsinane.   60

                    [*Exeunt all except Doctor*

DOCTOR Were I from Dunsinane away and clear,
   Profit again should hardly draw me here.   [*Exit*

SCENE IV. *Country near Dunsinane: a wood
in view*

Enter, with drum and colours, MALCOLM, *old* SIWARD *and
young* SIWARD, MACDUFF, MENTEITH, CAITHNESS, ANGUS,
LENNOX, ROSS, *and* Soldiers, *marching*

MALCOLM Cousins, I hope the days are near at hand
   That chambers will be safe.

MENTEITH   We doubt it nothing.

SIWARD What wood is this before us?

MENTEITH   The wood of Birnam.

MALCOLM Let every soldier hew him down a bough
   And bear't before him: thereby shall we shadow   5
   The numbers of our host and make discovery
   Err in report of us.

SOLDIERS   It shall be done.

SIWARD We learn no other but the confident tyrant
   Keeps still in Dunsinane, and will endure
   Our setting down before't.

MALCOLM   'Tis his main hope: 10
   For where there is advantage to be given,
   Both more and less have given him the revolt;
   And none serve with him but constrained things,
   Whose hearts are absent too.

MACDUFF   Let our just censures
   Attend the true event, and put we on   15
   Industrious soldiership.

SIWARD   The time approaches
   That will with due decision make us know
   What we shall say we have, and what we owe.
   Thoughts speculative their unsure hopes relate,
   But certain issue strokes must arbitrate: 20
   Towards which advance the war.   [*Exeunt, marching*

SCENE V. *Dunsinane. Within the castle*

Enter, with drum and colours, MACBETH, SEYTON,
                and Soldiers

MACBETH   Hang out our banners on the outward walls;
   The cry is still "They come": our castle's strength
   Will laugh a siege to scorn: here let them lie
   Till famine and the ague eat them up:
   Were they not forced with those that should be ours, 5
   We might have met them dareful, beard to beard,
   And beat them backward home.
                         [*A cry of women within*
                         What is that noise?

SEYTON   It is the cry of women, my good lord.   [*Exit*

MACBETH   I have almost forgot the taste of fears:
   The time has been, my senses would have cool'd   10
   To hear a night-shriek; and my fell of hair
   Would at a dismal treatise rouse and stir

As life were in't: I have supp'd full with horrors;
Direness, familiar to my slaughterous thoughts,
Cannot once start me.

Re-enter SEYTON

                Wherefore was that cry?   15
SEYTON The queen, my lord, is dead.
MACBETH She should have died hereafter;
There would have been a time for such a word.
To-morrow, and to-morrow, and to-morrow,
Creeps in this petty pace from day to day,   20
To the last syllable of recorded time;
And all our yesterdays have lighted fools
The way to dusty death. Out, out, brief candle!
Life's but a walking shadow, a poor player
That struts and frets his hour upon the stage,   25
And then is heard no more: it is a tale
Told by an idiot, full of sound and fury,
Signifying nothing.

Enter a Messenger

Thou comest to use thy tongue; thy story quickly.
MESSENGER Gracious my lord,   30
I should report that which I say I saw,
But know not how to do it.
MACBETH   Well, say, sir.
MESSENGER As I did stand my watch upon the hill,
I look'd toward Birnam, and anon, methought,
The wood began to move.
MACBETH   Liar and slave!   35
MESSENGER Let me endure your wrath, if't be not so:
Within this three mile may you see it coming;
I say, a moving grove.
MACBETH   If thou speak'st false,
Upon the next tree shalt thou hang alive,

Till famine cling thee: if thy speech be sooth,   40
I care not if thou dost for me as much.
I pull in resolution, and begin
To doubt the equivocation of the fiend,
That lies like truth: "Fear not, till Birnam wood
Do come to Dunsinane"; and now a wood   45
Comes toward Dunsinane. Arm, arm, and out!
If this which he avouches does appear,
There is nor flying hence nor tarrying here.
I gin to be a-weary of the sun,
And wish the estate o' the world were now undone.   50
Ring the alarum-bell! Blow, wind! come, wrack!
At least we'll die with harness on our back.
                              [*Exeunt*

SCENE VI. *Dunsinane. Before the castle*

Enter, with drum and colours, MALCOLM, *old* SIWARD,
        MACDUFF, *etc., and their* Army, *with boughs*

MALCOLM   Now near enough; your leavy screens throw
        down,
    And show like those you are. You, worthy uncle,
    Shall, with my cousin, your right-noble son,
    Lead our first battle: worthy Macduff and we
    Shall take upon's what else remains to do,   5
    According to our order.
SIWARD   Fare you well.
    Do we but find the tyrant's power to-night,
    Let us be beaten, if we cannot fight.
MACDUFF   Make all our trumpets speak; give them all
        breath,
    Those clamorous harbingers of blood and death.   10
                              [*Exeunt*

SCENE VII. *Another part of the field*

Alarums. Enter MACBETH

MACBETH　They have tied me to a stake; I cannot fly,
But, bear-like, I must fight the course. What's he
That was not born of woman? Such a one
Am I to fear, or none.

Enter young SIWARD

YOUNG SIWARD　What is thy name?
MACBETH　　　　　　　　　Thou'lt be afraid to hear it. 5
YOUNG SIWARD　No; though thou call'st thyself a hotter
name
Than any is in hell.
MACBETH　　　　　My name's Macbeth.
YOUNG SIWARD　The devil himself could not pronounce
a title
More hateful to mine ear.
MACBETH　　　　　　　No, nor more fearful.
YOUNG SIWARD　Thou liest, abhorred tyrant; with my
sword　　　　　　　　　　　　　　　　　　　　　　10
I'll prove the lie thou speak'st.
　　　　　　　　[*They fight, and young Siward is slain*
MACBETH　　　　　　　Thou wast born of woman.
But swords I smile at, weapons laugh to scorn,
Brandish'd by man that's of a woman born.　　[*Exit*

Alarums. Enter MACDUFF

MACDUFF　That way the noise is. Tyrant, show thy face!
If thou be'st slain and with no stroke of mine,　　15
My wife and children's ghosts will haunt me still.
I cannot strike at wretched kerns, whose arms
Are hired to bear their staves: either thou, Macbeth,
Or else my sword, with an unbatter'd edge,

I sheathe again undeeded. There thou shouldst be;   20
By this great clatter, one of greatest note
Seems bruited: let me find him, fortune!
And more I beg not.   [*Exit. Alarums*

Enter MALCOLM *and old* SIWARD

SIWARD   This way, my lord; the castle's gently render'd:
The tyrant's people on both sides do fight;   25
The noble thanes do bravely in the war;
The day almost itself professes yours,
And little is to do.
MALCOLM   We have met with foes
That strike beside us.
SIWARD   Enter, sir, the castle.
                            [*Exeunt. Alarums*

SCENE VIII. *Another part of the field*

Enter MACBETH

MACBETH   Why should I play the Roman fool, and die
On mine own sword? whiles I see lives, the gashes
Do better upon them.

Enter MACDUFF

MACDUFF   Turn, hell-hound, turn!
MACBETH   Of all men else I have avoided thee:
But get thee back; my soul is too much charged   5
With blood of thine already.
MACDUFF   I have no words:
My voice is in my sword; thou bloodier villain
Than terms can give thee out!   [*They fight*
MACBETH   Thou losest labour:
As easy mayst thou the intrenchant air

With thy keen sword impress, as make me bleed: 10
Let fall thy blade on vulnerable crests;
I bear a charmed life, which must not yield
To one of woman born.

MACBETH   Despair thy charm;
And let the angel whom thou still hast served
Tell thee, Macduff was from his mother's womb   15
Untimely ripp'd.

MACBETH   Accursed be that tongue that tells me so,
For it hath cow'd my better part of man!
And be these juggling fiends no more believed,
That palter with us in a double sense;   20
That keep the word of promise to our ear,
And break it to our hope! I'll not fight with thee.

MACDUFF   Then yield thee, coward,
And live to be the show and gaze o' the time:
We'll have thee, as our rarer monsters are,   25
Painted upon a pole, and underwrit,
"Here may you see the tyrant."

MACBETH   I will not yield,
To kiss the ground before young Malcolm's feet,
And to be baited with the rabble's curse.
Though Birnam wood be come to Dunsinane,   30
And thou opposed, being of no woman born,
Yet I will try the last. Before my body
I throw my warlike shield: lay on, Macduff;
And damn'd be him that first cries "Hold, enough!"
                    [*Exeunt, fighting. Alarums*

Retreat. Flourish. Enter, with drum and colours, MALCOLM,
old SIWARD, ROSS, LENNOX, ANGUS, CAITHNESS, MENTEITH,
and Soldiers

MALCOLM   I would the friends we miss were safe arrived. 35
SIWARD   Some must go off: and yet, by these I see,
So great a day as this is cheaply bought.

MALCOLM   Macduff is missing, and your noble son.

ROSS   Your son, my lord, has paid a soldier's debt:
   He only lived but till he was a man;   40
   The which no sooner had his prowess confirm'd
   In the unshrinking station where he fought,
   But like a man he died.

SIWARD   Then he is dead?

ROSS   Ay, and brought off the field: your cause of sorrow
   Must not be measured by his worth, for then   45
   It hath no end.

SIWARD   Had he his hurts before?

ROSS   Ay, on the front.

SIWARD   Why then, God's soldier be he!
   Had I as many sons as I have hairs,
   I would not wish them to a fairer death:
   And so, his knell is knoll'd.

MALCOLM   He's worth more sorrow, 50
   And that I'll spend for him.

SIWARD   He's worth no more:
   They say he parted well, and paid his score:
   And so, God be with him! Here comes newer comfort.

Re-enter MACDUFF, *with* MACBETH'S *head*

MACDUFF   Hail, king! for so thou art: behold, where
      stands
   The usurper's cursed head: the time is free: 55
   I see thee compass'd with thy kingdom's pearl,
   That speak my salutation in their minds;
   Whose voices I desire aloud with mine:
   Hail, King of Scotland!

ALL   Hail, King of Scotland! [*Flourish*

MALCOLM   We shall not spend a large expense of time 60
   Before we reckon with your several loves,
   And make us even with you. My thanes and kinsmen,
   Henceforth be earls, the first that ever Scotland

In such an honour named. What's more to do,
Which would be planted newly with the time,—   65
As calling home our exiled friends abroad,
That fled the snares of watchful tyranny;
Producing forth the cruel ministers
Of this dead butcher and his fiend-like queen,
Who, as 'tis thought, by self and violent hands   70
Took off her life; this, and what needful else
That calls upon us, by the grace of Grace,
We will perform in measure, time and place:
So, thanks to all at once and to each one,
Whom we invite to see us crown'd at Scone.   75

                    [*Flourish. Exeunt*

NOTES

G. = *Glossary*. Several other abbreviations used sometimes in the *Notes* are explained at the beginning of the *Glossary*, in which they occur more frequently. They should be observed; see p. 157.

ACT I

Scene 1

Enter three Witches. "In *Macbeth*, the poet's object was to raise the mind at once to the high tragic tone.... The true reason for the first appearance of the Witches is to strike the key-note of the character of the whole drama"—*Coleridge*. The Witches, in fact, introduce that atmosphere of guilt and evil which hangs as a pall over the whole play.

As the moment of their first appearance is significant, so is the scene. "They appear in a desert place, with thunder and lightning; it is the barren place where evil has obtained the mastery of things"—*Dowden*. And the storm (created, like that in *The Tempest*, by incantation) not only harmonises with them and their rites, it is a symbol also of the present convulsion in Duncan's kingdom, and of the still greater convulsion to come. A precisely similar effect is gained by the storm-scenes in *King Lear* and *Julius Cæsar*.

Abbott remarks: "The verse with four accents is rarely used by Shakespeare, except when witches or other extraordinary beings are introduced as speaking. Then he often uses a verse of four accents with rhyme." Cf. Puck's speeches in *A Midsummer-Night's Dream*, II. 2. 66–83, v. 378–97, 430–45. This 4-stressed metre is ordinarily of the so-called trochaic type (line 1) varied by the iambic (line 2); the trochaic lines often have a single, stressed syllable in the 4th foot—e.g. "Whén the | húrly|búrly's | dóne".

three; with its multiple *nine* (I. 3. 36), a mysterious number.

1. There should be no stop at the end of the line: "the question has regard to the *time*, not the *season*, of the witches' next meeting".

3. *hurlyburly*, uproar, tumult; referring to the turmoil of battle and rebellion (Scene 2). See G.

8–12. Probably each Witch in turn should be made to

address her attendant spirit or "familiar" (supposed to be impatiently awaiting her), while all join in the jingling couplet "Fair is foul" etc.

8, 9. *Graymalkin;* a common name for a gray cat; see G. *paddock,* a toad; cf. *Hamlet,* III. 4. 190, and see G. It was popularly supposed that the familiar spirits in the service of magicians and witches took the form of animals and other creatures, especially toads and cats. Ariel, the graceful spirit-attendant on Prospero in *The Tempest,* has a bird-form.

10. *Anon!* in a moment! coming!

11. *Fair is foul, and foul is fair,* i.e. in the eyes of the Witches. The line (which has a proverbial ring) is a sort of summary of their creed, and serves as a signal to us, a warning of what we must expect from them. Some think that primarily the line refers to the tempest as being favourable to witchcraft and its rites (line 2). When the Witches are alone, their language "displays a certain fierce familiarity, grotesqueness mingled with terror"; whereas with Macbeth it is "solemn, dark, and mysterious". They "blend in themselves the Fates and Furies of the ancients with the sorceresses of Gothic and popular superstition"—*Coleridge.*

Scene 2

Many critics consider that the text of this scene has been much mutilated. But in part, at any rate, the abruptness or exaggeration of style is accounted for by the circumstance that the Sergeant and Ross have each just come from the stress of battle—the one wounded. Some think that the style is intentionally epic rather than tragic—cf. the picturesque imagery of 8, 9, 25-8, 35-8—the epic manner being traditionally associated with narratives of battle; cf. the Player's Speech, *Hamlet,* II. 2. The quasi-historical element is due to Holinshed.

3. *sergeant;* scan as three syllables. "In ancient times *sergeants* were not the petty officers now distinguished by that title, but men performing one kind of feudal military service [viz. to guard the person of the king], in rank next to esquires." (F.).

4. *hardy,* brave; F. *hardi.*

5. *Hail;* scan as two syllables. Monosyllables containing diphthongs or long vowels, since they allow the voice to dwell on them, often take the place of a whole foot. See p. 193, footnote.

6. *the,* i.e. the knowledge you have; *thy* is a needless change.

broil, battle, literally 'confused struggle, turmoil'; cf. F. *brouiller*, 'to jumble, confuse'.

7. The marked pause due to the division of the line between two speakers makes up for the omitted medial stress or accent.

9. *choke their art*, render useless their skill in swimming; from *choke* = 'to suffocate', and so 'to destroy, nullify'.

10. *to that*, to that end, viz. "to be a rebel": he has many evil qualities which naturally fit him for the part.

13. *kerns...gallowglasses;* light-armed and heavy-armed Irish soldiers; see each word in G. Cf. v. 7. 17, 18. Holinshed says that "*out of the westerne Isles* there came vnto him [Macdonwald] a great multitude of people, offering themselues to assist him in *that rebellious quarell*, and out of Ireland in hope of the spoile came no small number of *Kernes and Galloglasses* offering gladlie to serue vnder him". *supplied of*, i.e. in respect of, 'furnished with'.

14, 15. I.e. Fortune showed herself as it were the mistress of the rebel and espoused his cause; but Macbeth, supported by a higher power, viz. Valour (19), made the aid of Fortune unavailing. Some think that *show'd* implies deception on the part of Fortune, i.e. that she smiled on him, but deceived him.

damned quarrel, detestable, accursed cause. Elizabethan writers sometimes use *quarrel* (Lat. *querela*, 'a complaint') in the sense 'cause, motive of dispute'. *Quarrel* is the word in Holinshed (see 13, note), and most editors adopt it. The 1st Folio has *quarry*, prey (see G.), which has been interpreted "the slaughter and depredations made by the rebel".

all's too weak; the historic present among preterites is certainly strange; but cf. *swells* in 28.

18. *execution*. Scan the *-ion* as *i-ön;* that is, sounding the *i* instead of slurring it into the next syllable, which is stressed lightly. In Shakespeare and in Milton's early poems the termination *-ion*, especially with words ending in *-ction*, such as 'perfe*ction*', 'distra*ction*', is often treated as two syllables, particularly at the end of a line. In Middle English poetry the termination *-ion* was always two syllables. See 25.

19. *minion*, favourite; usually contemptuous; see G.

20. "This irregular line [like 41] is explained by the haste and excitement of the speaker"—Abbott.

21. *Which*, who (i.e. Macdonwald); a common Elizabethan use; cf. the Bible often. *shook hands*. The line is considered to allude "to the formal hand-shaking which preceded a duel".

22. *unseam'd*, ripped open. *nave*, navel, middle. *Nave* means

commonly the boss or centre of a wheel and does not appear to be used elsewhere in the sense of its diminutive *navel*. *Nape* (i.e. of the neck) has been suggested, but the change is needless.

24. *cousin*. Holinshed says that Duncan and Macbeth were the sons respectively of the two daughters, Beatrice and Doada, of Malcolm, the predecessor of Duncan on the throne.

25–8. *As whence the sun* etc. "As storms often come from the east, the region of the dawn, so victory may be the starting-point for a fresh attack"—*Herford*.

28. *swells*. The word suggests a swoln destructive river, whereas we should have expected the idea '*wells* like a fertilising stream'. (F.)

30. *skipping;* appropriate to light-armed troops.

31. *the Norweyan lord*, Sweno (60). Having described the suppression of Macdonwald's rebellion and his death by suicide, Holinshed says that "Sueno king of Norway" invaded Scotland with a great army but was defeated, and that then a *second* army was "sent by Canute king of England in revenge of his brother Suenos ouerthrow". Shakespeare combines the two invasions for the sake of dramatic compression. Historians say that neither really took place.

surveying vantage, seeing a favourable opportunity.

34. *captains;* to be scanned as three syllables, like F. *capitaine*. Cf. 3 *Henry VI*, IV. 7. 30, "A wíse | stout cáp|(i)taín, | and soón | persuáded".

37. *cracks*, charges; properly the word describes the explosion of the charge. See IV. I. 117.

40. *memorize another Golgotha*, i.e. create by slaughter of the enemy another "place of a skull" as famous in tradition as that mentioned in Scripture (Matt. xxvii. 33, Mark xv. 22).

45. *thane;* see G.

46, 47. *So should*, so ought, so might that man ("he") be expected to. *seems to*, shows by his appearance that he is about to; has the appearance of being a messenger of strange tidings.

49, 50. *flout*, mock; it was an insult to the Scottish heavens that Norwegian flags should be flying there. *fan our people cold*, paralyse our countrymen with fear as they wave in the wind. Cf. *Henry V*, Prol. III. 6. The two verbs must be historic presents, describing the first stage of the contest when the Norwegians promised themselves victory over the Scots. The description is quite inapplicable to a defeated army. *Norway*, the king of Norway; cf. "England", IV. 3. 184.

52, 53. Holinshed does not mention Cawdor in connection

with Sweno at all; and he places Cawdor's deprival of his title, lands and offices "shortlie" *after* Macbeth's first meeting with the Witches. But Shakespeare associates Cawdor with Sweno, so as to account for Cawdor's deprival, and to make the news of it reach Macbeth at the first great crisis of the drama (I. 3. 104–7).

53. *began;* scan *'gan*, prefixes being often clipped thus, e.g. *'gainst* (56) for *against. dismal*, i.e. adverse to the Scots at first; see G.

54. *Bellona's bridegroom*, i.e. Macbeth, the very spouse of Bellona herself (the Roman goddess of war, *bellum*).

The phrase is a very strong term of admiration. The speaker feels that all would know to whom alone it could be applied: hence the omission of Macbeth's name—a suggestive touch.

lapp'd in proof, encased in impenetrable armour; see *proof* in G.

55. *him*, i.e. "Norway himself". *self-comparisons;* the plural implies 'points of comparison (i.e. equality) between their two selves', such as strength, skill, etc. Macbeth proved himself in all ways a match for the Norwegian king.

56. *Point*, weapon's point. *rebellious;* not strictly applicable to "Norway himself", but he was in league with the rebel Cawdor.

57. *lavish*, unrestrained, insolent. *Lavish* is from an obsolete verb meaning 'to pour out': whence the idea 'bounteous, unrestrained'.

59. *That*, so that.

60. *Norways'*, Norwegians'. *composition*, terms of peace, agreement. We speak of people 'composing their differences', i.e. settling.

61–3. All from Holinshed, who, however, is really speaking of the defeat of the *second* Danish army sent by Canute.

62. *Saint Colme's inch:* "the island of Inchcolm off the coast of Fife, in the Firth of Forth, once occupied by St Columba, the first teacher of Christianity to the Picts". There are remains there of an abbey dedicated to *St Colomba* (whence *Colme*). *Inch* is said to mean 'a small island' in the Erse (Irish) language.

63. *dollars;* see G.

65. *Our bosom interest*, our close affection for him; see I. 4. 13, 14. *present*, immediate; a very common use; cf. IV. 3. 140.

68. *noble Macbeth*. The scene closes on the note of Macbeth's glorification. It has given him already the first place in our thoughts, and we await his appearance with curiosity. And it is in relation to him that this war-element has been introduced.

For (1) through it we see the greatness of Macbeth as a soldier, and that greatness makes the tragedy of his fall so much more pitiful. Again, (2) the reward he receives for his services becomes, by his previous evil meditations, an impulse towards the crime (1. 3. 116, 117), and makes his ingratitude towards the generous Duncan all the more hateful.

Scene 3

Scene. A heath; cf. 1. 1. 6. Shakespeare "has altered the meadow-land, which Holinshed represents as lying around Inverness, into the heath which is really characteristic of the district": a change that heightens the "local colour" much— *Brandes.*

Enter the three Witches. Who are these malign beings (unmatched elsewhere in Shakespeare) for whom "Witches" is to modern ears a scarcely adequate term? They are *not* simply the embodiment of inward temptation. They are personifications of the evil forces at work in the world, of the active principle of evil in nature and in society; "instruments of darkness" (124). "They lead evil minds from evil to evil; and have the power of tempting those who have been the tempters of themselves"— *Coleridge.* That they may appeal to the popular imagination, Shakespeare makes them resemble externally the witches of popular superstition, and heightens this resemblance by all the usual symbols and signs of witchcraft.

2. A Scot writes that Shakespeare purposely assigned to the Witch a work peculiarly revolting to Celtic Highlanders, to whom the pig is an "unclean" animal—a thing "tabu" (forbidden).

6. *Aroint thee,* begone. *rump-fed,* pampered, literally, 'fed on the best joints'; rather than the opposite sense 'offal-fed'.

ronyon, scurvy creature. See *aroint* and *ronyon* in G.

7. *Tiger;* a not uncommon name; cf. *Twelfth Night,* V. 1. 65. A ship the *Tiger* traded regularly between London and Tripoli (in Syria), the port of Aleppo, where the Levant Company of Merchants had a settlement. Hakluyt mentions a special voyage in 1583.

Travel was one of the chief influences at work in Shakespeare's time. "We may trace everywhere in Elizabethan literature the impression made by the wonders told by the sailors and captains who explored and fought from the North Pole to the Southern Seas." Cf. Hakluyt's *Voyages* (1598–1600). See W. Raleigh: *Shakespeare's England* (1916), I. 170–223.

8. That witches could sail on the sea, however tempestuous, "in a riddle or sieve", cockle-shell or egg-shell; could assume the form of any animal minus the tail; had control over the winds, and made money of their power by selling favourable winds to sailors "in glasses" or through "tying of certain knots upon a rope"; could cause a person to pine away by making a waxen image of him and then sticking pins into it and dissolving it before a fire: these were all current superstitions, which Shakespeare mentions, whatever his own opinion about witch-craft may have been. For the references to the sea (8 and 11–17) see Introduction, p. viii.

10. *do*, work, i.e. gnaw through the bottom of the ship.

15. *blow*, blow *upon*. She exercises control over all the *ports* into which the winds might carry a ship, and so can prevent the ship reaching the port safely. An obvious suggestion is *points* (i.e. of the wind).

17. *the shipman's card;* "the circular card, marked with the 32 points of the compass, for the steersman's use"; commonly called the *compass-card*, to which the needle of the compass points. Cf. the phrase 'to speak by the card', i.e. with great precision, exactly—e.g. in *Hamlet*, v. 1. 148, 149.

18. *drain him dry;* "exhaust the moisture from his body".

20. *pent-house;* properly a shed or outhouse sloping down from a main building, much as the eyelid slopes when closed; see G.

21. *forbid;* some interpret 'cursed, blasted'; more probably 'excommunicated', i.e. forbidden the rites and benefits of the Church.

28. *pilot*, steersman; the man at the helm.

29. *homeward;* a pathetic touch, emphasising the Witch's malignity.

32. *The weird sisters;* literally 'the fate-sisters', hence 'those who are the ministers of Destiny'. The term is in Holinshed; it showed Theobald that the Folio's reading *wayward* was a mis-take for *weird* (= two syllables). 33. *Posters of*, swift travellers o'er.

35. *to thine*, to thy side. In the representation of a play a gesture often supplements and explains the spoken word; cf. II. 1. 5.

Enter Macbeth and Banquo. Macbeth had already contem-plated the murder of Duncan and spoken to his wife about it; see I. 5. 1–28, I. 7. 47–52. Hence there exists a guilty sympathy between Macbeth and the Witches. The soil has been prepared for the evil seed. He is surprised into premeditated crime by sudden temptation. Banquo on the other hand is the loyal soldier wholly free from these guilty thoughts. So while Macbeth is guiltily uneasy, Banquo is cool and collected. Banquo serves essentially as a foil or contrast to Macbeth.

38. *So foul and fair a day,* i.e. of sunshine and storm, the struggle of which answers to the moral strife in Macbeth's heart.

Macbeth's echoing of the Witches' parting cry in I. I. 11 is clearly meant to indicate the sympathy between tempters and tempted, and the *unconsciousness* of the indication is the first note of the "irony" (see p. 174) which characterises *Macbeth* above all Shakespeare's plays.

The whole interview is based on Holinshed's account of the meeting between Macbeth and Banquo and the Witches.

39. *Forres;* about midway between Elgin and Nairn, near the Moray Firth; the railway passes through it.

40. *wild in their attire;* "in strange and wild apparell", says Holinshed.

44–6. *choppy;* see G. *should;* cf. I. 2. 46. *beards.* It was a popular notion that witches were always bearded.

48–50. The Witches' salutations are direct from Holinshed. Note that they ignore Banquo's address and turn to Macbeth, their anticipated (I. I) victim. Coleridge says: "Superstition, of one sort or another, is natural to victorious generals; the instances are too notorious to need mention": the main reason being that "chance", or what seems chance, plays so large a part in warfare. A signal instance is Napoleon with his belief in his "star", lucky days, etc.

Moreover the ambitious promptings of the Witches come to Macbeth *just when* he is full of the elation of victory. This is one of Shakespeare's suggestive deviations from Holinshed, who places the meeting with the Witches a little time after the Norwegian invasions.

49. Again "irony" of situation, for we know what Macbeth does not yet know, viz. that Cawdor's title *has* already passed to him.

51. *why do you start...?* Such touches bring out the inner working of guilty thoughts. The prophecy of kingship is an echo of Macbeth's secret ambitions, and advances them a stage.

53. *fantastical,* imaginary; creations of the fancy. Holinshed says that afterwards Macbeth and Banquo, for a time, regarded the meeting as "some vaine *fantastical* illusion". See again 139.

54. *show*, appear; often intransitive in Shakespeare.

55. *present grace*, i.e. the title which Macbeth already enjoys as "thane of Glamis" (48).

56. *noble having*, possession; referring to the next "noble" title given him, "thane of Cawdor" (49).

57. *That*, so that; cf. I. 2. 59. *rapt*, transported; see G.

60, 61. I.e. "who neither beg your favours nor fear your hate".

62. *Hail;* an inferior salutation to "*All* hail!"

67. *get*, beget; a complimentary allusion to the tradition that the House of Stuart was descended from Banquo.

70. Some movement of departure by the Witches rouses Macbeth from his reverie.

71. *Sinel*, Macbeth's father. The name was *Finnlaec*.

72, 73. Macbeth must have known that Cawdor was a captured rebel: how then could he describe him as "a prosperous gentleman"? Some editors see in this a strong argument that Shakespeare did not write I. 2. 50–66, or Scene 2 at all. But Macbeth does not know who the Witches are or how much they can tell him: hence his subsequent enquiries (see I. 5. 1–3). He himself, coming straight from the battle, knows about Cawdor what the Witches, if mere mortals, are not likely to know; *so he feigns ignorance to test their knowledge* and perhaps spur them to say something more about the greater prophecy of kingship. He has had ample time to mature a plan since the Witches' three-fold salutation (48–50).

76. *owe*, have, possess; see G.

77. Milton remembered this line; cf. *Par. Lost*, I. 615.

81. *corporal*, corporeal; both forms were in current Elizabethan use.

82. *As breath;* Coleridge remarks on the appropriateness of the simile to a cold climate.

84. *the insane root*, the root that produces insanity; variously taken to mean hemlock, henbane, or deadly-nightshade. Possibly Shakespeare was thinking of a story in Holinshed—how "the Scots won the victory by drugging [Sweno's army], who incautiously accepted from Duncan a present of ale and bread, compounded with 'the juice of mekilwoort berries'". This "mekilwoort" seems from another Chronicler to be deadly-nightshade, the berries of which were thought to induce sleep. (F.) The writer on "Plants" in *Shakespeare's England* (1916) says henbane is the herb meant.

Scan *insane*, and see note on II. 3. 41.

92, 93. *Wonder* is that silent feeling of admiration of which *praise* is the inadequate expression. Duncan, as he hears of Macbeth's achievements, is moved by each to a fresh feeling of wonder (note the plural) which makes mere "praise" difficult and inadequate, though not to give praise will appear grudging and ungracious: thus he is tongue-tied with the conflict— "silenced with that".

Which should be thine or his, i.e. whether he should keep the "wonder" to himself, or give the expression of it ("praise") to you.

97, 98. *As thick as hail;* a simile very common in Elizabethan writers. The Folio's reading "as thick as *tale*" seems scarcely possible, though it has been interpreted, 'as fast as they could be told, i.e. counted'—from *tale* = 'number', as in "the tale of bricks", Exodus, v. 18. *post*, messenger.

104. *earnest*, pledge; cf. 132 and see G.

106. *addition*, title; cf. III. 1. 100. Literally "something annexed to a man's name, to show his rank, occupation...or otherwise to distinguish him".

107. *devil;* slurred into a monosyllable, as by the Scotch. Banquo refers to 49.

108, 109. Cf. v. 2. 20–2. How exactly does Macbeth say this?

111–14. Angus's ignorance is certainly hard to explain, since he has come with Ross, who knew the whole story of Cawdor's defection.

111. We must scan *whether* = *whe'er* (as often), and slur *he was* into a single syllable.

112. *line*, strengthen, support; the metaphor of putting a new *lining* into. Cf. *Henry V*, II. 4. 7, 8:

> To line and new repair our towns of war
> With men of courage and with means defendant.

118–20. Macbeth wants (cf. 86) to find out what Banquo thinks of the greater prophecy (50), though he only mentions the lesser (49).

120. *That, trusted home;* "such trust, pushed to its logical consequence"—*Herford*. *home*, to the full.

124–6. I.e. they win our trust by speaking the truth in trivial things so that they may deceive us in matters of vital importance.

The honest Banquo perceives straightway the fact which Macbeth cannot see (nor his wife) till he is face to face with doom (v. 8. 19–22).

128. *swelling*, grand, magnificent, from the literal sense

'inflated', as in *Henry V*, a play which has a "prologue" or introductory speech to each "Act"; cf. Prol. 1. 3, 4:

"A kingdom for a stage, princes to act
And monarchs to behold the swelling scene!"

130–42. This soliloquy shows Macbeth's supreme quality, viz. his imaginativeness, which makes him so liable to the influences of superstition, and by which Nemesis punishes him.

How does the "supernatural" (130) influence that assails Macbeth differ from the notion of Fate in Greek tragedy? The gist of the answer is that Shakespeare endows all characters with the free-will by which a man can withstand his so-called Fate, if he chooses. Banquo and Macbeth pass through the same ordeal: the one is unscathed, the other succumbs, because he chooses to dally with the thought of Duncan's murder.

130. *soliciting*, temptation.

134. *suggestion;* see G.

137. *fears*, causes of fear.

140. *my single state of man*, the very kingdom of my being. Shakespeare uses the expression *state of man* twice elsewhere, viz. in *Henry V*, 1. 2. 184, and *Julius Cæsar*, II. 1. 67. In each case the context shows that *state* has the notion 'body politic, kingdom'; man being regarded as a microcosm (Gk. μικρὸς + κόσμος, 'little world') or epitome of the 'state, body politic', just as he is often regarded as a microcosm of the universe.

I think that *single* might mean 'absolute', from the common meaning 'only, mere'. Some interpret 'my feeble body politic of man', from *single* in its depreciatory sense 'poor, weak', as in 1. 6. 16.

For the notion that man is a microcosm, a reproduction on a small scale, of the universe, cf. *Lear*, III. 1. 10, "his little world of man".

140–2. *function Is smother'd* etc.; the power of action is lost in speculations, and only the imaginary—that which my fancy pictures but which as yet has no existence—possesses for me any actuality.

147. *Time and the hour* etc., i.e. the roughest (= most unpleasant) day will come to an end at last and bring, early or late, the appointed hour; that is, the hour which will see some particular matter done or decided. Editors show that such forms of expression as *time and the hour*, *day and long time*, were proverbial. The rhyme is that of a proverbial saying. *runs;* singular because the two nouns really make up the single idea of the lapse of time.

149, 150. He apologises ('excuse me') for his disregard of the others and invents a reason for his musings. *wrought*, moved, agitated.

151. *where*, i.e. in his memory.

154. *The interim having weigh'd it;* either 'let us, having weighed it *in* the interval', etc., or absolutely, 'the interval having weighed it', i.e. given us time to weigh it.

Scene 4

2. *Those in commission*, those deputed to carry out Cawdor's execution.

3-11. Perhaps in describing Cawdor's treachery, confession and dignity in meeting his punishment, Shakespeare had in mind the case of the Earl of Essex. (F.) Essex was an exceptional figure in Elizabethan history, to whom Shakespeare refers very pointedly in *Henry V*, Prol. v. 29-34.

5. *confess'd;* cf. I. 3. 115.

7, 8. One of the numerous pieces of *Macbeth* that have become common quotations.

the leaving it. This idiom seems to represent a combination of (1) the verbal noun followed by *of*, and (2) the gerund without the article. Elizabethan usage with regard to the verbal forms in *-ing* was not fixed.

9. *studied;* i.e. as one who had rehearsed the act of meeting death. *Study* is the word used of an actor learning his part by heart.

10. *owed*, possessed; see G.

11. *careless*, not cared for, valueless; an illustration of the free Elizabethan use of adjectival and participial terminations.

11-14. Note the dreadful "irony" (for Duncan's words, said of Cawdor, apply equally to Macbeth, "the *deeper* traitor") and its peculiar appositeness. Macbeth's first meeting with the king after Scene 3 can be no ordinary meeting: we look for something—some touch of significance—and the "irony" just gives it. That the words should have their full effect Macbeth must be visible, approaching, as Duncan begins (11), and at the close Duncan should turn to greet him. The note of "irony" runs throughout the scene, e.g. "O *worthiest* cousin!" (14): "The sin of *my ingratitude*" (15).

19. *the proportion*, the right proportion, the due relation.

20. *mine*, i.e. mine to give you; in my power to render.

21. *More is thy due* etc.; your desert exceeds more than all I

can do to repay you; more than all I can do is due to you—aye,
even more than that. The rhyme in 20, 21 gives the effect of
terse summing up. Duncan wishes to put as strongly, yet as
briefly, as is possible those professions of gratitude which are
equally difficult to say and to receive.

23. *it*, i.e. what he owes. The service which he owes as a
loyal subject is recompensed in the very discharge of its duty.

27. *Safe toward*, i.e. 'with a sure regard to'; "everything that
is sure to show you love and honour". Note "the exceeding
effort of Macbeth's addresses to the king": the traitor has to
force himself to this lip-service, and the result is a strained
style. (F.)

28. *I have begun to plant thee;* alluding to the bestowal of
Cawdor's title on Macbeth. The metaphor is continued in 32, 33.

30, 31. *nor...No;* the use of double negatives, expressing
emphasis, is very common in Shakespeare.

34. *Wanton;* in its literal notion 'unrestrained'.

37. *establish our estate upon,* settle the succession to the throne
on. The nomination (which Holinshed puts later) just fits in at
this point, for the recent troubles would remind Duncan that an
uncertain succession to the crown is an incentive to rebellion.
It destroys Macbeth's hope that "chance may crown him"
(I. 3. 143), and forces a decision (48–53).

39. *The Prince of Cumberland.* Steevens says: "The crown
of Scotland was originally not hereditary. When a successor was
declared in the lifetime of a king (as was often the case), the
title of *Prince of Cumberland* was immediately bestowed on him
as the mark of his designation. *Cumberland* was at that time
held by Scotland of the crown of England as a fief." (F.) So
now the title of Prince of Wales marks its possessor as Heir-
Apparent.

43. *bind us further,* lay us under further obligations, as our host.

44. *The rest;* "the rest which is not spent in the king's
service is like severe labour"—*Hunter.*

45. *harbinger;* see G.

45, 46. His departure (really to concert a plot with her)
naturally carries our thoughts forward to Lady Macbeth (I. 5).
The stages in the unfolding of a plot form an interesting study,
especially in a tragedy like *Macbeth*, where the dramatic movement sweeps swiftly on, down a single straight channel, to
destruction. There is no by-plot to divert the current. Coleridge
characterised *Macbeth* as "the most rapid" in movement of all
Shakespeare's plays.

50–3. The deed, already visualised by his excited fancy, is done at night (II. 1, 2). The rhyme lends a melodramatic tone, as if he had made up his mind and were taking the final plunge.

52. *wink at the hand*, i.e. be blind to its deeds.

54. *he is full so valiant*, he is, indeed, as brave as you say. They have been speaking, apart, about Macbeth.

Scene 5

reading a letter. The letter shows us the impression which the meeting with the Witches made on Macbeth; also the close sympathy between him and his wife. Note too how here, as when he enters, he leaves it to her to broach openly what he has indirectly suggested.

2. *report*, intelligence, information; he has made enquiries.

6. *missives*, messengers; as in *Antony and Cleopatra*, II. 2. 74, the only other place where Shakespeare uses the word.

13–23. In studying the characterisation of a play we learn much by noting what the *dramatis personæ* say of each other. Now no one knows Macbeth so intimately as his wife, and every line of this analysis of his character should be weighed (and illustrated). She knows his weaknesses thoroughly, but she has not realised his extreme imaginativeness, and therefore totally miscalculates the effect which acted crime will have on Macbeth's temperament.

As the speech tells us much about Macbeth, so it tells us a good deal about her: for in analysing the character of others a speaker must reveal something of his own. She exemplifies in a high degree the influence of ambition as a force that sustains the will to a certain point, and overbears all scruples in self and others. Note that she never hints at personal animosity towards Duncan (though, as a matter of history, she had strong cause for it—see p. 171). It is Shakespeare's purpose to show that she acts solely for her husband's sake.

14. *fear*, fear for, i.e. fear the weakness of.

15. *too full o' the milk of human kindness*. We do not see this aspect of his character because we never see the natural Macbeth—the "peerless kinsman" of whom Duncan and all have spoken so well. We see a man mastered by a "supernatural" temptation which incites him to a crime that brings into play all the evil in him.

16. *the nearest way;* she grimly leaves unsaid the nearest way *to what*.

18. *illness*, evil, ill qualities; an unusual sense. *should*, i.e. which should. Omission of the subject relative where the sense is not obscured thereby is one of the commonest of Shakespearian ellipses. It is specially frequent when, as here, the verb follows the antecedent immediately. So in Chaucer.

19. *holily*, i.e. you would like to obtain it by innocent means; ignorant that to wish strongly for a thing is often to will the means of getting it: hence the danger of indulging idle fancies. (F.)

20–3. *thou'ldst have* etc. We might paraphrase:

'You would like, great Glamis, the thing (i.e. the crown) which as it were cries out to you "This is what you must do (i.e. murder Duncan) if you are to get what you desire (= *it*)", and you would like the deed (i.e. the murder) which you fear to do yourself but which if it *were* done you would not wish undone.'

I think that *have* (20) is used by a sort of zeugma, in two ways, and may be rendered by 'you would like'—thus; 'you would like (to possess) the crown, and you would like the deed, i.e. be glad that it should be done'. *it* = 'what you desire; your object'.

Most editors take *that which* (22) to allude to the crown, personified. Some refer it to Duncan's murder, and interpret *it* (21) of the crown. But different things seem intended by *which* in 21 and *which* in 22.

25, 26. *chastise*, i.e. drive away all the scruples and fears which may keep you from gaining the crown. Shakespeare always accents *chástise;* cf. *King John*, II. 1. 117, "And by whose help I mean to chastise it". *round;* cf. IV. 1. 88.

27, 28. *seem*. To her excited fancy Macbeth's attainment of the crown seems almost a thing accomplished.

metaphysical, supernatural; see G. Editors show that the word *metaphysics* is defined in Elizabethan dictionaries as meaning 'supernatural arts', 'things supernatural'. Marlowe's 2 *Tamburlaine*, IV. 3. 63, 64, describes a mysterious ointment,

Tempered by science metaphysical,
And spells of magic from the mouths of spirits.

29. *The king comes here to-night*. The surprise of this announcement throws her off her guard. It comes to her at a critical moment, as the announcement of his new title came to Macbeth (I. 3. 104–7). But she quickly recovers her composure and tries (30, 31) to account for her excitement, lest the Messenger should suspect anything.

31. I.e. sent us word, so that we might prepare.

34. *for breath*, i.e. for want of; literally, 'in respect of, as regards'. Cf. *Henry V*, I. 2. 114, "All out of work and cold for action". *more*, i.e. breath.

36. *The croaking raven.* She compares the Messenger to a raven. "The messenger, says the servant, had hardly breath 'to make up his message'; to which the lady answers, mentally, that he may well want breath: such a message would add hoarseness to the raven. That even the bird, whose harsh voice is accustomed to predict calamities, could not *croak the entrance* of Duncan but in a note of unwonted harshness"—*Johnson*.

For the raven regarded as a bird of ill-omen cf. *Hamlet*, III. 2. 264 (the Players' scene), "The croaking raven doth bellow for revenge".

37. *entrance;* scan as 3 syllables, *ent-e-rance*. We often find an intrusive *e*-sound before *r* and *l;* cf. *Richard II*, IV. 17, "Than Ból|ingbróke's | retúrn | to Éng|e-lánd". See III. 6. 8.

38. *my;* as if her husband were of no account! Note the pause in the middle, "wherein the speaker gathers and nerves herself up to the terrible strain that follows" (38–52).

Lady Macbeth has been justly characterised as a woman of extreme nervous sensibility. Here she knows that she must "bend up" (I. 7. 79) her will to the breaking-point, if she is not to fail in the middle of the work which now she means to do herself (cf. 65, 66), though afterwards she makes Macbeth do it. And this intense strain on her will, by the natural process of reaction, contributes greatly to her ultimate state (v. 1).

39. *mortal*, murderous, deadly; cf. III. 4. 81.

41. *make thick my blood;* so that she may go about the work in a dulled, numbed state, and thus feel the horror of it less.

42. Scan *accéss. remorse*, pity. See both words in G.

43. *nature*, natural feeling.

44, 45. *keep peace between*, i.e. interpose as peace-maker between the purpose (*it*) and the execution (*effect*) of it, so as to prevent the matter going any further.

46. *take my milk for gall*, i.e. as gall: 'nourish yourselves with my milk, which, through my being unsexed, has turned to gall'.

47. *sightless*, invisible; see note on I. 4. 11.

48. *wait on*, i.e. ready to carry out. *nature's mischief*, all that is cruel and destructive in Nature. Some, however, take *nature* = 'human nature', and interpret 'man's evil propensities'.

49. *pall*, wrap as in a pall (Lat. *pallium*, 'a cloak').

51. *peep;* implying that even a furtive glance at a deed so hideous would be all that Heaven itself could bear. Shakespeare uses *peep* of the sun (*Venus and Adonis*, 1088), and of the stars.

"The *blanket* of the dark" is a very common metaphor, especially where some dark deed has to be concealed. Cf. "night's black mantle", 3 *Henry VI*, IV. 2. 22. Here *blanket* is a strong term for a 'curtain, covering'. Homely metaphors of this kind are not uncommon in Elizabethan writers.

52. *cry "Hold";* cf. v. 8. 34.

53. *the all-hail hereafter.* It has been well observed that she speaks as if she had actually heard the Witch's salutation (I. 3. 50) and not merely read the letter, in which the word *hereafter* was not used. But note that Macbeth may have written her more than one letter (54).

55. *ignorant*, i.e. unconscious of what lies before us, of our future greatness; in a way she personifies the "present". Some, however, take *ignorant* passively = 'unknown', and so 'obscure' (i.e. compared with what is to come); a very doubtful sense.

Either *feel* or *now* (probably the latter, by antithesis) must be emphasised to form two syllables.

56, 57. How does Macbeth say this?

59. The short line makes a strong pause which clinches the matter: let him make up his mind to *that* without more ado!

60. Some change of expression on Macbeth's face at her last words prompts this warning.

61. *to beguile the time*, to deceive the world. Shakespeare often uses *the time* = 'the present time, the world, one's contemporaries'; cf. IV. 3. 10; so in Hamlet's (I. 5. 188) "The time is out of joint". In *Twelfth Night*, III. 3. 41, *beguile the time* has the more obvious sense 'to while away the time'.

65. *provided for.* This is surely the most ghastly euphemism in Shakespeare's works.

69. *We will speak further.* He can neither resist the dominating force of her personality nor yet "bend himself up" to definite assent. And so he half "saves his conscience" by deferring decision, as before (I. 3. 143, 144).

70. *To alter favour ever is to fear*, to change countenance is always equivalent to, i.e. a sign of, being afraid. *favour;* see G.

Scene 6

The singularly reposeful character of the opening of this scene makes a great contrast to what precedes and follows.

The time is evening, dark enough to make necessary the torches which heighten the picturesqueness of the scene, yet not so dark as to make it unnatural that the king and his companions should pause outside the castle and comment on its situation.

Note the "irony" of situation which lies in Duncan's praising the castle that is to be the place of his terrible end, also in his pointed use of such hallowed titles as "host", "hostess", "guest": each is an unconscious reproach to her who has planned to violate so hideously the sacred laws of hospitality and kinship.

1–10. A Scot says: "Shakespeare may have learned from the lips of some Highland chief in the Court of King James about the mild climate of Inverness to which he makes special reference in *Macbeth*."

3. *gentle,* calm, composed, i.e. made placid by the "air".

4. *martlet;* misprinted *barlet* in the Folio; see *The Merchant of Venice*, II. 9. 28–30. The word is a diminutive of *martin*, a large species of swallow; *martin* being the proper name *Martin*, applied to various birds and animals, e.g. F. *martin-pêcheur*, 'a kingfisher'. *approve*, prove, show.

5. *By his loved mansionry*, by making it his favourite abode. The description seems to imply the yearly return of the bird to its old haunt. The 1st Folio has *mansonry*. Some editors read *masonry* (= 'building', i.e. nest).

6. *jutty;* a part that projects like a *jutty*. A *jetty* (whence the corrupted form *jutty*) is literally 'a thing thrown forward', i.e. into the water; F. *jeter*, 'to throw'.

7. *coign of vantage*, convenient corner, i.e. for nesting in. The phrase has become a common quotation to signify 'any position that affords special facility for observation or action'. Properly *coign* means 'a projecting corner', being an obsolete spelling of *coin*, 'a corner-stone', hence 'a corner, angle'. F. *coin*, 'a corner'; literally 'a wedge' (Lat. *cuneus*).

11. *sometime*. The Elizabethans often treat *sometime* = *sometimes*.

13, 14. *God 'ild*, i.e. *yield* = 'may God reward, repay you'; an everyday form of thanks that got corrupted in various ways; thus the 1st Folio here has *god-eyld*.

Duncan means: the love of his subjects sometimes occasions him "trouble" (11), but he accepts the "trouble" with thanks for the sake of the love: so Lady Macbeth and her husband should accept with thanks the "pains" and "trouble" (14) which his visit occasions, and be grateful to him, for the sake of the feeling which his visit shows—namely, his great regard for them. Briefly, he would not be at their castle at all if he did not esteem them highly. (F.)

bid God 'ild us; practically equivalent to "thank us" (14).

your pains, the trouble caused to you. F. *peine,* 'trouble'.

14–19. She finds it easier to lie than Macbeth did (I. 4. 22–7).

16. *single,* poor, simple, unworthy; from the sense 'no more than, mere, only'; and the same mock-humility is seen in *business* = 'affair' (as we say colloquially).

20. *We rest your hermits,* we are your debtors still, bound to remember you in our prayers. *Hermit* here has the same notion as "beadsman", literally 'a man of prayer' (from A.S. *biddan,* 'to pray'), and so 'one who prays for his benefactor', e.g. as the inmate of an almshouse who prayed for the person that founded it.

22. *purveyor,* forerunner; literally the officer sent on in advance to provide (F. *pourvoir*) food for the king and his retinue. Scan as three syllables.

23. *holp;* the form of the pret. used for p.p. *holpen.*

26. *in compt,* under obligation to render an account; the metaphor of a steward of an estate who at the "audit"-day has to give an account of receipts and expenditure to the owner.

28. *to return your own,* to give you back what is yours.

31. *By your leave,* permit me; explained by 28.

Scene 7

Enter a Sewer; see *sewer* in the Glossary.

1–28. This famous speech should be analysed closely. It reveals a medley of feelings in Macbeth's heart, for and against the meditated crime. Note how the practical considerations (such as fear of consequences) preponderate over nobler motives.

It is his looking forward that mainly distinguishes Macbeth's attitude towards the murder from Lady Macbeth's. She does not look beyond the actual winning of the crown, and concentrates her whole strength on that. Cf. I. 5. 38–48.

1. *If it were done* etc.:

'If the deed were done with when once it is executed, then

the sooner it were executed the better. If the act of murder could catch in its toils (and so arrest) the evil results of murder, and thus in the moment of its completion secure successfully its object; so that just this blow might be the one thing necessary to do and the absolute conclusion of the matter in this life—just in this life, I say, this narrow bank in the mighty ocean of eternity; why, then, we would hazard the life to come with all its possibilities of punishment, and do the deed.' (F.)

The use of *done* in two senses is quite in Shakespeare's manner. Our text is substantially that of the 1st Folio. See also p. 176.

3. *trammel up*, to net up, to enmesh; the notion being that the consequence of the deed should be captured in the doing and so not escape to "plague" (10) the doer afterwards. See G.

4. *his*, its; referring to "assassination", certainly not to the unmentioned Duncan. *surcease*, cessation, conclusion; see G.

success, real attainment of one's purpose; not just to do the deed and afterwards be "plagued" with the consequences.

that, so that, as in 25. Abruptness well suggests broken meditations.

6. *But here*, only here. The line implies, 'all I ask is safety in this world—not much to ask, seeing how short our time here is'.

shoal. The 1st Folio has *schoole*. The emendation *shoal* (by Theobald) gives us one of the finest of images—the likening of "our little life" to "an isthmus between two eternities": an image that reminds us of Hamlet's comparison of this earth with "a sterile promontory" (II. 2. 310, 311). Quite possibly, *school* was simply an Elizabethan spelling of *shoal*.

7. *jump*, hazard. Cf. *Cymbeline*, v. 4. 188: "You must either be directed...or jump the after inquiry on your own peril." From the literal sense 'to skip over' comes the figurative sense 'to pass lightly over', hence 'to disregard, to chance, to risk'.

the life to come; contrast Hamlet's speculations on the "something after death" (III. 1. 64–82).

8. *We...have judgment here*, judgment on our deeds awaits us in this world. *still*, ever, always. *that*, so that.

8–10. *we but teach;* "we teach others to do as we have done, and are punished by our own example"—*Johnson*.

10. *this;* a rather tempting change is *thus*.

11. *Commends*, offers. Holinshed uses the same figure in describing Macbeth's fears after the murder: "least he should be served of the same cup as he had ministered to his predecessor". Shakespeare's audience would remember that it was

through "the poison'd cup" prepared for Hamlet that the
Queen died (*Hamlet*, v. 2. 303–21).

14. *Strong both*, i.e. two strong reasons, viz. kinship and
loyalty. It is one of the points in which Macbeth's character is
purposely blackened by the dramatist, that he is made to be
Duncan's host at the time of the murder. This belongs to the
Donwald-story. Really the circumstances under which Duncan
was slain by Macbeth at Bothgouanan ('the smith's bothy or
hut') near Elgin are obscure.

16. *this Duncan*. Shakespeare's idealisation of the character
(see Introduction) is his most striking deviation from Holinshed.

17. *faculties*, powers, prerogatives of office. The essential
idea of *faculty* is 'power of doing' (Lat. *facere*, 'to do'); and a
common meaning formerly was 'power, liberty, right of doing,
prerogative'—as here. The "Court of *Faculties*" is an ecclesias-
tical court with power to grant certain licences and permissions.

18. *clear*, i.e. of guilt; spotless, blameless.

20. *taking-off*, removal, i.e. murder; cf. III. 1. 105, v. 8. 71.
So in *King Lear*, v. 1. 64, 65:

> Let her who would be rid of him devise
> His speedy taking off.

The euphemism is very characteristic of Macbeth, and appropriate to the moment; for as he thinks of the king's goodness he
cannot, even to himself, speak plainly of the deed, and fact it.

21. Pity, personified, is compared with an object typically
suggestive of sympathy and compassionate feelings.

22. *cherubin;* a plural. Elsewhere in Shakespeare 'cherubin'
is the singular and 'cherubins' the plural form. But in this line
'cherubin*s*' would sound unpleasant, while the correct plural
'cherubi*m*' was probably not known to Shakespeare. See G.

The general conception here of the Cherubim is due to
passages in Scripture such as Psalm xviii. It was a medieval
belief that the Cherubim had a peculiar power of vision, and
wherever Shakespeare mentions them this power seems to be
referred to. Thus here they are made to direct "the *sightless*
couriers of the air".

23. *the...couriers of the air*, i.e. the winds. Cf. *Cymbeline*,
III. 4. 38, where it is said the "breath" of slander "Rides on the
posting winds". Cf. F. *avant-coureur*.

24. *blow...in every eye;* and so cause it to fill with tears.

25. *tears shall drown the wind;* i.e. so many tears will be shed
that, like a shower of rain, they will cause the wind to fall.

25, 26. *I have no spur* etc. "I have nothing to *stimulate* me to the execution of my purpose but ambition, *which is apt to overreach itself.*" (F.)

Macbeth has no motive other than ambition for murdering Duncan. He can plead neither private grievances, nor public duty (the usual plea of regicides, e.g. of Brutus in *Julius Cæsar*). For Duncan has lavished honours on Macbeth—so lately—and been a good king.

27. *o'erleaps itself;* a phrase like 'to overreach oneself'. The second metaphor is that of a rider who in mounting on to his horse takes too great a leap and falls on the other side of the animal. (F.)

The first metaphor of the rider spurring a steed has led to the second. Swift transition from one piece of imagery to another is one of the great characteristics of Shakespeare's mature style.

28. *on the other,* i.e. side. The insertion of *side* would be wrong. It is omitted because the word has occurred in 26, and is still present to the speaker's eye of imagination; and it is not essential to the meaning, because on the stage a gesture by the actor would make the point quite clear. Nor again does the metre require *side,* because Lady Macbeth's entrance compensates for the omission of a stressed syllable.

32. *bought,* won, acquired.

34. *would,* should.

35–9. The passage plainly refers to a period before the commencement of the play. It is a proof, therefore, that Macbeth had contemplated the crime before he met the Witches.

36. *dress'd;* carrying on the metaphor suggested in 34.

37. *green,* with the after-effects of intoxication (35). *pale,* with fear.

39–45. Compare carefully with I. 5. 13–23. *Such,* i.e. as valueless, because as fickle and inconstant as your conduct in this matter.

43, 44. "Would you remain such a coward in your own eyes all your life as to let your paltry fears, which whisper 'I dare not', control your noble ambition, which cries out 'I would'?" (F.)

45. *the...cat i' the adage,* i.e. in the old Latin proverb ("adage") which said *catus amat pisces sed non vult tingere plantas.* An old English version of it was "The cate would eate fishe, and would not wet her feete". (F.)

Well might Lady Macbeth say (I. 5. 25) that she would "chastise" Macbeth into doing the deed. For she ridicules his courage and his love for herself (the two things most precious

in his eyes), and adds mockingly that *she* would not hang back!
It has been well said that Lady Macbeth is to him a fourth and
worse Witch, within his castle.

47. *beast;* in contrast to "man" (46); she harps on his words;
cf. 49 and 51. If, though "a man", Macbeth is unwilling now
to do the deed which he himself proposed to her, he cannot
(she says) have been "a man", when he first suggested it:
something—a "beast"—must have possessed him.

48. *break*, impart, disclose; commonly 'to break *with*', as in
The Two Gentlemen of Verona, III. 1. 59, "I am to break with
thee of some affairs", i.e. have some matters to tell you about.

50. *to be*, by being, i.e. by making yourself king.

52. *adhere*, favour (i.e. agree with his plan).

54, 55. These lines and the reference to her father (II. 2. 13,
14) are the chief indications of that gentler side of her character
which makes Macbeth address her in endearing terms (I. 5. 56,
III. 2. 45).

56, 57. It is wrong to regard this as a proof of "a merciless
and unwomanly nature" in Lady Macbeth. She means that
rather than break such a pledge (58, 59) *she* would have done
that which was *most revolting* to her feelings.

59. *If we should fail?* Macbeth's opposition is beginning to
weaken.

We fail. Her famous reply can be regarded in three ways:
(1) as an exclamation of disdain at the very notion of their
failing; (2) as a surprised question, implying that she had never
thought of failure; (3) as a quiet acceptance of the consequences
of failure, implying 'well, if we fail, we do, and must bravely
pay the penalty'. The first rendering seems to me best; it
harmonises with her mocking, goading tone: she drives him into
the deed by her scorn. (F.)

60. *But*, only, just; said with bitter emphasis.

screw...sticking-place. "A metaphor perhaps taken from the
screwing up the chords of string-instruments (e.g. the harp) to
their proper degree of tension, when the peg remains fast in its
sticking-place, i.e. in the place from which it is not to move."
This was done with a screw called a "wrest". (F.)

63. Holinshed, in his story of the murder of King Duff,
describes how the King's *two chamberlains* were plied with
"sundrie sorts of drinks" by the murderer and his wife till they
were sunk in "drunken sleep", and how Donwald slew them
and laid guilt on them (cf. II. 3. 83–101). See Introduction, p. xx.

64. *wassail*, carousing, revelling; see G. *convince*, overpower,

overcome; from the literal meaning of Lat. *convincere*, 'to overcome' (Lat. *con*, implying 'wholly'+*vincere*, 'to conquer').
Cf. IV. 3. 137. Now, *convince* is limited to overcoming in
argument.

65–7. Two ideas are present to her: they shall not remember
what happens—indeed, they shall not understand it at the time.

Shakespeare has in view the old anatomical theory of the
brain being divided into three sections, in each of which certain
functions are discharged: thus "reason" understands, and
"memory" retains the impression of, an incident. Here the
notion is that the fumes of intoxication first overpower the
"memory", the lowest-placed of the three sections, and then are
drained up as through an alembic into the receptacle ("receipt")
of "reason" and overcome it also. (F.)

65. *the warder of the brain*. Memory is so described either
because it is the keeper of the secrets of the brain, or because,
being the outer section of the brain, it is pictured as a sentinel
or outpost.

66. *Shall be a fume*, i.e. shall become like, no better than, a
noxious vapour bred of intoxication. Milton several times speaks
of the "fumes" that arise from excess in eating or drinking.

67. *limbeck;* see G.

71. *spongy;* strictly active, 'imbibing as readily as a sponge';
but here perhaps passive, 'drenched, full of liquor as a soaked
sponge'.

72. *quell*, murder; A.S. *cwellan*, 'to kill', cognate with *kill*
and *quail*.

73. *mettle;* see G.

74–7. Now he in his turn suggests details of the plot!

78. *As*, seing how.

79. *bend up;* the metaphor of stringing a bow.

81. *the time*, those about us; cf. I. 5. 61, 62.

ACT II

Scene 1

The scene "must be in the inner court of the castle, which
Banquo might properly cross in his way to bed"—*Johnson*.

The introduction here of Banquo serves to indicate the time,
and gives us a final glimpse of the king, gracious to the last
(13–16).

4. *husbandry*, thrift, economy.

5. Shakespeare compares the stars with candles more than once; cf. *Romeo and Juliet*, III. 5. 9, "Night's candles are burnt out".

Take thee that too; handing him something else, e.g. his shield.

13–17. Shakespeare makes the wife, not the husband (as Holinshed mentions), the recipient of a gift; the change intensifies the "irony" since she (as we know) has proved herself Duncan's deadlier foe. Indeed, it is all "irony" (13–17)— Duncan's "unusual pleasure", his present "measureless content", his graciousness.

14. *largess;* F. *largesse*, 'bounty'; from Lat. *largiri*, 'to bestow'.

offices; the servant's part of a house, on the ground floor, at the back, such as kitchen, pantry, store-rooms, cellar; still used thus.

Here *to your offices* might be rendered colloquially 'to the servants' hall' (i.e. to the servants). See *Richard II*, I. 2. 67–9.

16. *and shut up;* supply *is:* 'and he *is* lapped in a sense of boundless satisfaction'. Some, however, take *shut* as a preterite, meaning literally 'shut himself up, retired to rest'.

17–19. A laboured apology for his inadequate reception of the king. Macbeth's will, which would have had free play if he had known sooner of Duncan's coming, was limited in ways that could not be helped. *the servant to,* subject to.

25. *my consent,* i.e. agreement with me. Macbeth speaks vaguely on purpose. What he really means is: 'if you will support me, throw in your fortunes with mine'.

when 'tis, i.e. then: 'when we meet and talk'. We cannot refer *it* to any particular noun, though some refer *'t* to "business" (23), which seems too far off.

26. *So,* provided that, on condition that.

28. *franchised,* free (i.e. from guilt). *clear;* cf. I. 7. 18.

31. *drink;* the night-cup or posset (II. 2. 6).

32. *strike upon the bell;* the preconcerted signal; cf. 61.

33–49. Note how his hallucination grows; from the uncertainty of "Is this a dagger?" to particularisation of details (46, 47). His imaginings are the outlet of a perturbation which borders on insanity.

36. *sensible To,* perceptible by. The primary sense of the word is 'perceptible through the bodily organs'; F. *sensible*, Lat. *sensibilis*.

39. *the heat-oppressed brain;* the same idea of 'feverishly excited' as in "Lovers and madmen have such seething brains", *A Midsummer-Night's Dream*, V. 4.

40. *palpable;* Lat. *palpabilis*, 'that may be felt'; *palpare*, 'to feel'.

41. "Macbeth may be supposed to draw his dagger after this short line"—*Abbott*.

44, 45. *made the fools o'*. The common sense of this phrase is 'deceived by, made the dupe of', but here the meaning must be 'are ridiculed by'. Macbeth's "eyes" tell him that the dagger is real, his "other senses", e.g. touch (36, 37), tell him that it is not real: if the "eyes" are right, they are obviously "worth all the rest"; if the eyes are wrong, then the laugh is with "the other senses", which deny the reality of the dagger and thereby ridicule the eyes.

46. *dudgeon*, haft; in Shakespeare's time a common word, especially in Scotland, for the handle of a dagger; generally made of box-wood for its hardness. The etymology is unknown.

gouts, thick drops. *Gout* (F. *goutte*, Lat. *gutta*, 'a drop') means properly any 'drop of liquid', but now is used especially of blood, implying a 'large drop, a clot'.

48, 49. *informs Thus to*, takes this form before; or perhaps 'creates this vision before'.

49, 50. I.e. "over our hemisphere all action and motion seem to have ceased"—*Johnson*.

51. We may scan "The cúr|tain'd slé|ep; witch|craft cél|ebrates"; *sleep* being prolonged into two syllables. To insert *now* or *while* would be quite wrong. Milton imitates this line in *Comus*, 554, "close-curtain'd Sleep".

52. *Hecate's*. The scansion of the name as two syllables = *Hecat'* is very common. Cf. III. 2. 41, III. 5. 1; and *King Lear*, I. 1. 112, "The mysteries of Hecat', and the night". In medieval superstition Hecate is *the* goddess of witchcraft.

wither'd, ghastly, spectre-like; cf. "like a ghost", 56.

53. *Alarum'd*, summoned to his work; see *alarm* in G.

54. *his watch*, i.e. murder's means of telling how the night is going; as though murder, being wolf-like, could judge from the wolf's howl what the hour was; cf. "his sentinel".

55. The reference is to the story of Sextus Tarquinius, told in Shakespeare's *Lucrece*. Pope corrected the Folio's reading *sides*.

57. The form of expression is like "I know thee who thou art".

58. Editors note the reference to Luke xix. 40: "if these should hold their peace, the stones would immediately cry out".

59. *take the present horror*, i.e. by breaking the awful silence which increases so much the horror of the moment.

60. *it*, the "time" (59), or possibly the deed; certainly not the place ("whereabout", 58).

61. *too cold breath gives*, chills; in talking about a deed one's ardour for it often cools: "strike while the iron is hot". Like Hamlet, Macbeth, if he is to act against his inclination, must act on impulse.

words...gives. The 1st Folio has many similar cases, without rhyme, of an apparently singular verb after a plural subject; but for the most part, being unrhymed, they have been silently changed by editors. We may either (1) regard *gives* as singular and explain the anomaly "words... gives" by the theory that the verb is attracted to the *sense* = 'speech' or to the nearer noun 'breath'; or (2) treat *gives* as an example of the "northern plural" in *s*. This question of the survival in Elizabethan English of the three plural inflexions *es* or *s* (northern dialect of Middle English), *eth* (southern) and *en* (midland), is very difficult.

63. *knell;* "alluding to the passing-bell, which was formerly tolled as the person was dying"—*Elwin*. The rhyme of this couplet marks the close not merely of the scene, but of Duncan's life. It has the effect of an epitaph.

Scene 2

"The scene is written with a pen of fire, and we seem eye-witnesses of the deed of death, though it is transacted off the stage"—*Boas*.

And how appalling are the accessories of horror: the strange sounds and voices unaccounted for; the hoot of the owl without and cry of the crickets within, as if all nature were conscious of the crime; the sleeping servants—for sleep is a mystery, as of an intermediate state 'twixt life and death; and the unconscious alarm of Duncan's sons in the adjoining chamber (19–30). The "note" of the whole tragedy is Terror, and in this scene Terror reaches its climax.

3. *the fatal bellman*. "The owl, as a bird of ill omen, is compared to the 'bellman' sent to condemned persons the night before they suffer." There was an old ballad, exhorting to repentance, entitled "The Bellman's Good Morrow" (*Shake-*

speare's England, II. 522). The bellman was the night-watchman in Shakespeare's time, like the linkman of the 18th century. One of his duties was to call out the hour and the weather.

It has been shown that in *Macbeth* II. 2. 3, 4 ("the fatal bellman" etc.) Shakespeare alludes to "a certain Newgate custom" of his time, and that the passage illustrates the probable date (1606) of *Macbeth*. For "in 1605 Robert Dow, merchant taylor, gave a sum of money to provide for or fee such an official as Shakspeare is believed to allude to in Lady Macbeth's speech. Dow died in 1612, but his endowment was given to the parochial authorities of St Sepulchre's seven years before. Many London handbooks give an account of this benefaction and of another connected with it. Thus, to quote from what is at hand, Pennant:

'A solemn exhortation was formerly given to the prisoners appointed to die at Tyburn in their way from Newgate. Mr Robert Dow, merchant taylor, who died in 1612, left 26s. 8d. yearly for ever that the bellman should deliver from the wall to the unhappy criminals, as they went by in the cart, a most pious and aweful admonition; *and also another in the prison of Newgate on the night before they suffered.* I give them in the note, as they are affectingly good.'

I quote the opening sentences of the address that illustrates Shakspeare's allusion:

'You prisoners that are within,
Who for wickedness and sin,

after many mercies shown you, are now appointed to die to-morrow in the forenoon, give ear and understand that to-morrow morning the greatest bell of St Sepulchre's shall toll for you, in form and manner of a passing bell as used to be tolled for those that are at the point of death, to the end that all godly people, hearing that bell and knowing it is for you going to your deaths, may be stirred up heartily to pray to God to bestow his grace and mercy upon you whilst you live, &c.'

One cannot doubt that this formal appointment of such a monitor would be much talked of just at the time Shakspeare was writing 'Macbeth', and might very well be in his mind" (Professor Hales).

6. A *posset* was "hot milk poured on ale or sack [light wine], having sugar, grated bisket, and eggs, with other ingredients, boiled in it, which all goes to a curd". (F.)

9. *Who's there? what, ho!* Macbeth makes this exclamation at the "noise" he afterwards mentions (15); as he is returning

(17) *from Duncan's chamber.* It is to this exclamation that she refers (17).

11. *the attempt and not the deed,* i.e. an unsuccessful attempt.

12. *Confounds,* ruins; a stronger word in Elizabethan E.

13, 14. *Had he not resembled* etc. Dramatically some revelation (as here and in I. 7. 54, 55) of her better and gentler nature, from which she had deliberately (cf. I. 5. 38–52) cut herself off, is necessary; otherwise we should regard her an absolute monster, incapable of feeling any remorse afterwards.

16. *the crickets cry;* proverbially a sign of death. Commonly the white owl "screams" or screeches, the brown owl hoots.

21. Here again (cf. II. I. 41) the action shown in the stage-directions accounts for the short line.

23, 24. *one did;* for the omission cf. I. 5. 18. *That,* so that.

28. *As,* as if. *hangman,* executioner.

29. *Listening;* transitive, as in *Julius Cæsar*, IV, I. 41, "Listen great things" = 'hear important news'.

33. *thought,* i.e. thought *on;* but there is no need to add the *on.*

34. *it will make us mad.* This, like line 67, is one of those utterances to which after-events lend a dreadful significance and irony.

36–9. Another famous description of Sleep in Shakespeare is Henry IV's (2 *Hen. IV*, III. I. 5–31), ending "Uneasy lies the head that wears a crown".

37. *the ravell'd sleave,* the tangled skein. *sleave = sleave-silk,* i.e. soft floss silk; silk in a raw, coarse, unwrought state. The word is cognate with Germ. *schleife,* 'a loop, knot'; from the root of *slip.*

39. *second course;* the metaphor is shown by the next line.

56. *gild.* "Though there is no real resemblance between the colour of blood and that of gold, it is certain that *to gild with blood* was an expression not uncommon in the 16th century; and other phrases are found which have reference to the same comparison.... Gold was popularly and very generally styled *red.* So we have 'golden blood' II. 3. 95"—*Nares.*

57. *guilt.* The quibble on *gild* and *guilt* occurs in 2 *Henry IV*, IV. 5. 129, 130, where the sick king says bitterly that his prodigal son ("England") when *he* comes to the throne will welcome every "ruffian" to court and reward him:

> England shall double gild his treble guilt,
> England shall give him office, honour, might.

See also *Henry V*, Prol. II. 26. In each case the context is tragic.

Shakespeare makes his characters jest thus in moments of great emotion—especially bitterness or horror—as a relief to the feelings—and we can imagine partly what Lady Macbeth's are! The dying Gaunt, angry with Richard, puns on his own name ("Old *Gaunt* indeed, and *gaunt* in being old"), *Richard II*, II. I. 73–83, just as in the *Ajax* of Sophocles the miserable Ajax (Αἴας) puns on Αἴας and αἰάζειν, 'to cry alas!' It is like a man joking under great pain. The thing gives a sort of relief to anguish, mental or physical.

61–3. A very similar passage has been found in the *Hippolytus* (723–6) of the Latin dramatist Seneca.

It is quite likely that Shakespeare read some of Seneca's works in the original as a schoolboy, the tragedies being a favourite school-book. In any case they had been translated into English (1581) and had a great influence on the Elizabethan drama. But here, as so often in poetry, what counts is the *expression* of the thought, not the thought itself, which may occur to many minds.

62. *multitudinous*, innumerable and infinite. *incarnadine*, dye red; see G. Note (67, 68) her quiet, contemptuous reply.

63. *Making the green one red*, turning the green into one mass of red. *Green* and *red* are both nouns = the green colour and the red colour. "The imagination of Macbeth dwells upon the conversion of the *universal green* into *one pervading red*." It is impossible to take *green* and *red* as adjectives, with *sea* or *seas* understood.

65. *Knocking within;* explained by the following scene. Here, as in the banquet scene (III. 4), it is her self-control and alertness of brain that save them from discovery.

68–70. *Your constancy* etc.; your usual courage has deserted you.

nightgown; what we call a dressing-gown; a loose garment worn in the bedroom, not in bed; cf. V. I. 5.

71. *watchers*, i.e. still up, awake; not gone to bed.

73. *To know my deed.* Better, he means, to be "lost in my thoughts" and so "know" neither myself nor my deed than be recalled to a consciousness of *both:* if knowing (i.e. being made fully conscious of) what I have done *is the price* of knowing what I am, it were better to remain "lost" (71).

74. *Wake Duncan with thy knocking!* addressed to the invisible knocker. Some editors would like to have it addressed to Duncan himself, and read: "Wake, Duncan, with *this* knocking."

Scene 3

What may be called "the Porter's scene" (1–25) has been
rejected by some critics as unauthentic. The following features
stamp it, to my mind, as absolutely Shakespearian: (1) the *relief*
it gives in relaxing the tragic tension; (2) the *contrast* which
makes us feel in how abnormal a world of horror the action has
been moving: this is brought home to us by the note of normal
life which the scene re-introduces; (3) the "*irony*"—for Macbeth's castle *is* a hell, and the man "devil-porters" (17) without
knowing it. Moreover, (4) certain phrases have an indisputably
Shakespearian ring, and (5) some scene is necessary to the
structure of the play. Macbeth and his wife must have time to
remove the traces of his crime; and the "knocking" was
mentioned in the last scene. The principle involved in (1) and
(2) is of course essentially Shakespearian.

Note the allusions which throw light on the date of the play.
In Elizabethan plays there is a considerable element of what has
been called "topical allusion"—allusion, that is, to topics and
events of the time, literary customs, pastimes, fashions, current
jokes, etc. It is generally through such characters as the Porter
that this "topical" element is introduced. The Porter occupied
the gate-house (Lat. *porta*), like the "Porter's lodge" of a
college. The Porter in *Henry VIII*, v. 4, has a busy time with
the crowd pushing into the courtyard.

2. *old*, abundant; no stint of it; an emphatic colloquial use,
somewhat similiar to the slang phrase 'a high old time of it'.

4, 5. *a farmer* etc. This is commonly thought to allude to the
exceptionally abundant harvest of 1606, and the consequent
lowness of the price of corn. Editors quote from Hall's *Satires*
a description of a speculating farmer who hoards his grain in the
hope of a rise of prices, "And hangs himself when corne
grows cheap again". It was a common grievance in S.'s time
that wealthy men would hoard or buy up crops at cheap rates,
to sell in dearer times; but the speculation did not always pay!

8–11. *an equivocator;* see p. 177. *the scales*, of Justice.

13, 14. *an English tailor...stealing out of a French hose;* a
double hit—at the tailor who skimps his cloth (yet charges his
customer for the full amount), and at the English practice of
aping foreign fashions. The latter is a stock subject of Elizabethan satire. Compare Portia's jesting description of her
English suitor, the young baron (*The Merchant of Venice*, 1. 2.
79–81). There were too kinds of French *hose* (i.e. knee-breeches),

one made very long and full (cf. "round"), the other very tight and short. It is obvious which a pilfering tailor would prefer to make. (F.)

15. *goose*, the tailor's smoothing-iron, shaped somewhat like a goose.

18. *the primrose way*. Compare "the primrose path of dalliance" in *Hamlet*, I. 3. 50.

23. *till the second cock;* "about 3 o'clock in the morning". Cf. *King Lear*, III. 4. 120, 121: "This is the foul fiend Flibberti-gibbet: he begins at curfew, and walks till the first cock."

30. *a joyful trouble;* an instance of *oxymoron*, i.e. the close combination of antithetic words. It is a figure of speech which Milton, with his classical tastes, uses more than Shakespeare; cf. "With wanton heed and giddy cunning", *L'Allegro*, 141, and "In willing chains and sweet captivity", *Vacation Exercise*, 52.

32. *physics pain*, is a remedy for the trouble (F. *peine*) it involves. Cf. *The Tempest*, III 1. 1, 2, for the general sentiment that pleasure and labour often go together.

34. *limited*, appointed; it was Macduff's duty to "call" Duncan. This was a legal use of *limited*.   36. *lay*, lodged.

40. *combustion*, social conflagration; see G.

41. *New hatch'd to*, just born to the unhappy age. Of course, what is already born cannot, strictly, be foretold ("prophesied"), but its operations can, and the age can be warned of what is ahead.

hatch'd to; so we speak of a child being 'born to' the parents.

the obscure bird; cf. II. 2. 3. *obscure*, living in the dark; that loves the night. The screech-owl is meant.

Scan *óbscure*. This is an illustration of the rule that in Shakespeare and Milton words like *obscúre, extréme, compléte* throw the accent on to the previous syllable when they are followed immediately by an accented syllable, e.g. a mono-syllable like *bird*. Cf. *Lucrece*, 230, "And éxtreme fear can neither fight nor fly".

Clamour'd, wailed. The noun often means 'loud wailing'; cf. *Hamlet*, II. 2. 538, "The instant burst of clamour that she made".

43. *feverous*, i.e. like a man stricken with ague; cf. *Coriolanus*, I. 4. 60, 61.

46, 47. The inversion of the natural order expresses his emotion. For the double negative cf. I. 4. 30, 31.

48. *Confusion...hath made his masterpiece*, destruction (cf. III. 5. 29) has achieved his deadliest work.

50. *The Lord's anointed temple.* "A blending of two Scriptural phrases: 'the Lord's anointed' (as in *Richard III*, IV. 4. 150) and 'ye are the temple of the living God'"—*Herford*. The latter is from 2 Corinthians vi. 16: so in 1 Cor. iii. 16, 17.

54. *a new Gorgon.* "There were three Gorgons, but the reference is to Medusa, whose head, fixed on Minerva's shield, turned all beholders to stone"—*Herford*.

60. *The great doom's image!* a picture of the Judgment-day itself. The metaphor is continued in 61. *doom;* see G.

The strong pause in the line (which compensates for the lack of a stressed syllable) indicates that Macduff waits a moment for their reply to his summons.

62. *To countenance,* to look with your own eyes on.

67. *repetition,* recital, narration.

75. Primarily part of his purpose to deceive by feigning grief; but in its inner meaning, for Macbeth himself, a deadly truth. He had repented the deed in the very doing, and knows that for him the joy and "peace" of life have perished (III. 1. 67). *mortality,* human life and all that composes it.

76. *toys,* trifles; see G. *renown and grace is dead;* for Duncan possessed both, yet they availed him naught: why then should men trouble any more about them? His death was their death-blow.

is. We often find a singular verb with two singular nouns as subject, especially where the two nouns express kindred ideas and therefore make up one general idea which forms the real subject. Cf. *Troilus and Cressida*, IV. 5. 168, 170, "faith and troth ..bids", where 'loyal obligation' is the general idea. The idiom is not peculiar to English. Here *renown and grace* = goodness with the good fame it brought.

77, 78. "A metaphorical comparison of this world vaulted by the sky, and robbed of its spirit and grace, with a vault or cellar from which the wine has been taken and the dregs only left"—*Elwin.* (F.)

And the metaphor of the "drawn wine" is suggested to Macbeth by the sight from which he had just come in Duncan's chamber.

79. *You are,* i.e. "amiss".

92. *amazed;* a stronger word in Elizabethan English; 'distracted'.

92, 93. *a,* one, the same. *expedition,* haste.

95. *laced,* adorned as with bands of lace. "The allusion is to the decoration of the richest habits [i.e. dress] worn in the age of

Shakespeare when it was usual to *lace* cloth of *silver* with *gold*, and cloth of *gold* with *silver*." (F.)

97. *ruin's*, destruction's. *wasteful*, devastating.

99. *breech'd*, covered; literally 'covered as with breeches'. "A metaphor must not be far-fetched nor dwell upon the details of a disgusting picture.... There is but little, and that far-fetched, similarity between *gold lace* and *blood*, or between *bloody daggers* and *breech'd legs*.... Language so forced is only appropriate in the mouth of a conscious murderer dissembling guilt"—*Abbott*.

101. *Help me hence, ho!* There seems no reason to doubt the genuiness of Lady Macbeth's faint. It is an intimation of the "natural reaction of her overtaxed powers". The second deed of bloodshed is unexpected by her, and a shock at such a moment turns the scale. Macbeth, with a man's superior physical strength, is playing his part well, in the presence of danger.

103. *argument*, subject, i.e. on which to exercise their "tongues"; Lat. *argumentum*, 'subject, theme'.

105. *in an auger-hole*, literally 'in a hole as small as that bored by a carpenter's auger', i.e. in some imperceptible spot. (F.) Donalbain feels that danger surrounds them: *their* fate too may be lurking in some obscure quarter which they would never suspect.

107, 108. *Our...our;* contrasted ironically with Macbeth's and his wife's carefully prepared outbursts. *Upon the foot of motion*, ready to manifest itself. Holinshed says that Macbeth over-acted his part, so that some of his lords began to have their suspicions about him.

109, 110. They have rushed from their rooms scantily clad, and the place is cold (II. 3. 16).

111. *question*, discuss. The noun often means 'conversation'.

114. *the undivulg'd pretence*, the secret designs, aims; cf. II. 4. 24. Yet Banquo does nothing.

116. *manly readiness;* "the equipment and mood of battle"— *Herford*. They must be ready to "fight" against any further machinations that treason may have in store, and the first step is to "hide their naked frailties" by donning their clothes and armour.

120, 121. *to England...To Ireland;* from Holinshed.

123, 124. *the near in blood* etc.; the nearer to us in blood, the more likely to prove bloodthirsty (i.e. to murder them); meaning Macbeth.

For *near* = *nearer* cf. the proverbial phrase *ne'er the near*, implying that after all you were still no *nearer* getting what you wanted. See G.

125, 126. *Hath not yet lighted*, i.e. not yet reached its final mark. Naturally Malcolm, Duncan's nominated but powerless successor (I. 4. 37–9), fears that he and Donalbain, as the next heirs, will be the next victims. But their flight diverts suspicion from Macbeth to themselves (II. 4. 24–7) and leaves him free to claim the throne.

Scene 4

This scene illustrates a very instructive feature of Shakespeare's dramatic method: his side scenes. Hitherto we have been, as it were, amid the rush of tragic incidents; now we view them retrospectively, some way off, as when one turns to look back on a plain; we see them as they appear to the non-actors. And we learn the immediate after-effects (24–35) of the occurrences at which we have been present.

The omens and signs really belong to Holinshed's description of the murder of King Duff. The Elizabethan stage was hung with black curtains to mark a tragedy; cf. lines 5–10.

4. *trifled*, made trifling, dwarfed; a noun = verb, as often.

5. *act*, deed; with a quibble however on the dramatic sense.

7. *the travelling lamp*, the sun; a phrase like II. 1. 5 ("candles"). The 1st Folio has *travailing*, an old spelling of *travelling*.

8. *predominance;* an astrological word for the superior "influence" (also an astrological term) of the stars.

the day's shame; as though the daylight were ashamed to reveal such work to the world. Cf. III. 2. 47.

11. *On Tuesday last;* one of those touches of circumstantial accuracy by which an effect of reality is given to fiction, as in *Robinson Crusoe*. Holinshed's narrative is quite indefinite.

12. *towering.* A term of falconry, used when the hawk soars spirally to a great height (her "pitch"), preparatory to swooping down, with closed wings (technically "stooping"), on the prey. Shakespeare had a thorough knowledge of country life and sport, and is especially fond of hawking-terms, which he uses with perfect accuracy. Here, for instance, he says *her* because in all breeds of hawks (the favourite English species for hawking was the peregrine falcon) the female bird is larger and more powerful than the male, and used for bigger game, e.g. herons and ducks.

15. *minions;* literally 'darlings', and so 'the very pick of'.

race; then a special term for 'a breed of horses'.

24. *pretend*, intend, aim at; cf. II. 3. 114.

27. *'Gainst nature still;* another piece of "unnatural" (10) conduct! Cf. 16, "Turn'd wild in *nature*".

28. *ravin*, devour; see G. *up;* signifying completeness, as in 'to eat up', 'to burn-up'.

31. *Scone:* "The ancient royal city of Scone, supposed to have been the capital of the Pictish kingdom, lay two miles northward from the present town of Perth. It was the residence of the Scottish monarchs as early as the reign of Kenneth M'Alpin, and there was a long series of kings crowned on the celebrated stone enclosed in a chair, now used as the seat of our sovereigns at coronations in Westminster Abbey,...[to which] it was transferred by Edward I in 1296"—*Knight.* Cf. v. 8. 74, 75. (F.)

33. *Colme-kill;* Iona, one of the Western Isles; the burial-place of the ancient kings of Scotland, constantly mentioned as such by Holinshed. The word is said to mean 'the *cell* or chapel of St Columba', by whom Christianity was first preached there in the sixth century (about A.D. 563). We have already mentioned St Colomba (I. 2. 62).

36. Macduff's refusal is a foretaste of the part he afterwards plays.

38. *Lest our old robes* etc; i.e. lest the new order of things prove not so easy for us as the old, under Duncan. Macduff means that he will say "adieu" now, as no one can tell how matters are likely to go, and they may not meet again.

ACT III

Scene 1

7. *shine*, are conspicuous in their truth; some interpret 'prosper'.

Sennet; a set of notes played on the trumpet; see G.

13. *all-thing*, altogether, quite; Dr Murray compares the adverbial use of *nothing*, e.g. in '*nothing* loath'.

16. *the which*, i.e. Macbeth's "commands".

22. *still*, ever, always. *grave*, weighty (Lat. *gravis*, 'heavy').

23. *we'll take to-morrow;* to-morrow will serve; we will defer it till to-morrow. Of course, the needless change *talk* has been suggested.

26. *the better;* implying 'faster than usual', because of having to be back for supper.

28. *twain;* A.S. *twegen,* "The A.S. forms show that the difference between *two* [fem. and neut., A.S. *twā*] and *twain* [mas.] was originally one of gender only"—*Skeat.*

30. *are bestow'd,* have taken refuge, are lodged; cf. III. 6. 24.

32. *parricide;* applied to both the deed (as here) and the doer.

33. *strange invention;* a glance at the reports of his own guilt which he knows are in circulation.

Macbeth's repeated mention of "to-morrow" (cf. 23) is a blind to deceive Banquo and the others—as the latter part of the scene proves. The plot against Banquo follows Holinshed's account closely.

34, 35. *cause of state,* matters of state, state-affairs, that require our joint attention. *cause,* questions; cf. *Henry V.* I. I. 45, "Turn him to any cause of policy" (i.e. put him to, try him on).

44. *while,* till; an Elizabethan use. *God be with you;* slurred into *God b' wi' you;* whence the familiar contraction *Good-bye.*

49. *But to be safely thus;* an obvious *aposiopesis* (i.e. breaking-off in the middle of a sentence): 'but to be *safely* established in this position *is everything'. fears in,* fears in respect of.

50. *royalty,* nobleness, natural fitness to be king.

52. *to,* in addition to.

55-7. A reminiscence of North's translation of Plutarch's *Lives,* which Shakespeare used in writing *Julius Cæsar* (1600) and *Antony and Cleopatra.* North narrates how Antony consulted an Egyptian soothsayer who told him that his (Antony's) Genius or "good angel" was "afraid of his" (Cæsar's), and became "fearful and timorous" when near the other. Cf. the scene in *Antony and Cleopatra,* II. 3, where Antony interrogates the soothsayer.

56. *Genius.* Shakespeare almost always uses this word in allusion to the classical belief that every man is watched over by a guardian spirit who directs his actions—what the Greeks called a δαίμων ('demon') and the Romans a '*genius*'. Cf. *Troilus and Cressida,* IV. 4. 52:

> Hark! you are call'd: some say the Genius so
> Cries 'come' to him that instantly must die.

57-60. Cf. I. 3. 54-61.

60. *a line of kings;* the "line" we see later; cf. IV. I. 117.

63. *with an unlineal hand,* by the hand of one who is no heir to me.

65. *filed*, defiled. A.S. *fȳlan*, 'to make *foul*, render *filthy*'. The word was in common use (but more in pre-Shakespearian English) in the literal sense 'to make foul' and the figurative 'to defile, corrupt'.

68. *eternal jewel*, immortal soul; or perhaps 'eternal happiness'.

69. Cf. *Twelfth Night*, II. 2. 28, 29:

> Disguise, I see, thou art a wickedness,
> Wherein the pregnant enemy does much;

i.e. the ever-ready foe of man, viz. Satan ('the adversary').

64–70. No passage makes more strongly in favour of the view which attributes to Macbeth something of the real remorse of the conscience-stricken.

71. *come, fate, into the list*, etc. Macbeth accepted what he thought the will of Fate (as voiced by the Weird Sisters) in relation to himself, but rebels against the will in relation to Banquo and his heirs, and challenges Fate to do her worst against him in deadly combat.

the list, the space enclosed by movable barriers wherein a combat took place; more often in the plural.

72. *champion me*, fight *against* me, as one champion against another; a very unusual sense; it would naturally mean 'fight *for* me'.

to the utterance; F. *à outrance*, 'to extremity, to the death'; from F. *outre*, Lat. *ultra*, 'beyond'.

The *medieval* system of single combat (the 'Duello') is fully illustrated in the last scene of *King Lear* (V. 3. 91–151), where, as here, the allusion to its customs and terms is strictly an anachronism.

79, 80. *this I made good to you* etc., I proved all this to you at our last meeting which was spent in demonstrating to you how etc. Some interpret *pass'd in probation* = 'I proved to you in detail'.

81. *borne in hand*, duped with false hopes. *To bear in hand* meant originally 'to *maintain* a statement, or charge against someone' (being a literal rendering of the legal word *manutenere*, 'to maintain a charge against'); then 'to maintain a false statement' etc.; then 'to pretend, to delude with false hopes, to deceive'. In the last senses it is a common Elizabethan phrase.

83. *notion*, mind, intellect; its only Shakespearian sense.

88. *Are you so gospell'd...?* this is thought to refer to Matt. V. 44.

91, 92. They meant 'we are but human—and so will have

revenge'; Macbeth affects to misunderstand them and replies
that they represent the very lowest class of "manhood" (103),
if they let Banquo's treatment of them pass unrequited (88).
go for, pass as.

93, 94. There is a similar "catalogue" of dogs, well-bred and
other, in *King Lear*, III. 6. 71–3.

94. *Shough*, a kind of shaggy dog. *water-rug*, a rough water-
dog; *rug* means rough, entangled hair, from Swedish *rugg;*
cf. "*rug*-headed" = with shaggy hair, *Richard II*, II. 1. 156.

demi-wolves, a cross-breed. *clept*, called; see G. The word,
except in the participle, was almost obsolete even in Shakespeare's day.

95. *the valued file;* the "catalogue (of hounds) graded according to their relative value"—*Herford*.

97. *housekeeper*, house-dog, watch-dog; one kept to guard
the house.

100. *Particular addition*, some special title (1. 3. 106), such as
"the housekeeper", "the hunter", etc.

100, 101. *from the bill* etc., apart from the general list ("catalogue") in which they are all entered indiscriminately as "dogs".

102, 103. *if you have a station* etc.; if you claim to have some
position of you own, and that not at the very bottom of the
ladder among the nameless herd of mankind.

105. *takes your enemy off;* cf. 1. 7. 20.

112. *tugg'd with fortune*, dragged this way and that; perhaps
a metaphor from wrestling.

116. *bloody distance*, a hostility that must lead to bloodshed.
O.F. *destance*, Lat. *distantia*, 'a standing apart'; hence 'separation'; hence 'discord, dispute, quarrel', the earliest sense of
distance in E. Cf. "to set at distance", i.e. 'at enmity', in
Bacon's Essay *Of Seditions*.

117, 118. i.e. every moment he lives is as a stab to the very
principle of my being. *my near'st of life*, that thing on which
more than on anything else my very existence depends.

120. *avouch it*, be responsible for the deed.

122. *may not*, cannot; the old sense of *may;* cf. Germ. *mag.*
but wail, i.e. but I would have to ("must") bewail the fate of
him whom etc.

123. *Who*. The neglect of the inflexion is very common,
especially in interrogative phrases; see IV. 3. 166. Cf. modern
colloquialisms like 'Who did you see?'

128. Macbeth cuts short their assurances.

130. *the perfect spy o' the time;* "probably = the result of

perfect spying, the fit moment as determined by the closest scrutiny"—*Herford*. We must make *spy* = '*spying out*, discovery by spying'. Some would change "*the* perfect" to "*a* perfect" as though Macbeth meant, 'I will put some very competent man to spy out the favourable moment and will then get him to tell you'.

132. *always thought;* an absolute construction, 'it being of course not forgotten that'; 'always remembering that'.

133. *clearness*, i.e. from all suspicion.

134. *rubs...botches;* metaphors for imperfect and clumsy work. *rubs;* unevennesses, e.g. on a board not properly planed; commonly used of obstacles on a bowling-green, such as an uneven bit of ground or a stone, whence the figurative sense 'difficulty, impediment', as in "there's the rub" (*Hamlet*, III. 1. 65).

A *botch* is a 'flaw or blemish resulting from unskilful workmanship'.

136, 137. *absence...embrace the fate*. Euphemisms like 141, 142, and "takes off" in 105. *absence* = removal.

Scene 2

4. *For a few words*. Was *she* going to propose the "taking off" of Banquo, even if Macbeth had not led up to the subject? Cf. 38.

4–7. Proverbial sayings and maxims are often rhymed.

8. *why do you keep alone?* Partnership in guilt has begun to produce its inevitable result, separation "between the two who dare not meet each other's eyes"; and events widen the chasm more and more.

10, 11. *Using*, harbouring; so to "use discontent" in *Much Ado About Nothing*, I. 3. 41, is to harbour, cherish it.
those thoughts; cf. II. 2. 33, 34.

11. *without*, beyond, literally 'outside of'; see III. 4. 14.

13. *scotch'd*, cut with shallow incisions; slashed with wounds that will soon "close" again and not prove deadly. Cf. *Antony and Cleopatra*, IV. 7. 10, where a soldier, making light of his wounds, says that he has "Room for six scotches more", i.e. a few more shallow cuts. See G.

15. *tooth;* cf. the now proverbial words in *King Lear*, I. 4. 310, "sharper than a serpent's tooth". See III. 4. 31.

16. *the frame of things*, the whole fabric of the universe—the heavens and the earth ("both worlds").

The irregular rhythm reflects Macbeth's great passion.

6

20. *our peace;* the bliss which they had promised themselves in the attainment of the crown: for both there could have been no "peace" of mind while the prophecy of the Witches remained unfulfilled. The jingling, ironical repetition of *peace*, in two senses, viz. 'peace of mind' and 'the peace of the grave', is the same sort of grim jesting that we had in II. 2. 56, 57. Note too the antithesis ("peace") to 21, 22.

The later Folios have "our *place*", one of those tame too-obvious changes. Note that such verbal repetition as *peace... peace*, though it may not please modern taste, is thoroughly Elizabethan; see V. 3. 44.

21. The metaphor of a prisoner being "broken" on the rack (a method of torturing).

22. *ecstasy;* see G. "Restless ecstasy" describes Macbeth's state to the very life. Imagination, which might have restrained him from crime (I. 3. 130–7) by picturing vividly its results, now fills him with a fever of fear that drives him into new crimes.

22–6. For the whole sentiment—the peace of the grave—cf. the song in *Cymbeline*, IV. 2. 258–81, "Fear no more the heat o' the sun".

23. *he;* emphatic; in antithesis to 17–19.

24, 25. We have seen Duncan assailed by each (except "poison").

his, its; or "treason" may be personified.

27. *Gentle my lord;* the adjective is often transposed thus (perhaps to give it emphasis) in short phrases of address.

sleek..rugged; the metaphor of smoothing roughened hair. Cf. Tennyson's description of the shepherds tending the dead Paris, "One raised the Prince, one sleek'd the squalid hair" (*Death of Œnone*).

28, 30. Scan *'mong* and *rememb(e)rance* (4 syllables).

30, 31. *Let your remembrance* etc.; 'you have reminded me of my duty towards my guests; see that *you* do your share as hostess, especially as regards Banquo; treat him with particular distinction'.

Macbeth has not told her of the plot, but her hint in 38 encourages him to a half-confidence (43–6), which perhaps enables her to play her part better at the banquet scene.

32, 33. *Unsafe the while* etc.: 'during the time that we, in our insecurity, are forced to bathe our dignities in these streams of flattery to others (i.e. influential men like Banquo) as the only way of keeping them in vigour (or unsoiled)'. Macbeth expresses the insecurity of their new-won "honours" by likening them to something which must be invigorated by fresh water if it is to keep sound and wholesome. But the sense is forced, and the passage corrupt.

34, 35. Cf. I. 5. 61–4, I. 7. 81, 82. *vizards*, masks.

35. *leave this*, dismiss such thoughts, cf. 10, 11.

38. *nature's copy*, i.e. the *copyhold* of tenure by which they hold their lives from nature, as a man holds a farm from the owner. *Copyhold* "was a form of land tenure which differed from freehold in being terminable".

Some interpret 'the form of man' or 'of human nature', from *copy* = 'reproduction' (F.). The adj. *eterne* (Lat. *æternus*) gives us the Elizabethan verb *eternise*, 'to make immortal'.

39. *they are assailable*. Yet the Witches had prophesied to Banquo also (I. 3. 65–7); and Macbeth might have reflected that as they had proved correct in his own case, so would they in regard to Banquo and Fleance.

41. *cloister'd*, within cloisters. "The bats wheeling round the dim cloisters of Queens' College, Cambridge, have frequently impressed on me the singular propriety of this original epithet" —*Steevens*. (F.)

to, in obedience to. *Hecate's;* for the scansion cf. II. 1. 52.

42. *shard-borne*, borne through the air upon scaly wing-cases.

The word *shard* or *sherd* (see G.), literally 'a fragment', commonly meant 'a fragment of pottery', as in Isaiah xxx. 14. Being hard, shiny and brittle, the wing-cases of the beetle might well be likened to bits of pottery and called *shards*. Cf. *Cymbeline*, III. 3. 20, "The sharded beetle" (i.e. furnished with shards). The technical name for the wing-cases is *elytra*; their hard, horny substance protects the delicate wings inside. (F.)

42, 43. Gray, probably with these lines in his memory, marks the fall of night in the same way, *The Elegy*, 5–8.

43. *yawning*, drowsy. *peal;* a metaphor suggested by the old custom of ringing the curfew at dusk. We might paraphrase 'his nightly curfew that bids to slumber'.

44. *note*, notoriety; often = 'distinction', whether good (cf. V. 7. 21), or bad, as here. Some interpret 'stigma, brand' (= Lat. *nota*, 'a mark of censure').

46–53. Contrast her great address (I. 5. 38–52) to night and the powers of darkness and evil: hers rings with a fierceness that corresponds precisely with her hard, imperious will; his is steeped in sentiment and fancy, and alive with imagery and observation of nature; more poetical, in short, more emotional, more imaginative. It is from him that we have the play's most wonderful speeches; and the greater his feeling, the higher rises the wave of his eloquence. Lady Macbeth overshadows him because sheer power of doing tends to overshadow thought or speech.

46. *seeing night*, night that closes the eyes; see G.

47. The same thought as in II. 4. 8, viz. that the deed is too terrible for daylight. Day in its "pity" would warn Banquo. *Eye of day* often (but not here) means the sun.

49. The legal metaphor is the outcome of the image suggested by her speech (38). Macbeth likens himself to a man whose safety depends on the cancelling of some "bond"; the "bond" here being that by which Banquo and Fleance hold their tenure of life. Editors compare *Richard III*, IV. 4. 77, 78, where Queen Margaret prays for Richard's death: "Cancel his bond of life, dear God, I pray."

Shakespeare's partiality for legal terms and accuracy in using them indicate a considerable knowledge of law, which gave rise to the conjecture that as a youth he may have been in an attorney's office. But his use of technical terms in general is very correct. *King Lear* shows that his medical knowledge was great; yet the medical profession have not claimed him as a doctor.

51. *the rooky wood*, the wood which is the haunt of rooks or "crows" (50). "Crow" was (and is) used quite commonly of the *rook*, though strictly it denotes the carrion crow.

Some editors make a difficulty about taking *crow* = 'rook', and interpret *rooky* = 'misty', *rooky* or *roky* being a north-country variation of *reeky*, 'vaporous, misty'. But is it likely that Shakespeare, a midlander by birth and Londoner by residence, would use a north-country dialect word?

The short line marks a pause during which Macbeth looks out.

53. *preys*, i.e. their respective kinds of prey; the plural often has this notion 'respective'.

55. This striking thought has been traced back to the *Agamemnon* of Seneca, whose philosophy (especially his pithy commonplaces on life), no less than his style, strongly affected the Elizabethan dramatists.

Dowden calls this line the motto of the play. "*Macbeth* is the tragedy of the twilight and the setting-in of thick darkness upon a human soul."

Scene 3

It has been argued that Banquo's fate is simply "poetic justice" because he had acquiesced in the sovereignty of Macbeth whom he suspected to be guilty (III. 1. 1–3): as he took the risk (not to mention the shame) of doing so, he must take the consequence.

2. *since he delivers* etc.; seeing that he reports correctly.

4. *To the direction just*, i.e. just as we have been directed.

7. *timely*, in time.

9, 10. I.e. all the other guests expected at the banquet. *note*, list. *expectation*, people expected; abstract for concrete. Banquo is a little late (11), as he anticipated (III. 1. 25–8).

11. *about*, i.e. round, by the longer way.

18. Tradition said that Fleance escaped into Wales, married a Welsh princess, and had a son Walter, who became Lord High Steward of Scotland, took the name of *Walter Steward*, and was the ancestor of James I. But we are now told that Banquo and Fleance are simply fictitious persons, the invention of the old chroniclers.

19. *the way*, the best way, the right thing to do.

Scene 4

1. *degrees*, ranks.

1, 2. *at first And last*, from the beginning to the end of the feast.

5. *keeps her state*, remains in her chair of state, i.e. a raised, canopied throne. No doubt, *state* in this common Elizabethan sense was originally short for 'chair (or 'seat') of *state*' (= 'dignity', 'honour'). Sometimes the word was used of the canopy alone, as in *Paradise Lost*, x. 445.

6. *require her welcome*, ask her to bid you all welcome.

9. *encounter*, meet, respond to.

14. *'Tis better* etc.; "a daringly ungrammatical way of saying that the blood is better on the murderer's face than in Banquo's veins"—*Herford*. For *without* = 'outside' see III. 2.

11. Some interpret *than he within* = 'than that he should be within this room'.

19. *nonpareil*, one who has no equal (F. *pareil*—cf. Lat. *par*).

22, 23. Three metaphors: his kingship would have been sound in itself to the very core, as solid marble; firmly based as the rocks of the coast not far off; unfettered and free in its range as the air that surrounds (encases) us.

24. *cabin'd, cribb'd*, imprisoned as in some cabin or cell, shut up in a crib. The noun *cabin* often signified 'a cell, a small room'. *Crib* was used similarly, but suggests still more the idea 'cramped space'. This line of *Macbeth* is now a frequent quotation.

25. *saucy*, petty but vexatious. *safe*, safely dispatched. A colloquial use, as in our phrase 'safe out of the way'. So in *The Tempest*, III. 1. 21, Miranda bids Ferdinand take a rest, as Prospero will not know: "He's safe for these three hours."

27. *trenched;* F. *trancher*, 'to cut'; see v. 8. 9.

29. *worm*, snake; reptiles (cf. IV. 1. 8, 14–17) were considered venomous. *Worm* is used in *Antony and Cleopatra* of the asp (serpent) with which Cleopatra killed herself (v. 2. 243, 256). A.S. *wyrm* means indifferently 'worm' and 'snake'.

32. *We'll hear, ourselves, again;* we (the regal 'we') will hear your report to-morrow when we are alone, by *ourself*.

33–7. Lady Macbeth rebukes her husband for not playing the part of a host (forgetful of his promise and of his own instructions to her, III. 2. 29–31). 'You do not bid the company welcome; a feast is no feast—'tis a mere inn-meal—if during its course the host does not often assure his guests how glad he is to see them: mere eating can best be done at home: away from home people look for that ceremonial courtesy (such as the pledging of toasts) which is a relish to the food and without which a gathering is cold and incomplete.'

To *make* or *do* or *give cheer* was a common phrase = 'to give a kindly welcome, to receive hospitably'.

36. Scan *c'rémony*.

37. *remembrancer;* cf. III. 2. 30.

39. It is a strange notion that Macbeth sees two ghosts— first Banquo's and then (92) Duncan's, or *vice versa*. Lines 50 and 81 (cf. 27) *must* refer to Banquo, and if a different ghost had been intended after 92 the fact would have been indicated by a stage-direction.

in Macbeth's place; symbolising, practically, what Macbeth himself said (III. 1. 64–70).

40. *Here had we now...roof'd;* all the rank and distinction of our country would be assembled under this roof.

41. *graced*, gracious. In Elizabethan E. we often find *-ed* = *-ful;* cf. "guiled shore", i.e. guileful, treacherous, in *The Merchant of Venice*, III. 2. 97.

42. *who;* cf. III. 1. 123. *may I,* I can.

43. *mischance,* his ill luck in not being here.

55. *upon a thought;* literally 'following upon'; in a moment or two.

57. *extend his passion,* increase his agitation.

58. *Are you a man?* An echo of her previous taunts (I. 7. 49–51).

60. *proper,* fine! Of course, said ironically.

62. *This is the...dagger;* this is another of your apparitions, like that visionary dagger! *air-drawn,* drawn in the air, unreal.

63. *flaws,* bursts; see G.

64. *to,* compared with; from the notion 'in relation to'. A very common use; cf. *Hamlet,* I. 2. 139, 140:

> So excellent a king: that was, *to* this,
> Hyperion *to* a satyr.

65. I.e. a "Winter's Tale"; cf. *Richard II,* V. 1. 40–2. *The Old Wives' Tale* is the title of a comedy by Peele (1558–98).

66. *Authorized by;* literally 'vouched for by', hence 'told on the authority of'. For the scansion cf. *Sonnet* 35, "Authórizing thy trespass with compare"; and *chástise* in I. 5. 25. These verbs in *-ise* or *-ize* (the syllable now accented) still showed in Elizabethan E. the French influence, e.g. *authórize* = F. *autōrīser.*

72, 73. I.e. we must leave the dead unburied so that birds of prey may devour them and thus serve as their tombs.

76. *húmane;* this is Shakespeare's invariable accentuation of the word, except in *The Winter's Tale,* III. 2. 166. Cf. *Lucrece,* 571, "By holy humane law, and common troth". The present distinction between *húman,* 'of or pertaining to man', and *humáne,* 'worthy of a man, benevolent', did not then exist. The 1st Folio always has *humane* for either sense. As late as Dryden and Pope we find *humane* = *human.*

purged the gentle weal; "purged the state of violence and hence made it 'gentle'"—*Herford.* We had the same proleptic use of the same adjective in I. 6. 3. *weal;* cf. *commonwealth* = 'state'.

81. *twenty;* cf. 27.

83, 84. Critics note the resourcefulness and tact of Lady Macbeth's method of dealing with her husband at this crisis. First she seeks by angry taunts to shame him into self-control; failing, she addresses him in an ordinary tone (a device that often succeeds with disordered brains).

85. *muse,* wonder; see G.

92. *And all to all,* and pledge all good wishes to all.

95. *speculation*, intelligence; that which is absent from the eyes of a blind man, though they may show no external defect. Some, however, take *speculation* = power of sight

101. *Hyrcan*, *Hyrcanian*; from "*Hyrcania*, a province of the ancient Persian Empire, on the S. and S.E. shores of the Caspian or Hyrcanian Sea", famous as a breeding-place of tigers. "*Hyrcanian* beast" in *Hamlet*, II. 2. 472, means 'tiger'.

102. *nerves*, sinews (= Lat. *nervi*); never used by Shakespeare in the modern sense. Milton (*Sonnet* 17) calls money 'the nerve' —where we say 'the sinews'—of war (*nervi belli pecunia*).

105. *If trembling I inhabit*. Some interpret 'if I harbour fear', from an old use of *inhabit* = 'to give a habitation to'; others 'if I stay at home skulking', instead of going forth "to the desert" (a strange, intransitive use of *inhabit*); others 'if I display trembling', literally 'if I *vest* myself in trembling, if I put on trembling as an outward *habit* or *garb*' (a still stranger use of *inhabit*).

The first explanation seems best. Probably, as a scholar points out to me, it is the real clue to "knowledge ill-*inhabited*" in *As You Like It*, III. 3. 10, i.e. ill-lodged. *protest me*, i.e. declare me *to be*.

106. *baby;* perhaps in the ordinary sense, implying here a weak, sickly child; but most interpret it = 'doll', with the notion, 'call me a mere puppet' (a common Elizabethan use).

110. *admired*, strange, wonderful; cf. "wonder" in 112. See G.

111. *overcome us*. "Can such wonders as these *pass over us* without wonder, as a casual summer cloud passes over us?"— *Johnson*. Editors show that this literal use of *overcome* was then not uncommon.

112, 113. *You make me strange* etc.; literally 'you make me seem a stranger to my natural disposition': that is, 'you fill me with wonder and confusion', 'I hardly know myself'. Hitherto he has always thought himself a brave man, yet now he is over-come by something which moves no fear at all in his wife: hence he does not know what to make of himself, whether to consider himself a coward or not.

owe = 'possess'. He is addressing Lady Macbeth alone. "Strange" carries on the idea of "wonder" suggested in her speech (110) to which he has been replying (110–12).

117. She interposes instantly because the question (116) may lead to Macbeth's betraying himself.

119. *Stand...upon*. Cf. 3 *Henry VI*, IV. 7. 58, "Why,

brother, wherefore *stand you on* nice points?" i.e. why are you so particular about, attach so much importance to, subtle points like these?

123. *Stones,* i.e. under which the murdered have been buried. *trees;* Steevens refers to the story in *Æneid* III of the bleeding tree that revealed the muder of Polydorus.

124–6. *Augures and understood relations* etc. 'Divinations and perception of the inner connection of things and incidents, by means of magpies, jackdaws and rooks, have exposed murderers whose deeds were done in the utmost secrecy.'

Editors show that *augure* (the 1st Folio's reading) was an Elizabethan form (used here for the sake of the metre) of the common abstract word *augurie*, 'divination'. Here the abstract word goes well with the other abstract word "relations". Some substitute *augurs;* but "*Augurs* and relations" is awkward. Others read "*Augurs that* understood".

Lat. *augurium* (observation of the flight and notes of birds and other signs) is supposed by some to be connected with *avis*, 'a bird', and *gar*, from the root of *garrire*, 'to talk'; cf. *garrulus*.

"To *understand relations* as *an augur*, is to know how those things *relate* to each other, which have no visible combination or dependence"—*Johnson;* and also how they relate to the matter concerning which the soothsayer is making enquiry.

125. *magot-pies,* magpies; see G. *choughs,* jackdaws; see G.
127. *at odds with,* at variance with.
128. *How say'st thou, that,* what say you to the fact that?
denies, refuses to come. No doubt, Macduff had been invited to the banquet. In the latter part of *Macbeth* he fills the same part of prominence as Banquo in the earlier.

132. *fee'd.* Holinshed says that Macbeth "had in everie noble man's house one slie fellow or other *in fee* with him" (i.e. in his pay).

133. Scan *'times* and *wei-rd* (2 syllables), as in I. 3. 32, IV. 1. 136.

133–5. The forces of evil seem now to be threatening Macbeth himself. He is being driven to that pitch of desperation in which suspense is torture, and knowledge of the worst a relief: hence his recourse to the Witches.

136. *All causes,* all considerations; every scruple and obstacle.

139. *Strange things;* the murder of Macduff.

141. *the season,* the seasoning; "that which *preserves* nature, and keeps it *fresh* and *lasting*". (F.) Lady Macbeth utters no

word of reproach to him. His welfare is still her first thought and care.

142. *My strange and self-abuse* etc.; my strange self-deception is (= is due to) the fear of the novice inexperienced in crime,— the fear that attends first attempts at crime and lacks the hardening of experience. See *abuse* in G.; and for *self* cf. v. 8. 70, note.

143. *initiate;* used actively = 'initiatory', of or belonging to initiation'. Macbeth himself recognises that the vision was unreal.

144. *deed;* another of his euphemisms (= 'crime').

Looking back on the whole scene we feel that, as has been well said, Macbeth has already touched the extreme of torture—and through that imagination which his wife had not taken into account!

How far either of them is conscience-stricken by genuine remorse is a matter which each student must try to determine for himself. Fear is, at least, a considerable element of Macbeth's unrest. Still, the repentance is there: "Macbeth retained enough of goodness to make him a haggard, miserable criminal": though "never enough to restrain him from a crime".

Scene 5

1. *Hecate;* scan *Hecat'*, as before (II. 1. 52).

7. *close contriver*, secret plotter.

13. Middleton makes his Hecate say (*The Witch*, I. 2), after the disconsolate suitor Sebastian has come to consult her, "I know he loves me not, nor there's no hope on't".

15. *Acheron;* properly, one of the four rivers of the infernal world of classical mythology; the 'stream of pain' (Gk. ἄχος, 'pain'+ῥεεῖν, 'to flow'). Shakespeare, however, seems to have regarded *Acheron* as a burning lake. Here it must be meant as a poetical title for some mountain-pool or lake (gloomy as the infernal Acheron), where the Witches are wont to assemble, near Macbeth's castle. (F.)

20. *I am for the air.* Similarly Middleton's Hecate says "I'm for aloft" (*The Witch*, I. 2). Many illustrations of this notion of Hecate and witches riding through the air might be quoted from Elizabethan writers. See *Comus*, 135; *Paradise Lost*, II. 663.

23. *corner.* Some interpret in its etymological sense 'horn' (Lat. *cornu*); but there does not seem to be any evidence for this use; yet the word certainly suggests the classical *cornua lunæ* (cf. *Georgic* III. 433). Milton imitates the line in *Comus*, 1017.

24. *There hangs* etc. "Classical magic ascribed to the moon certain exudations (*virus lunare*) which, under the spells of the enchanter, we shed upon earthly objects"—*Herford*.

profound; either literally, 'deep, hence ready to fall', or figuratively, 'having hidden qualities or meaning'. The literal sense seems better.

27. *artificial sprites;* the "Apparitions" of Act IV, Scene I.

29. *confusion,* destruction; cf. II. 3. 48.

30. *He shall spurn fate;* cf. Macbeth's own challenge to destiny, III. 1. 71, 72.

32. *security,* carelessness, false confidence; the state of a man whose "hopes" make him deaf to the warnings alike of wisdom, conscience, and fear (31).

33. "*Come away, come away*"; see p. 181.

34. *my little spirit,* i.e. her attendant familiar spirit.

Scene 6

Another of those valuable side-scenes (cf. II. 4) of comment and preparation. It shows—as we see in the cautious but ironical speech of Lennox—how the destruction of Banquo is working to Macbeth's own destruction. Great nobles such as "Lennox and another Lord" are now alarmed for themselves (32–9); Macduff has fled to England, and the "suffering country" but waits for its deliverer. As regards the dramatic structure, the scene serves to bridge the interval between the appearance of the Witches and Macbeth's promised visit to them.

3. *borne,* managed; cf. 17.

gracious; cf. 10, I. 7. 16–20, II. 3. 76 ("grace").

4. *he was dead;* when pity cost Macbeth nothing!

6, 7. An ironical reference to the way Macbeth had interpreted the flight of Duncan's sons.

8. *Who cannot want the thought...?* who can fail to think? The double negative form has the same intensive force as in the cases of two negatives or of a negative after some verb which implies negation. Strictly, Lennox should have said *who cannot have the thought* or *who can want* [= lack] *the thought*. But the combination of the two forms of expression is perfectly clear in its emphasis. This tendency to repeat a negative is a general principle of language.

monstrous; for the intrusive *e*-sound (*monst-e-rous*) cf. *rememb-e-rance*, III. 2. 30; *child-e-ren*, IV. 3. 172.

10. *fact,* deed (Lat. *factum*); especially in Shakespeare an

evil deed, as here. The same word as *feat* (O.F. *fait*, Lat. *factum*).

13. *thralls;* see G.

21. *broad*, free; implying 'free-spoken'. Cf. III. 4. 23.

22. *tyrant*. There seems no valid ground for supposing that Shakespeare used this word in the Greek sense of τύραννος = 'a usurper'.

24. *bestows himself;* cf. III. 1. 30.

28, 29. i.e. in no wise lessens the high respect paid to him.

30. *upon his aid*, in aid of him (Duncan's son, Malcolm).

31. *wake*, raise, call to arms.

35. *Free*, remove. "He is thinking of the Murderer who appeared at Macbeth's banquet to report Banquo's assassination." (F.)

36. *faithful*, loyal, i.e. to the rightful king. *homage;* O.F. *homage*, Late Lat. *homaticum*, 'the service of a vassal or man (Lat. *homo*) to his lord'. *receive...honours;* cf. v. 8. 62–4.

40. I.e. having received from Macduff a positive refusal.

41. *cloudy*, i.e. vexed, angry; cf. 2 *Henry VI*, III. 1. 154, 155. *turns me;* the so-called ethic dative; cf. *Julius Cæsar* (also a descriptive passage), I. 2. 265–8: "Marry, ...when he perceived the common herd was glad he refused the crown, he plucked me ope his doublet and offered them his throat to cut." In such passages the pronoun has the force 'look you!' 'mark this!'

42. *as who should say*, i.e. 'like *one* or *he* who'; cf. F. *comme qui dirait*, i.e. *celui qui*.

44, 45. I.e. to get as far as possible out of Macbeth's reach.

48, 49. I.e. our country *suffering under* a hand, etc. Such inversions are common; cf. *Richard II*, III. 1. 9, "A happy gentleman in blood and lineaments", i.e. a gentleman happy in. So in Milton; cf. *Paradise Lost*, I. 567, "With fixed anchor in his scaly rind".

ACT IV

Scene 1

This scene, like the first and third (to line 37) scenes of the play, is a remarkable exemplification of the rites of witchcraft. The ingredients of the Witches' caldron naturally consist of things venomous or loathsome.

1, 2. *brinded*, brindled, streaked; see G. *hedge-pig*, hedgehog.

3. *Harpier;* the name of some demon; suggested perhaps by the word *harpy* (a winged monster of classical legend). Many of these names of demons are taken from the Talmud or Hebrew commentaries on the Bible.

6. *cold;* equivalent to two syllables. The needless insertion of *the* disarranges the inverted (or "trochaic") rhythm; *coldest* would be a preferable change metrically.

8. *venom;* Shakespeare several times speaks of toads as venomous (and there seems to be still some doubt on the point); cf. the familiar lines in *As You Like It*, II. 1. 12–14. Lee says that many of the "ingredients" (34) come from the description of Medea's caldron in Ovid's *Metamorphoses* (IV), familiar to S. through Golding's translation and similarly drawn upon in the famous "Ye elves" passage of *The Tempest*, V. 33.

12. *fenny,* from a fen, marsh.

14–16. Neither the *newt* (a kind of lizard—see G.) nor the *blind-worm* (i.e. slow-worm) is harmful; but both were then thought to be.

Adder's fork, i.e. forked tongue. When Titania goes to sleep, her fairy attendants sing (*A Midsummer-Night's Dream*, II. 2. 9–12):

> You spotted snakes *with double tongue,*
> Thorny hedgehogs, be not seen;
> *Newts and blind-worms, do no wrong,*
> Come not near our fairy queen.

17. *howlet,* owl (traditionally associated with witchcraft); see G.

21. *Fire;* a dissyllable, as often; cf. *Richard II*, I. 3. 294, "O, whó | can hóld | a fí|re ìn | his hánd". Scan here "Fí-re | búrn and | cáldron | búbble".

22. *dragon;* a fabulous sort of winged serpent; Lat. *draco.* The chariot of the Night was supposed to be drawn by dragons.

23. *mummy;* "a preparation for magical purposes, made from dead bodies"—*Schmidt.* Another writer notes that "Egyptian mummy, or what passed for it, was formerly a regular part of the *Materia Medica*". There appear to have been various kinds of *mummy* used in medicine, for different purposes, e.g. to stanch blood. (F.)

maw...gulf; alternative words for the stomach of animals. *Gulf* = 'maw' is simply a figurative use of *gulf* = 'an abyss; something that engulfs or swallows, like a whirlpool or the gullet'. O.F. *golfe*, Gk. κόλπος. Probably *gulf* is not connected with *gulp*, 'to swallow'.

24. *ravin'd.* The verb always means in Shakespeare 'to devour greedily' (II. 4. 28): hence *ravin'd* can hardly mean 'glutted with prey'. Probably it is active = 'ravenous'. Cf. III. 4. 41, note. See G.

28. *Sliver'd,* torn off; see G. An eclipse was proverbially of evil omen, the precursor of troubles. Being an unlucky moment for beginning any lawful design, it was thought favourable to wicked schemes.

32. *slab,* slimy, glutinous. From *slab,* 'a puddle'; whence *slabby,* 'sloppy, dirty'; akin to *slobber.*

33. *chaudron,* entrails; see G.

37. Shakespeare accents *báboon* and *babóon,* as suits the metre.

43. "*Black spirits*"; see p. 180.

44. "It is a very ancient superstition that all sudden pains of the body, which could not naturally be accounted for, were presages of something that was shortly to happen"—*Steevens.*

50–61. *I conjure you* etc. Macbeth cares nothing for anybody or anything: his desire for knowledge must be gratified at all costs.

52, 53. For the power exercised over the winds by witches cf. I. 3. 11–17. *yesty,* foaming; see G.

54. *navigation;* abstract for concrete; 'all ships and sailors'.

55. *bladed;* 'in the blade', i.e. at the leaf-stage—*not* 'in the green ear'; for *blade* means the green shoot or leaf before the corn is in ear.

lodged, beaten down, laid almost flat; cf. 2 *Henry VI,* III. 2. 176, "Like to the summer's corn by tempest lodged". The modern term is 'laid'.

59. *nature's germens,* all the seeds (Lat. *germina*) of life in the world. The 1st Folio has *germaine;* the correction *germens* is certain. Cf. the similar passage in *King Lear,* III. 2. 8, where Lear, buffeted by the storm, apostrophises the thunder thus: "Crack nature's moulds, all germens spill [= 'destroy'] at once".

tumble; plural because *treasure* is treated as = 'riches'.

60. *sicken,* i.e. grow weary of its own work of destroying.

65. *farrow,* litter; akin to Germ. *ferkel,* 'a young pig'.

68. *The Apparitions.* "The 'armed head' represents symbolically Macbeth's own, struck off by Macduff (see *stage-direction* v. 8. 53); the 'bloody child' represents Macduff (see v. 8. 15); the 'child crowned with a tree in his hand' represents Malcolm, who gives the order to the soldiers to cut down the boughs of Birnam Wood (v. 4. 4)"—*Herford.*

Thunder accompanies the apparition of Ariel "like a harpy" in *The Tempest*, III. 3. 52.

70–2. An injunction to silence is customary in all scenes of incantation; and it was an ancient belief that spirits summoned to earth by means of spells were reluctant to answer questions and eager to be "dismissed". (F.) Cf. the Epilogue to *The Tempest*.

71–94. Holinshed describes how "certeine wizzards" told Macbeth that he "ought to *take heed* of Macduffe"; and how another time "a witch" told him that "he should *neuer be slaine with man borne of anie woman, nor vanquished till the wood of Bernane came to the castell of Dunsinane*", which prophecy made him "put all fear out of his heart...and doo manie outragious things". The rhyme in the speeches of the Apparitions gives them the effect of riddles.

74. *harp'd*, touched aright, hit; as a harpist touches the right string.

84. *a bond of*, a pledge from; so that he may have a hold over fate and feel sure of the fulfilment of the prophecy (80, 81).

88, 89, *round;* cf. I. 5. 26. *top;* used with the same figurative notion that 'crown' often bears, viz. 'summit, culminating point'. Perhaps *round* is intended to suggest the lower, encircling part of the crown, and *top* the upper, ornamental part. (F.)

93. *Dunsínane* is the accentuation here, but *Dunsináne* elsewhere in the play. Both accentuations have the authority of Scots writers.

94–101. Rhymed because phrased in the same key as the supernatural speeches that have just gone before.

95. *impress*, force to take military service. Cf. the old system of '*press*-gangs' for the navy. Shakespeare uses *press* and *impress* several times with this idea, e.g. in I *Henry IV*, I. I. 21.

97. *Rebellion's head;* another of Theobald's fine corrections; the 1st Folio has *rebellious dead*. *Rebellion* is precisely what a usurper would fear; cf. lines 90, 91. Some think that the metaphor may be suggested to Macbeth by the "armed head" he has lately beheld. To retain *dead* and interpret it of Banquo is very far-fetched.

99. *the lease of nature*, i.e. his allotted term of years. For the legal metaphor cf. 84 and III. 2. 49.

106. *noise;* Elizabethan writers often use *noise* = 'music', and it is thought to have that sense here; cf. the stage-direction. The *hautboy* is a wood instrument (F. *haut + bois*).

111. *A show of Eight Kings.* "Banquo is reputed to have been an ancestor of the Stuarts. Walter Stuart married the

grand-daughter of Robert Bruce, and their son was Robert II. His descendants, who sat upon the throne, were Robert III and the six kings called James. Mary, daughter of James V, is omitted in the vision, as the Witches' prophecy related only to kings"—*Herford*. The purpose of the "show" is to introduce the famous complimentary reference (120, 121) to the accession of King James. S. may have had in mind an official proclamation (extant) exhibiting the pedigree of the Stuarts and James's descent from Banquo (*Shakespeare's England*, 1916, II, 536).

112. *the spirit of Banquo;* the apparition at the banquet-scene, which usurps in Macbeth's memory the place of Banquo as he had known him in life.

116. *Start, eyes!* He has already said that the sight of *one* king alone scorches his eyeballs (113): well may he, after seeing four, wish to be rid of his eyes altogether.

117. *the crack of doom;* "the thunder-peal of the day of judgment". Cf. passages descriptive of the Judgment-day in The Revelation, e.g. in xi. 19, xvi. 18. *Crack* was often applied to a loud noise, e.g. the roar of cannon (I. 2. 37), a thunder-clap, trumpet-blast. Some think (less probably) that "the crack of doom" here means the last trump.

The verse "could not fail to be a most acceptable prediction to King James", but the course of history gave it a grim "irony".

119. Mirrors and crystals, and glasses so cut as to produce an illusion when looked into, play an important part in magic. By this use of the "glass" Shakespeare suggests to the imagination the long line of other kings whom it would have been tedious to bring on the stage.

121. The *ball* is "the globe, part of the king's insignia. In 1542 Henry VIII. took the title of King of Ireland. When James VI. of Scotland came to the English throne the three sceptres were united. Thus he alone of the eight could carry 'two-fold balls and treble sceptres'"—*Herford*.

Cf. *Henry V*, IV. 1. 277, 278, where Henry enumerates all the emblems of sovereignty, "the balm, the sceptre, and the ball", etc.

Why the distinction "*twofold* balls...*treble* sceptres"? Maybe that the sceptre, being the easier to bear of the two emblems and therefore used on occasions when the ball was not produced, was regarded as typical of all aspects of kingship; while the ball was specially associated with the greatest event in a monarch's career, namely, his coronation. If this be so, then "*twofold* balls" refers to the double coronation of James, at Scone and at

Westminster. Some, however, think that the "*twofold* balls" =
the two islands, Great Britain and Ireland, and the "*treble*
sceptres" = the three kingdoms, England with Wales, Scotland
and Ireland. (F.)

123, 124. *blood-bolter'd*, having his locks matted with clots of
blood; see *bolter* in G. *for his*, as *his* descendants, not Macbeth's.

126. The only line where the accentuation *Mácbeth* occurs.

127. *sprites*, i.e. *spirits* = feelings, state of mind.

130. *antic round*, a fantastic round-dance. *antic;* see G.

132. Said, of course, in mocking irony; see 48 for Macbeth's
"welcome" of them.

138. *Infected;* as with the plague. In Shakespeare *infect* and
its derivatives often have this notion of plague.

144. *anticipate*, forestall, prevent.

145. *flighty*, swift to take flight beyond one's reach. We have
seen what his "purpose" was (83, 84).

148. *The firstlings*, the first product of, signifying here the
first thoughts or deeds of. *Firstling*, like Germ. *erstling*, means
literally 'the first of its kind to be produced...the first product'.

153. *trace*, follow; the metaphor of following footsteps.

155. *sights!* i.e. the "apparitions", "shows" and "sights"
(122). Macbeth has cursed his intercourse with the Witches
(133-5, 138, 139), and now renounces all further dealing with
them.

Scene 2

The scene is important as bringing out the utter savagery into
which Macbeth has deteriorated. Also, its tone of domestic
calm is a contrast. The part with the child is the one bit of pure
pathos in the play: "a pathos which clings about all Shake-
speares' portraits of children"—*Symons*. Compare Prince
Arthur in *King John*. In Holinshed's narrative Macbeth goes
himself to besiege Macduff's castle, believing him to be there,
and causes "the wife and children of Makduffe, with all other
whom he found in that castell, to be slaine".

1. Macduff's flight appears at first sight to merit his wife's
censure. But we see later that he acted from patriotic motives.
He felt that the time was ripe for rebellion and that he must go
to England to summon Malcolm. Cf. IV. 3. 207.

7. *titles*, possessions; literally 'the things to which he has a
title' (i.e. a title of ownership).

9. *the natural touch*, natural affection, i.e. for his wife and
children. *Touch* in Shakespeare sometimes means 'sensation,

feeling', the context defining the particular feeling—here affection. Cf. *The Two Gentlemen of Verona*, II. 7. 18, "Didst thou but know the inly touch of love".

17. *fits;* perhaps 'crises'; some interpret 'caprices'. The metaphor (i.e. from some illness) is shown by *Coriolanus*, III. 2. 33, "The violent fit o' the time craves it as physic".

19. *know ourselves,* i.e. to be traitors. Macduff had been forced by national circumstances to act in a way which made him appear a "traitor" (44–50) to his family (3, 4): yet he did not "know himself" to be a "traitor", did not feel himself to be one.

19, 20. *when we hold rumour* etc.; when we interpret every report in the light of (or 'under the influence of') our fears, yet cannot define those fears and say what it is that we dread.

On the eve of some national crisis, like a Revolution, the atmosphere is charged with a vague alarm, and this condition colours men's view of everything and makes them interpret unfavourably every fresh rumour.

hold; not 'hold true', but simply 'judge, estimate' and so 'interpret'.

22. *Each way and move;* literally 'every way and with every movement' (of the sea); that is, 'in every direction, according to the current'. It is the picture of a rudderless ship drifting about at the sport of the waves. Shakespeare does not elsewhere use *move=movement*. No change, such as "*And each way* move", is wanted.

29. I.e. he would give way to his feelings.

30. *Sirrah;* not always, though commonly, a contemptuous word.

35. *pitfall;* usually for catching animals, not birds. *gin;* short for *engine;* lit. 'something *ingeniously* made'—hence 'a trap, snare'.

36. *Poor;* emphatic.

65, 66. I.e. though I am perfectly acquainted with your noble name and position. *doubt*, fear.

70. *To do worse,* i.e. by not warning her.

77. *womanly,* womanish; the word could not now be used thus.

82. *shag-ear'd,* with shaggy, hairy ears; "shag-*hair'd*" (2 *Henry VI*, III. 1. 367) is an obvious but not necessary change.

Scene 3

No dramatic theme remains except the great avengement, which is to fall in different ways on husband and wife in accordance with the different operation of crime in their lives. But to bring about the avengement suddenly would violate probability. Rebellion takes time to work. The climax, therefore, must be led up to gradually; and this long scene, as it were, fills the period in which the storm-clouds gather. Time-illusion is one of the essentials of dramatic construction.

Note the terrible "irony" which springs from Macduff's ignorance of the fate of his own wife and children.

In the interview between Malcolm and Macduff, Shakespeare has followed Holinshed very nearly. There are more verbal similarities than in any other part.

3. *Hold fast the...sword*, i.e. resolutely take up.

4. *Bestride*, defend; the metaphor of a soldier standing over a fallen comrade and defying the enemy to touch him. Cf. *2 Henry IV*, I. 1. 207, "Tells them he doth bestride a bleeding land".

birthdom, inheritance, birthright; it can hardly mean 'land of our birth, mother-country'.

8. *Like syllable of dolour*, a similar cry of pain (Lat. *dolor*, 'pain').

10. *to friend*, friendly, favourable. Cf. *Julius Cæsar*, III, I. 143, "I know that we shall have him well to friend" (meaning that Antony will not oppose the conspirators). From *to* = 'equivalent to', 'for'. Cf. the *Prayer-Book*, "I take thee to my wedded wife".

14, 15. *something You may deserve*, i.e. you may win Macbeth's favour for yourself by betraying me.

and wisdom, and *it is* wisdom, wise policy. The omission is awkward because there is no preceding verb from which *is* can be easily understood.

19, 20. *A good and virtuous nature* etc.; "a good mind may *recede* from goodness in the execution of a royal commission" (office order)—*Johnson*. The idea in *recoil* is 'to fall off, grow degenerate, go back'.

21. *transpose*, change. Macduff *may* be honest in spite of Malcolm's suspicions: the fact that he suspects Macduff does not make Macduff a traitor, does not change his character, if he is honest. Cf. 30, 31.

22. *the brighest*, Lucifer (Satan); of whom "bright" (or an

equivalent) is essentially *the* Miltonic description, based on medieval tradition; cf. indeed the name *Lucifer* ('Light-bringer').

23, 24. *Though all things foul* etc.; Virtue could not change her appearance even if all things base chose to assume the appearance of Virtue (and thereby made that appearance hateful to Virtue herself and distrusted by men).

24. *my hopes;* "i.e. hopes of welcome from Malcolm, who withholds it from distrust, aroused by Macduff's abandonment of wife and children"—*Herford*.

25. *there;* in that action of yours (cf. 26) which has excited my suspicions about you.

26. *in that rawness*, so precipitately; without taking thought for the safety of your family. So the soldier William in *Henry V*, IV. 1. 147, speaks of the "children rawly left", i.e. left unprovided for by their fathers who have fallen in battle.

27. *motives*, influences.

29, 30. *Let not my jealousies* etc.; I pray you see in my suspicions the wish, not to discredit you, but simply to guard my own safety in all points. For *jealousies* cf. *Hamlet*, IV. 5. 19, 20.

33. *wear thou thy wrongs*, enjoy the fruit of your crimes, enjoy your ill-won gains; the person addressed being "tyranny", not the remoter noun "poor country". The metaphor perhaps is 'dress yourself out in your ill-gained plumes'.

34. *The title*, i.e. the title (= claim) you put forward to them. *affeer'd*, confirmed; see G. To speak, in legal language, of a "title" to that which has been gained wrongfully is an *oxymoron*.

43. *England*, the king of England.

46–9. Malcolm dissembles thus because he is afraid Macduff comes as a spy from Macbeth, with intent "to betraie him" (Holinshed).

49. *What*, what sort of man? *should*, could.

52. *open'd;* like buds; the metaphor is suggested by "grafted" (51).

55. *confineless harms*, boundless vices.

58. *Luxurious*, lustful; see G.

59. *Sudden*, capricious; or 'violent, passionate'.

62. *continent*, restraining; the metaphor of river-banks; cf. *A Midsummer-Night's Dream*, II. 1. 92, "That they have overborne their continents", i.e. banks (where "they" = flooded rivers).

65. *In nature;* the words probably go with "intemperance", the sense being 'intemperate indulgence of the appetites'.

69. *Convey*, secretly manage, stealthily indulge in. *Convey*

often has a bad sense in Shakespeare, e.g. as a colloquial word for 'steal'; and we find *conveyance* = 'dishonesty'.

70. *the time;* cf. I. 5. 61.

72. *ill-composed affection,* inordinate desires.

75. *his,* one man's.

77. *that,* so that.

80. *Sticks,* is rooted; cf. III. I. 50.

81. *summer-seeming lust;* literally 'lust that seems like a summer', hence 'that may be likened to a summer', i.e. in shortness of duration. The short-lived plant lust is contrasted with the deep-rooted avarice which, like some tree, grows stronger with age. The other obvious point of likeness between "lust" and "summer" may also be implied.

83, 84. *foisons,* plenty, abundance, implying not harvests alone but wealth in general, resources. *mere,* very, absolutely. See each in G.

Malcolm's own wealth will be enough to satisfy his avarice, however great, without his needing to filch other people's possessions.

84, 85. i.e. all these evil qualities ("evils", 57) are endurable if counterbalanced by other and good qualities.

87. *temperance;* contrast 64, 65.

88. Shakespeare always spells and accents *perséver,* and *perséverance.*

91. *In the division of,* in all the different shades of.

93. *the sweet milk of concord;* cf. I. 5. 15.

94. *confound,* destroy; as in II. 2. 12.

99. *bloody-scepter'd;* referring to "nation". We might paraphrase: 'ruled by the blood-stained sceptre of a usurper'.

103. *blaspheme;* literally 'to speak profanely, utter impiety' (= Gk. βλασπημεῖν), hence 'to speak evil of, to calumniate, cast a slur on'.

106. *Died,* i.e. prepared herself for death by a life that was dead to the vanities of the world. It is the same idea of self-mortification as in v. 2. 5. The form of the expression is thought to be due to I Cor. xv. 31, "I die daily". *Fare;* two syllables.

109. *passion;* cf. III. 4. 57, and see G.

113. *trains,* lures, artifices; see G.; a hawking metaphor.

114. *modest,* moderating, i.e. restraining.

120. *For,* as.

129, 130. "In the meane time, Malcolme purchased [won] such fauor at king Edwards hands, that *old Siward earle* of Northumberland, was appointed *with ten thousand men* to go with him into Scotland, to support him in this enterprise, for recouerie of his right" (Holinshed).

130. *at a point;* said to be simply a variation of the not uncommon phrase *at point* = 'ready equipped, fully prepared for any emergency' (F. *à point*). Goneril says that they cannot let *Lear* keep "At point a hundred knights" (I. 4. 347).

131, 132. *and the chance of goodness* etc.; and may the future of virtue be in accordance with the justice of our cause; *we*, he means, represent the cause of goodness (for has he not just claimed to be a *good* man?), and may that cause prevail in proportion to its justice.

I think that *chance* means simply 'fortune: how goodness fares in the struggle, whether well or ill': and that *goodness* means 'virtue, right', exactly as in Macduff's speech (33), which may linger unconsciously in Malcolm's thoughts.

Some interpret 'our chance of *success*'. But that is not a Shakespearian sense, nor is it clear that *goodness* was ever used = 'success'. Its nearest meaning (very rare) is 'general prosperity'.

135–51. The King referred to is Edward the Confessor. The description of Edward's gifts of healing and prophecy, and of his bequeathing to his successor the power of "touching", is due to Holinshed. Shakespeare, however, really means the passage to be another (cf. IV. I. 120, 121) compliment to King James, and has obviously gone out of his way to introduce it. See p. 178. The gift or "virtue" was thought to come from the unction of a monarch's hands at his coronation with the consecrated oil—the "balm" of *Richard II*, IV. I. 207.

137, 138. I.e. baffles the utmost efforts of medical skill. For *convince*, see I. 7. 64. *assay;* literally 'attempt', hence 'effort'; see G. and cf. the old Chaucerian phrase 'to do his *assay*' = to do his very best.

140. *presently*, at once; cf. I. 2. 65.

144. *solicits;* not merely 'petitions' but 'moves by his petitions', so that his prayers on behalf of the afflicted ("visited") prevail. (F.)

147. *mere*, utter, absolute; see G.

surgery; in the wide sense 'the curing art'; or perhaps abstract for concrete = 'doctors', like "medicine" in V. 2, 27.

148. *Hanging a golden stamp.* Each person touched received a gold coin, in King James's time an "angel" worth 10s.; afterwards a gold medal was substituted.

149. *holy prayers;* a form of service for the ceremony of "touching" appeared in the *Prayer-Book* as late as 1719.

151. *The healing benediction,* the blessed gift, the grace of healing. From the primary sense 'the utterance of a blessing' *benediction* comes to mean 'blessing carried into practical effect, blessedness; kindly favour, grace'. *virtue,* power, efficacy.

155. *My countryman;* judging by Ross's dress—*Steevens.*

159. *where it did,* i.e. is (= "stands") it in as unhappy a state as when Macduff fled?

163. *rent;* an Elizabethan form of *rend.*

165. *A modern ecstasy,* quite a commonplace disturbance of mind; great perturbation of spirit such as you may see any day of the week. *modern;* see G.

166. *for who;* grammatically this must be classed as an instance of the omitted inflexion; but the form of the question may be affected by the idea '*who* is it?'

168. *or ere;* see G. *relation,* report, account; cf. the verb *relate.*

169. *nice,* particular, precise; Ross has described the situation so *very* precisely, e.g. in the last lines, where the time is fixed to within an hour or so. See G.

170. *doth hiss,* i.e. causes him to be hissed for telling stale news.

174. *at peace;* so Macbeth, speaking of Duncan, III. 2. 20. Of all the examples of verbal "irony" in the play this seems to me the most terrible.

176. Note how he still delays to speak the fearful tidings.

178. *out,* up in arms, in the field; literally 'away from their homes'. Scots writers constantly use the expression "were out" in speaking of those who took part in the 1745 rebellion.

180. *power,* army; more often *powers.*

184. *gracious England;* cf. 43.

187. *gives out,* tells of; some interpret 'shows'.

189. *would,* should, ought to be,

190. *latch,* catch; see G.

191. *The general cause,* the public weal. *a fee-grief;* a sorrow peculiar to one person: literally "a grief held 'in fee' by a single owner"—*Herford.*

197. *possess,* fill.

201. *on the quarry of;* the literal idea is 'on top of the heap made by the bodies of these slaughtered deer'. Ross means that to describe how it all was done would be to kill Macduff himself and thus increase the heap of slain by another body. Cf. the

close of *Hamlet*, V. 2, where Fortinbras, pointing to the dead bodies of Hamlet and the others, speaks of them as "this quarry" (375). See *quarry* in G.

204, 205. Another of Seneca's sayings. Cf. the *Hippolytus*, 607: "*curæ leves loquuntur, ingentes stupent* (or *silent*, 'are silent')". Probably Shakespeare had in mind a free rendering of Seneca's line which occurs in Florio's translation of Montaigne's *Essays*, I. 2:

> Light cares can freely speake,
> Great cares heart rather breake. (F.)

Gonzalo's picture of an ideal "commonwealth" in *The Tempest*, II. 1. 147–64, is from Montaigne, who influenced Elizabethan writers much.

211. *He has no children*, i.e. Malcolm; a *father* would not offer vain comfort to a father at such a moment. See p. 179.

215. *Dispute it*, fight against it; do not be overcome by.

220, 221. *naught;* see G. *demerits;* an ambiguous word, like 'deserts'; here it has a bad sense ('faults, misdeeds'), but in *Coriolanus*, I. 1. 276, and *Othello*, I. 2. 22, a good sense. Lat. *demereri*, 'to deserve', well or ill.

224. *Convert*, change; intransitive.

227. *intermission*, delay, i.e. in their meeting.

230. *Heaven forgive him too!* if he is fortunate enough to escape my sword, let him enjoy a second blessing, viz. Heaven's forgiveness.

232. *Our lack is nothing but*, all we now need is to take leave.

234. *Put on*, incite, encourage. *their instruments*, i.e. himself and his supporters, who are to be the instruments by which Providence executes vengeance on Macbeth.

ACT V

Scene 1

The three main features of Lady Macbeth's delirium have been characterised as: (1) "the mere reproduction of the horrible scenes she has passed through": (2) "the struggle to keep her husband from betraying himself": (3) "the uprising of her feminine nature against the foulness of the deed". And we may add her fear of the after-death: "Hell is murky." As regards the prose see p. 197.

4. *went into the field*, took the field, i.e. at the outset of the

troubles in his kingdom: now he has had to fall back on his castle (v. 2. 12).

5. *nightgown;* cf. II. 2. 70.

6. *paper;* perhaps a reminiscence of Macbeth's letter (I. 5). (F.)

10. *the effects of watching,* deeds which she would do in her waking hours.

20. *stand close,* i.e. keep concealed; Lady Macbeth might chance to wake and then discover that she was being watched.

25. *their sense is shut;* the 1st Folio has *are,* probably a mistaken repetition of *are* just above. Some consider the plural verb attracted to the plural notion "*eyes*" (cf. "their"). Shakespeare's doctors are few. The one we know best is this. Cerimon (*Pericles*) and Cornelius (*Cymbeline*) are alike. Shakespeare's elder daughter married a well-known Stratford doctor (Hall).

42. How hideous a contrast to II. 2. 67 ("a little water" etc.)!

43, 44. *you mar all;* a recollection of the banquet-scene (III. 4. 63).

50. *Arabia;* traditionally in poetry the land of perfumes and spices.

61, 62. Cf. II. 2. 65–72.

64. *Even so?* An exclamation of surprise at her revelation of the second crime.

75, 76. *annoyance,* harming herself; see G. *still,* constantly. His warning, apparently, was disregarded (v. 8. 70, 71).

77. *mated,* bewildered, confounded; see G.

Scene 2

The rest of the play is occupied with Macbeth's actual downfall. In its main outlines the story follows Holinshed.

1. *power,* army; cf. IV. 3. 180.

3. *dear,* grievous, heart-felt; causes that touch them closely; see G.

4. *bleeding...alarm,* the summons (see G.) to arms and bloodshed.

5. *the mortified man;* even the ascetic, dead to all passions, such as the feelings of revenge that burn in Malcolm and Macduff. Most editors take *mortified* figuratively, not in the literal (and very rare) sense 'dead', 'slain'. Cf. *Love's Labour's*

Lost, I. I. 28–31, where the courtier Dumain, withdrawing from the world, says to the King:

> My loving lord, Dumain is *mortified:*
>
> ...To love, to wealth, to pomp, I pine and *die.*

So in an old play *Monsieur D'Olive* (1606), "He like a mortified hermit sits". (F.)

7, 8. This was probably suggested by the fact that Holinshed does not mention Donalbain in connection with Macbeth's overthrow. Lines 7 and 8 give a touch of circumstantiality to the narrative.

8. *file;* III. I. 95, 102.

10. *unrough*, smooth-faced, hairless.

11. *Protest their first of manhood*, i.e. for the first time give evidence of it; show that they have reached man's estate.

15, 16. *He cannot buckle* etc.; he cannot keep his cause in hand; his side or party is so deranged ("distemper'd") as to be beyond his control: hence the desertion of his nominal followers (18).

buckle; the notion 'to fasten in, confine', leads naturally to the general idea 'to control, keep in hand'. (F.)

18. *minutely*, every moment.

23. *pester'd*, troubled. The line describes Macbeth's madness (cf. 13), under a metaphor like 'mentally unhinged'.

24, 25. *When all that is within him* etc.; "when all the faculties of the mind are employed in self-condemnation"— *Johnson.*

27–9. *Meet we the medicine of* etc.; let us go to meet the physician (Malcolm) who comes to cure the nation's sickness, and with him let us shed every drop of our blood to purge our country of the tyrant. For *medicine* = 'physician' cf. *All's Well That Ends Well*, II. I. 75, 76.

Scene 3

1. *let them fly all;* cf. 7, 8 and v. 2. 18.

3. *taint*, be infected with; the metaphor of catching a disease.

8. *epicures*, men given to luxury of all kinds. A hardy northerner might well speak thus of the more luxurious nation south of the Tweed.

Shakespeare obviously had in mind passages in Holinshed that speak of "those superfluities which came into the realme of Scotland with the Englishmen"—such as "fine fare" and English likerous delicats"—*Steevens.*

epicure; from the name of *Epicurus,* the Greek philosopher whose teaching was misinterpreted as inculcating the pursuit of sensual pleasures.

9. *sway by,* am moved by; or 'rule by'.

10. *sag,* sink, droop; see G.

11. *loon;* a word used more by the Scots than the English. Middle E. *lown,* 'a base fellow'.

15. *lily-liver'd.* So we find *milk-livered* and *white-livered.* The liver was regarded as the seat of courage, and a white, bloodless liver as a sign of cowardice. The idea is part of the belief that the redness of the blood is a test of courage; so a coward is called a '*milk*sop', i.e. '*white*-livered'. As with many old medical notions, there is an element of truth in this belief; for courage generally goes with strength, and strength depends on the quality of the blood. *patch,* fool; see G.

20. *push,* attack, onset, from the literal sense 'thrust'; or 'crisis'.

21. *cheer...or disseat.* (1) The 1st Folio has *dis-eate,* whence the commonly accepted correction *disseat;* the later Folios *disease.* The only objection to *disseat* is that it does not give a good antithesis to *cheer.* Still the general sense is fair, viz.: 'this crisis (or attack) will bring comfort to the rest of my days (i.e. in the event of his gaining a decisive victory), or it will *un*throne me now, once for all'.

Some (2) change *cheer* to *chair* and read "*chair* me...or *disseat* me"; others, (3) keeping *cheer,* follow the later Folios and read "*cheer* me or *dis-ease* me".

The merit of (2) and (3) lies solely in the verbal antithesis: neither gives good sense. *Chair* might mean 'to *en*throne', but Macbeth is already on the throne.

Disease = 'to trouble, disquiet, render uneasy', is a good antithesis to *cheer* and good Elizabethan English. But so mild a word could not describe the fate which awaited Macbeth if defeated.

22. *my way of life,* the course of my life. To say that the course of one's life has reached the downward point ("fallen"), has declined into the autumn-stage, is surely a natural mode of expression. The metaphor in "way" is continued in "accompany" (24). Editors quote the phrase *way of life* from *Pericles,* I. I. 54.

Johnson's famous emendation "my *May* of life" is attractive at first sight because of the vivid antithesis it yields between spring-time and autumn ("the sear, the yellow leaf"); and of course the figurative use of *May*, to denote the spring-time of life, is very common. But it is a sentimental phrase, that hardly fits the grim, weary Macbeth; and there is no need for any change.

23. *sear*, dry, withered; see G. The metaphor is illustrated by *Sonnet* 73.

33. *Give me my armour.* "The Setons of Touch were (and are still) hereditary armour-bearers to the kings of Scotland; there is thus a peculiar fitness in the choice of this name." (F.)

35. *moe*, more; see G. *skirr*, scour; see G.

37. *your;* used here simply for euphony, whereas Macbeth afterwards addresses the Doctor by *thou* (40, 51, 53, 56). The normal Shakespearian usage is that a master uses *thou* in speaking to anyone in his service, while the latter replies by *you*, to mark the distinction of rank. Cf. *your* in the Doctor's answer (57).

40. *minister to a mind diseased.* This also seems to be from Seneca; cf. the *Hercules Furens*, 1269, 1270: "*nemo polluto queat | animo mederi*".

43. *oblivious*, causing forgetfulness; see G.

44. *stuff'd...stuff.* To substitute *grief* or *load* for *stuff*, or *fraught* for *stuff'd*, is simply to ignore the fact that such repetitions are thoroughly Elizabethan. See v. 2. 19.

perilous; scan *per'lous*, like the colloquial form *parlous*. Cf. *Julius Cæsar*, I. 3. 47, "Submitting me unto the perilous night".

47. Self-absorbed, he forgets that *she* is the patient.

48. *staff;* more probably 'lance' (v. 7. 18) than 'general's baton'.

54. *Pull't off*, i.e. his armour, which in his disturbed state he puts on and off—*Herford*. Here, as when Banquo is taking off his armour (II. 1), the sense is made perfectly clear in the acting.

55. *senna.* The 1st Folio has *cyme*, a word which does not resemble the name of any known drug and may be supposed to be a misprint for *senna*. *Senna* is a word of Arabic origin, and its forms in Elizabethan E. are diverse.

59. *bane*, destruction; see G.

Scene 4

1, 2. I.e. I hope the time is at hand when a man can lie down to rest and be safe. He is referring, surely, to his father's terrible fate.

4–7. *hew him down a bough;* Macbeth, retreating before Malcolm, had "fortified" himself "at the castell of Dunsinane". Meanwhile "Malcolme following hastilie after Makbeth, came the night before the battell vnto Birnane wood, and when his armie had rested a while there to refresh them, he *commanded every man to get a bough* of some tree or other of that wood in his hand, as big as he might *beare*, and to march foorth therewith in such wise, that on the next morrow they might come closelie and without sight in this manner within viewe of his enimies" (Holinshed). It is said that this stratagem was used by the Japanese in their war against Russia (1904–5).

6, 8. *discovery*, i.e. the enemy's scouts. *other*, i.e. report.

9, 10. *endure Our setting down*, i.e. stand a siege by us.

11. *advantage*, a favourable opportunity, viz. of leaving Macbeth's side. *to be given*, i.e. to them; that is, 'open to them, within their reach'. But the sense is forced, and probably *given* is a printer's error (due to line 12) for some word like *ta'en* or *got* or *gain'd*.

12. *more and less*, great and small, high and low; all classes alike.

13, 14. Cf. v. 2. 19, 20. *things;* very contemptuous.

14, 15. *Let our just censures.* Older and more cautious than Malcolm, Macduff hints that a soldier's part is to make every preparation and not fall into over-confidence. 'To judge aright' (he says), 'let us wait for the issue, which will show how things really are.' He and old Siward (16–21) speak with some ambiguity to avoid seeming to rebuke the young prince whom they hope to see soon on the throne.

censures, judgments, opinions; see G. *event*, issue, result (Lat. *eventus*). Both "just" and "true" have a proleptic force, e.g. 'in order that they may be just (i.e. correct)'.

Attend; F. *attendre,* 'to wait for'.

18. *What...we have, and what we owe;* what we have won and what we have lost; our gains and our penalties (in the case of defeat). Put colloquially his meaning is—we shall soon know 'how we stand'.

The rhyme gives the effect of elderly moralising, as in II. 4. 40, 41.

19. *Thoughts speculative;* surmise may express its uncertain hopes, but the conflict is the arbitrator that decides.

Scene 5

5. *forced*, reinforced.

10, 11. *The time has been;* cf. II. 2. 58. *fell of hair*, scalp.
Fell generally means (as here) a skin with the hair or wool on;
closely related to *pell*, 'a skin, hide', Lat. *pellis*.

12. *treatise*, story.

17. *She should have died hereafter*. This is all he has to say: a
callous remark on the inopportuneness of her death: and she was
once his "dearest partner of greatness", his "dearest love"
(I. 5. 10, 56).

18. *such a word*, such intelligence; as in 'to send *word*'.

19–21. *To-morrow, and to-morrow...Creeps* etc.; one morrow
after another creeps on in this trivial daily progress, till the last
word is reached and the Book of Time closed.

recorded time. While Time lasts a record of it is kept, and the
record will only cease when Time itself ceases, merged in
Eternity. We must paraphrase freely as above, or 'to the last
letter of the volume of Time's record'.

23. *dusty death*. "Earth to earth, ashes to ashes, dust to
dust" (The Burial of the Dead).

brief candle! short-lived flame of existence; recurring to the
metaphor of 22. "How oft is the candle of the wicked put out!"
Job xxi. 17; see also xviii. 6; Psalm xviii. 28.

24, 25. *Life's but...a poor player;* a favourite metaphor with
Shakespeare, himself a player as well as playwright; cf. the
famous passage "All the world's a stage, etc." in *As You Like
It*, II. 7. 139–43.

26–8. *a tale;* cf. *King John*, III. 4. 107–9:
> There's nothing in this world can make me joy:
> Life is as tedious as a twice-told tale
> Vexing the dull ear of a drowsy man.

28. *Signifying nothing;* not simply bad, but absolutely
nothing: such is the final conclusion to which all his and her
schemes and ambitions and crimes have brought him; the last
word of pessimism!

34, 35. Dr Ward says that stories similar to this of the
moving wood have been found in Arabic legend and elsewhere.

40. *cling thee*, cause thee to shrivel up. The original meaning
of *cling*, an intransitive verb, was 'to stick fast, shrink together'.
In pre-Shakespearian English it was quite a common word in
the sense 'to shrivel up from cold, hunger' and similar causes,

like dead animal or vegetable matter exposed to the air. Hence its transitive use here = 'to make to shrivel up'.

42. *pull in*, rein in, restrain. Macbeth "had permitted his courage (like a fiery horse) to carry him to the brink of a precipice, but, seeing his danger, resolves to *check* that confidence to which he had *given the rein before*". *Pale* ('grow pale, falter') is a needless change. (F.)

51. *wrack;* see G. under *wreck*.

52. *harness*, armour; see G. Much of the rhyme in this last Act is due to the number of scenes, the divisions between which could not be indicated in any other way on the Elizabethan stage than by rhymed couplets. Moreover, here the rhyme in itself has a fine effect of melodramatic defiance and desperation.

Scene 6

1. *leavy;* Milton uses the *v*-form, not *leafy;* cf. *Comus*, 278. V in place of *f* in many words characterised the southern dialects.

4. *battle*, division of an army; here 'the foreguard, vanguard'.

7. *Do we but*, if we but.

Scene 7

1–4. At the last Macbeth "fights not like 'Bellona's bridegroom', but with a wild and animal clinging to life". In the degradation of his nature through crime, his courage has degenerated into a "dull ferocity". Scenes of combat and wrestling were evidently very popular with Elizabethan audiences.

2. *the course*, the technical term in bear-baiting for the onset of the dogs. Shakespeare refers to this cruel pastime several times. Cf. *King Lear*, III. 7. 54, "I am tied to the stake, and I must stand the course". The chief scene of these exhibitions was the Bear Garden on the Bankside in London, close to the Globe Theatre. See *Shakespeare's England* (1916), II, 428.

3, 4. Deceived in one of the prophecies which he thought so "good" (IV. 1. 96), he falls back on the other, with the true desperation and superstition of the gambler.

12, 13. The rhyme is merely an echo of IV. 1. 79, 80.

17. *kerns;* here a contemptuous word = 'boors'.

18. *staves*, lances. *either thou;* the sentence is not completed; a sign of the speaker's excitement.

22. *bruited*, announced; see G.

24. *gently render'd*, surrendered without resistance.

29. *beside us*, i.e. so as to miss us; not really trying to slay us.

Scene 8

1. *play the Roman fool*, by committing suicide to avoid capture. Cf. *Julius Cæsar*, v. 3. 89, where Titinius, as he kills himself, says, "this is a Roman's part". In that play Brutus and Cassius, typical Romans, both commit suicide when they see that their cause is hopeless and only the disgrace of capture awaits them. There need not be a reference here to any particular Roman (like Nero). Shakespeare's own recognition of the sin of "self-slaughter" is expressed, one may think, by Hamlet (I. 2. 131, 132), and in *King Lear*, IV. 6.

2. *lives*, living men; on whom it is "better" to exercise his sword than on himself (3).

4. Repeated almost in *Coriolanus*, IV. 5. 87, 88.

5, 6. A humanising touch: he has *some* feeling still.

7, 8. I.e. thou villain bloodier than any words can describe you.

9. *intrenchant*, invulnerable, not to be cut; literally 'not cutting' (cf. III. 4. 27). Cf. *Hamlet*, I. 1. 146, "For it is, as the air, invulnerable" (referring to the Ghost), and IV. 1. 44, "the woundless air". (F.)

12. *charmed*. The word would have more significance in times nearer to "the days of chivalry, [when] the champions' arms being ceremoniously blessed, each took an oath that he used no *charmed* weapons". (F.) *must not*, is not destined to.

14. *angel*, evil angel; referring to the idea of a man's 'genius', a 'demon'. See III. 1. 56, note.

15, 16. At last the real force of *born* in the fatal couplet becomes clear to Macbeth—and to us: 'born naturally, brought forth in the normal manner of childbirth'.

16. "The untimely birth of Macduff is shown to be a feature which in Germanic mythology invariably indicates heroic strength"—Ward. *ripp'd;* the word is Holinshed's.

18. *my better part of man*. Some interpret 'the better part of my soul' or 'the mind'. So here I think Macbeth means 'my very soul'. Milton remembered this scene when he wrote *Paradise Lost*, XI. 494–8.

20–2. Cf. v. 5. 43, 44. Banquo, the honest-minded, knew the truth from the very first (I. 3. 123–6). *palter*, equivocate, quibble.

24–7. Shakespeare is referring to the shows and fairs of his own "time". Cf. *The Tempest*, II. 2. 28–34, where Trinculo, finding the queer-shaped Caliban, says that were he in England,

"and had but this fish painted", he would make a fortune out of it at fairs.

Painted, i.e. as an advertisement outside a booth, so as to tempt people to pay for going inside to see the "monster". *upon a pole*, i.e. on a cloth suspended from a pole. The public love for "monsters" was a stock-joke in Elizabethan plays.

34. *Exeunt, fighting.* From some inconsistency in the stage-directions of the Folio it seems likely that after Shakespeare's retirement from the stage, the actors, in order to make the end of the piece more sensational, had the "fighting" between Macduff and Macbeth (and his decapitation) done on the stage, before the audience.

36. *go off*, be killed; another euphemism for death. It is the play's last flash of "irony" that the words should be put in the father's mouth, after we have witnessed the son's fate.

by these; pointing to the many round him, who have not fallen.

41. *prowess;* slurred into one syllable; see G.

46–53. The story of young Siward's death and of his father's bearing is told in Holinshed. (F.) "Had he his hurts before?" is essentially the classical spirit. It might be an extract from some classical story of Spartan or Roman fortitude.

52. *parted;* cf. the Hostess's description of Falstaff's death: "a' parted...even at the turning o' the tide" (*Henry V*, II. 3. 12, 13).

paid his score; a common colloquial phrase = 'paid his debt'. *score;* properly a notch cut on a tally or piece of wood, then 'an account kept by notches', and so 'any account, reckoning'. Icelandic *skor*, 'a score, cut'; cf. the cognate A.S. *scéran*, 'to cut, to shear'.

54, 55. *behold, where stands,* i.e. *on a pole.* Compare Holinshed: "Then cutting his head from his shoulders, Makduffe set it vpon a pole, and brought it vnto Malcolme."

the time is free, the age has regained its freedom.

56. *pearl,* choicest representatives; the flower of your subjects, i.e. the great nobles who are assembled round their king.

64. *to do;* the gerund; cf. phrases like 'a house *to let*', 'water *to drink*'. This was the old idiom.

66. *As,* namely, to wit. *exiled friends;* in particular, his brother Donalbain, from Ireland (II. 3. 121).

68. *Producing,* bringing to justice.

70. *self;* in its adjectival use = 'own, pertaining to self'. Cf. *Richard II*, III. 2. 166, "Infusing him with self and vain conceit", i.e. vain self-conceit. This use underlies the expression "My

strange and self-abuse" in III. 4. 142, where *self* is a quasi-adjective in relation to "strange", yet a part of the compound. Strictly the form of expression there should be either "my strange and self abuse", or "my strange self-abuse".

71. *Took off her life;* cf. I. 7. 20, III. 1. 105.

72. *the grace of Grace.* Editors quote *The Two Gentlemen of Verona*, III. 1. 146, *All's Well That Ends Well*, II. 1. 163.

75. *at Scone.* Cf. II. 4. 32. The historical date of Macbeth's defeat by Siward (either the maternal uncle or cousin of Malcolm) is 27 July 1054. Siward's victory "enabled him to establish Malcolm as king of Cumbria...Macbeth still maintained his power north of the Mounth, but three years later, after the death of Siward, Malcolm himself succeeded in defeating and slaying Macbeth at Lumphanan in Mar on 15 Aug. 1057"—*Dict. of Biog.* Shakespeare, therefore, has again combined two campaigns. Malcolm, commonly called Malcolm Canmore, crowned 1057, was the first great King of Scotland. He died 1093.

The clouds have lifted at last, and the tragedy closes with the hope that under the rule of its young King the dawn of a happier era for Scotland is close at hand. The end of *Macbeth* is very similar to that of *Hamlet*, where the sceptre for which Hamlet himself was ill-fitted passes into the strong grasp of "young Fortinbras", at Hamlet's own bequest. Even *King Lear* ends on the notes of duty and optimism: that the world's work must go forward, and that there are men to do it. The quiet closes of Shakespeare's tragedies are a notable point. "Like the Greeks, he ends his plays, not with the crash of catastrophe, but...with a slight continuation of the action which [unites] the eddying of the play to the vast flow of the river of continuous life." Contrast the method of making the curtain fall on the *dénoûment*. The difference is that between true tragedy and melodrama.

GLOSSARY

Abbreviations

A.S. = Anglo-Saxon, i.e. English down to about the Conquest.
Middle E. = Middle English, i.e. English from about the Conquest to about 1500.
Elizabethan E. = the English of Shakespeare and his contemporaries (down to about 1650).
O.F. = Old French, i.e. till about 1600. F. = modern French.
Germ. = modern German. Gk. = Greek.
Ital. = Italian. Lat. = Latin.
New E.D. = the *New English Dictionary*.
Cent. Dict. = the *Century Dictionary*.

NOTE: In using the Glossary the student should pay very careful attention to the context in which each word occurs.

Abuse, II. 1. 50, 'to deceive', like F. *abuser*. See *Cymbeline*, III. 4. 123, "my master is abused", and I. 4. 124, "you are abused" = 'mistaken, deceived'. Lat. *abuti*.

Access, I. 5. 42. Many words retained in Elizabethan E. the French accent, derived from the original Latin words. Thus Milton wrote "By policy and long *procéss* of time" (*Paradise Lost*, II. 297); cf. F. *procès*, Lat. *processus*. So Shakespeare scans *accéss, edíct, exíle*, when it suits him.

Admired, III. 4. 110, 'strange, astonishing'. Elizabethan writers constantly use *admire*, and its derivatives, in the sense of Lat. *admirari*, 'to wonder, be astonished at'. Cf. Revelation, xvii. 6, "And when I saw her, I wondered with great admiration".

Affeer, IV. 3. 34; strictly a legal term = 'to fix or settle the amount of an amercement, i.e. a fine, to assess': hence 'to settle, confirm'. Certain cases were tried before assessors or jurors entitled *affeerors*. O.F. *aforer*, later form *afeurer*, from Late Lat. *afforare*, 'to fix the price or market-value' (Lat. *ad*, 'to'+*forum*, 'market', in Late Lat. 'market-price'). See *New E.D.*

Alarm, V. 2. 4, 'a summons to take up arms', from Ital. *all' arme*, 'to arms'—Lat. *ad illa arma*. Now the other form *alarum*, common in stage-directions, keeps the idea 'a loud summons, call', while *alarm* indicates the fear which such a summons indicates.

Annoyance, V. I. 75, 'hurt, harm'. Shakespeare always uses *annoy* in this strong sense. Cf. *Julius Cæsar*, I. 3. 20–2:

> Against the Capitol I met a lion,
> Who glared upon me, and went surly by,
> Without annoying me.

O.F. *anoi*, 'vexation' (F. *ennui*), from Lat. *in odio*, as in the phrase *est mihi in odio*, 'it is *odious* to me'.

Antic, IV. I. 130, 'quaint, fantastic'; especially said in Elizabethan E. of carving and stonework. What is old (*antique*) often appears odd (*antic*) to later generations; Lat. *antiquus*. Cf. Gray's *Progress of Poesy*, 30, 31:

> With antic Sports, and blue-eyed Pleasures,
> Frisking light in frolic measures.

Aroint, I. 3. 6, 'avaunt'. The phrase "aroint thee, witch" was evidently proverbial; cf. **King Lear**, III. 4. 125–9. Editors refer to Ray's *North Country Words* (1691), which has: "*Ryntye*, by your leave, stand handsomely. As '*Rynt you, witch*, quoth Bessie Locket to her mother'; Proverb, *Cheshire*". Seemingly this *rynt* is short for *aroint*. The sense of *aroint* is clearly 'avaunt, begone!' and probably it is the same as, or closely connected with, an old word *arunt* (etymology unknown) which occurs in a tract of Wycliff, and elsewhere, in the senses 'avoid' and 'drive away', each of which is kindred to the notion 'begone' in *aroint*. (*New E.D.*)

Assay, IV. 3. 138. Except in *King Lear*, I. 2. 47, and *Sonnet* 110, Shakespeare, like Milton, uses *assay*, not *essay*. Now *assay*, except as a poetical form, is used only of the analysis of metals. O.F. *essai* or *assai* = Lat. *exagium*, 'a weighing, *trial* of weight'.

Balm, II. 2. 39; properly the aromatic oily resin of the *balsam*-tree: hence any fragrant oil or ointment for anointing, or soothing pain; especially the consecrated oil used at the coronation of a monarch.

Bane, V. 3. 59, 'destruction'. Cf. *Measure for Measure*, I. 2. 133, "Like *rats* that *ravin* down their proper *bane*", i.e. devour greedily the poison put for them. So *baned* = 'destroyed', *The Merchant of Venice*, IV. 1. 46.

Boltered, IV. I. 123, 'having the hair matted with clots' (of blood). The verb *bolter*, older form *balter*, is of Scandinavian origin; cf. Danish *baltre* or *boltre*, 'to wallow, welter'. It meant (1) 'to tumble about', hence (2) 'to tangle or mat the hair' by tumbling it about, 'to clot or clog with anything sticky', as by tumbling about in mud. With this general idea 'clotted, matted', *balter* or *bolter* survives in the dialects of various counties, especially Warwickshire. Thus in Warwickshire snow is said to *bolter* on a horse's hoof, likewise dirt that collects in the hairs of an animal's legs and forms into hard masses; while *baltered* or *boltered* is used of ill-mixed, lumpy flour. For the alternative forms in *a* and *o* compare *choppy = chappy*. The dialect words in S. are associated mainly with Warwickshire and the adjacent counties, as might be expected. See *Shakespeare's England* (1916), II. 571–3.

Boot. From *boot*, 'advantage, good' (A.S. *bót*); the root being that which we get in *better, best*. Hence *to boot* (IV. 3. 37) means 'to the good', i.e. in addition.

Brinded, IV. 1. 1; an older form than *brindled*; it means literally 'marked as with a *brand*', and generally indicates stripes of dark colour on the tawny coat of an animal. Cf. "the brinded lioness", *Comus*, 443; "brinded mane", *Paradise Lost*, VII. 465.

Bruit, V. 7. 22, 'to announce with noise'; more often 'to report, noise abroad', as in 1 *Henry VI*, II. 3. 68, "I find thou are no less than fame hath bruited". The noun *bruit*, 'a rumour', is from F. *bruit*, 'noise'.

Carouse, II. 3. 23; originally an adverb used in 'to drink *carouse'* = 'all out'; from German *gar-aus*, 'quite out', i.e. with no liquor left in the glass. It was a stock piece of Elizabethan satire that the Germans were great topers; cf. *The Merchant of Venice*, I. 2. 90–108.

Censure. The original sense, common in Elizabethan E., of the verb was 'to judge' = Lat. *censere*. So *censure* = 'judgment, opinion' (V. 4. 14); cf. *Hamlet*, I. 3. 69, "Take each man's censure, but reserve thy judgment". As we are apt to judge others unfavourably, *censure* comes to mean 'blame'. Words tend to deteriorate in sense.

Charm, I. 3. 37; from Lat. *carmen*, 'a song or incantation'; like *enchant* from Lat. *incantare*, it still kept the notion of 'spell, magical power'. The force of the two words weakened as the belief in magic declined.

chaudron, or **chawdron,** IV. 1. 33, 'the entrails of an animal', especially the parts used for food; cf. the cognate Germ. *kaldaunen*, 'entrails'.

Middle E. *chaudoun* is from O.F. *chaudun*, 'entrails', from Lat. *caldunum*, the first part of which is from Lat. *calidus*, 'hot', while the latter part (*-unum*) is doubtful. *Chaudoun* got confused with *chaldron*, the old form of *cauldron* (the food being cooked in a *cauldron*), and old writers often use *chaldron* = 'entrails'; the *r* in *chaudron* or *chawdron* is a relic of this confusion.

Cherubin, I. 7. 22; a rare plural, as probably in the *Te Deum*. The word 'cherub' comes directly from the Heb. *kherūbh*, and makes its true plural 'cherub*im*' = *kherūbīm* (so always in Milton). The form 'cherub*in*' comes through the French (Lat. *cherubinus*) and makes its plural 'cherub*ins*'; cf. Wyclif, Exodus, xxv. 18, "two golden cherubyns". In the Bible of 1611 we have a hybrid form 'cherub*ims*', changed in the Revised Version to the correct Heb. 'cherub*im*'.

Choppy, I. 3. 44, i.e. *chappy*; cf. *Julius Cæsar*, I. 2. 246, "the rabblement hooted, and clapped their chopped hands". Middle E. *choppen* or *chappen* = 'to cut'; hence, 'to gape open', like a cut.

Chough, III. 4. 125, applied formerly to any sort of crow, but especially the jackdaw; cf. *A Midsummer-Night's Dream*, III. 2. 21, "russet-pated choughs", i.e. 'grey-headed', an epithet precisely suitable to the jackdaw, which has greyish plumage about the head and neck. Now *chough* is used strictly of the red-legged crow which frequents sea-cliffs, e.g. in Cornwall. Cognate with O.F. *choue*, Dutch *kauw*, formed in imitation of the bird's note.

Clept, III. 1. 94, 'called'. A.S. *cleopian*, 'to call'. Cf. *Hamlet*, I. 4. 19, "They clepe us drunkards". The word, which is very common in Chaucer and early writers, is most familiar now through Milton's lines (*L'Allegro*, 11–3):

> But come, thou Goddess fair and free,
> In Heaven yclept Euphrosyne,
> And by men heart-easing Mirth;

where *y* = the old participial prefix **ge**.

Combustion, II. 3. 40; properly 'conflagration', from Lat. *comburere*, 'to burn up': hence metaphorically 'utter social confusion'. It is one of the high-sounding, Latinised words dear to Milton: Satan was flung from Heaven "With hideous ruin and combustion down" (*Paradise Lost*, I. 46).

Dear, v. 2. 3, 'grievous, heart-felt'. The general Elizabethan sense of *dear* (cognate with Germ. *theuer*) is 'that which affects us closely, whether in a good or bad way'. In Shakespeare it often has a bad sense. Cf. *Hamlet*, I. 2. 182, "my dearest foe", i.e. worst enemy; and *Richard II*, I. 3. 151, "The dateless limit of thy dear exile". So in *Lycidas*, 6, "Bitter constraint and sad occasion dear". The sense may have been partly due to confusion with A.S. *dēor*, 'grievous'.

Dismal, I. 2. 53; O.F. *dis mal*, 'unlucky days', Lat. *dies mali*, 'evil days'. "The phrase was misunderstood, and *dismal* was treated as an adjective, with the addition of *days*; and later, of other substantives"—*Skeat*.

Dollar, I. 2. 63, derived through Dutch *daler* from Germ. *thaler*, which is short for *Joachimsthaler*, the name of a coin originally made from silver found in *Joachimsthal* (Joachim's *dale*) in Bohemia, early in the 16th century. Now, of course, *dollar* is mainly associated with the American coin (about 7*s.*) of that name. There were no dollars in Macbeth's time.

Doom, II. 3. 60, 'judgment'. Cf. *doomsday* = A.S. *dōmes dæg*; A.S. *dēman*, 'to judge'. We get the same root (= 'to lay down, hence 'decide') in Gk. θέμις, 'law', from τίθημι, 'I lay down, set'.

Earnest, I. 3. 104, 'a pledge', literally 'money paid beforehand as a pledge'. Lat. *arrha*, from Gk. ἀρραβών, 'earnest-money, pledge'.

Ecstasy, III. 2. 22. Gk. ἐκ, 'out'+στάσις, 'a standing'; so that the literal notion is 'being beside (i.e. outside) oneself'. It is used similarly of extreme mental torture in *The Tempest*, III. 3. 108.

Favour; often = 'face, features' (I. 5. 70). So *well-favoured* ='of good looks, handsome', as in Genesis, xxix. 17, "Rachel was beautiful and well favoured"; and *ill-favoured* = 'ugly'. *Favour* meant (1) 'kindness', (2) 'expression of kindness in the face', (3) 'the face itself'.

Fee, IV. 3. 191; much used as a legal term in connection with the possession or tenure of land. Thus *fee-simple* = hereditary land, held without any conditions and 'for ever'. A.S. *feoh* (cf. Germ. *vieh*) meant (1) 'cattle', (2) 'property'—cattle being the chief kind of property in a primitive state of society. Cf. Lat. *pecunia* from *pecus*.

Flaw, III. 4. 63, 'a burst of passion', literally 'a sudden and violent gust of wind'. Cf. *Hamlet*, v. 1. 239, "the winter's flaw"; and Tennyson, *Marriage of Geraint*, "Like flaws in summer laying lusty corn". The same as flaw, 'a crack' = Swedish *flaga*, 'a crack', also 'blast of wind'. Perhaps 'sudden burst' is the radical notion.

Foison, IV. 3. 83, 'plenty, abundance'. F. *foison*; Lat. *fusio*, 'a pouring out'; cf. '*profusion*'.

Gallowglass, I. 2. 13; Irish *galloglach*, 'a foreign soldier'; the *gallowglasses* being originally soldiers in the service of the Irish and other Gaelic chiefs; heavy-armed after the manner of the

English military settlers in Ireland. Irish *gall*, 'foreigner, stranger'+*óglách*, 'a youth, servant, warrior'. Spenser in his *View of the Present State of Ireland* (1598) describes the equipment of the *gallowglass*, and speaks of the light-armed *kern* as "the proper [i.e. native] Irish souldiour"; see 'Globe ed.' p. 640

Graymalkin, I. 1. 8; a name for a grey cat, commonly corrupted into *grimalkin*. The name *Malkin* means 'little *Mald*' (whence the softened form *Maud*), *not* 'little *Mary*'.

Groom, II. 2. 50, formerly any 'servant'; compare some of the titles of court-officials, e.g. 'Groom of the Chamber'. Its original sense was simply 'a man-child, boy; a male'. Dutch *grom*, 'offspring'. Through confusion with *groom* we get the *r* in *bridegroom*, which should be *bridegoom* = A.S. *brȳd-guma*, 'bride-man'.

Harbinger, I. 4. 45; used here in reference to its original sense, viz. 'an officer who went in advance of an army or prince to make provision for the night's shelter'. Hence 'forerunner' (v. 6. 10). The Middle E. form is *herbergeour*, and the *n* is intrusive, as in *passenger*, *messenger*. From Icelandic *herbergi*, 'an army shelter'; cf. the cognate German words *heer*, 'army'+*bergen*, 'to shelter'.

Harness, v. 5. 52, 'armour'; a common Elizabethan usage, revived by Tennyson: "Dry clashed his harness in the icy caves", *Morte d'Arthur*. So *harnessed* = 'dressed in armour'. Cf. *Troilus*, I. 2. 8, "Before the sun rose he was harness'd light". O.F. *harneis*, 'armour'.

His; this was the ordinary *neuter* (as well as masculine) possessive pronoun in Middle E. and remained so in Elizabethan E. Cf. Genesis, iii. 15, "*it* shall bruise thy head, and thou shalt bruise *his* heel'. There was also a use, not common, of *it* as a possessive, though uninflected; especially in the phrase *it own*. Cf. *The Tempest*, II. 1. 163, "of *it* own kind", and the Bible of 1611 in Leviticus, xxv. 5, "of *it* owne accord".

Then from the possessive use of *it* uninflected there arose, about the close of the 16th century, the inflected form *its*, in which *-s* is the usual possessive inflection, as in *his*. This new form *its* came into use slowly, the old idiom *his* being generally retained by Elizabethans. There are no instances of *its* in Spenser or the Bible (1611), and only three in Milton's poetical works (*Paradise Lost*, I. 254, IV. 813, *Nativity Ode*, 106). *Its* does not occur in any extant work of Shakespeare printed prior to his death: hence it seems not improbable that the nine instances in the 1st Folio (five in a single play, *The Winter's Tale*) were due to the editors or printers.

Howlet, IV. 1. 17, 'an owl'; from F. *hulotte*, 'an owl', which Littré connects with our word *owl*, Germ. *eule*, Lat. *ulula*. An *owl* is so called because it *howls*, and in old writers we find a form *howle = owl*.

Hurlyburly, I. 1. 3, 'uproar, tumult'. It is a "reduplicated word, the second part being an echo of the first. The simple form *hurly* is the original". F. *hurler*, 'to howl, yell', from Lat. *ululare*. Colloquial compounds (like *helter-skelter*, *hugger-mugger*, *tag-rag*) are common in Elizabethan English.

Incarnadine, II. 2. 62. Shakespeare seems to have been the first to use *incarnadine* as a verb = 'to dye red'; from F. *incarnadin*, Ital. *incarnadino*, 'carnation-coloured', literally 'flesh-colour'; Lat. *incarnatus*, 'clothed with flesh'.

Kern, I. 2. 13; a corruption of Irish *ceatharnach*, 'a soldier'. These *kerns* were light-armed, and in Elizabethan writers are often mentioned together with the *gallowglasses* (I. 2. 13). Cf. *Richard II*, II. 1. 155, 156, and 2 *Henry VI*, IV. 9. 24–7:

> The Duke of York is newly come from *Ireland*,
> And with a puissant and a mighty power
> Of *gallowglasses* and stout *kerns*
> Is marching hitherward in proud array.

Latch, IV. 3. 190, 'to catch'; A.S. *læccan*, cognate with *clutch*. Cf. *Sonnet* 113. *Latch* is probably a quite different word in *A Midsummer-Night's Dream*, III. 2. 36:

> But hast thou yet latch'd the Athenian's eyes
> With the love-juice, as I did bid thee do?

Apparently, *latch* there means 'to moisten', and is cognate with A.S. *leccan*, 'to wet'; cf. '*latch*-pan' (= 'a *dripping*-pan'), so called because it is used to drip liquid fat on meat.

Liege, I. 4. 2, 'lord, sovereign'; properly 'free', O.F. *lige*, from the Teutonic root seen in Germ. *ledig*, 'free'. "A *liege* lord was a lord of a free band, and his *lieges* were privileged free men, faithful to him, but free from other service" (Skeat). Gradually *liege* lost the notion 'free', and came to mean 'subject'.

Limbec, I. 7. 67; short for *alembic*, 'a vessel for distilling'. It is one of those hybrid words of Arabic + Greek origin which came into Spain through the Moors and then passed into European languages. Arabic *al*, 'the' + *anbik*, 'a still', from Gk. ἄμβιξ, 'a cup'. For the Arabic definite article *al*, 'the', cf. '*al*chemy', '*al*gebra', '*al*cohol'.

Luxury; Shakespeare always uses *luxury* = 'lust', the sense of *luxuria* in Late Lat.; and **luxurious** (IV. 3. 58) = 'lustful', *luxuriosus*.

Magot-pie, III. 4. 125, 'magpie'; O.F. *magot* = F. *margot*, 'a magpie—a talkative woman', +O.F. *pie*, Lat. *pica*. Variant forms of *magot-pie* were *maggoty-pie*, *magot o' pie*, *maggaty-pie*.

Marry, corrupted from the name of the 'Virgin *Mary*'; cf. "Lady" and "by'r *lady*" = 'by our Lady', i.e. the Virgin. Such expressions dated from the pre-Reformation times in England. The common meanings of *marry* are 'indeed, to be sure', and 'why!'

Mate, v. I. 77, 'to bewilder, confound'. Cf. *The Comedy of Errors*, v. I. 281, "I think you are all mated or stark mad". Sometimes it has the stronger sense 'to overcome, subdue', as in Bacon's Essay *Of Death*, "there is no passion in the minde of man so weake, but it mates and masters the feare of Death". "O.F. *mat*, 'weak', was orig. a chess term, like our *mate* in check-mate, which represents the Pers. *sháh mát*, 'the king is dead'." Chess came from the East.

Mere, 'absolute, utter'. Cf. "his mere enemy". *The Merchant of Venice*, III. 2. 265; "the mere perdition of the Turkish fleet", i.e. complete destruction, *Othello*, II. 2. 3, 4. Lat. *merus*, 'pure, unmixed'.

Metaphysical, I. 5. 27, 'supernatural'. Gk. μετὰ τὰ φυσικά (whence Lat. *metaphysica*, 'metaphysics') meant properly 'after the *Physics*', and was a title applied to certain of Aristotle's works the study of which came after his *Physics*. But the prefix (μετά) got to be regarded as meaning 'beyond', 'above', and *metaphysics* acquired the notion 'a science that is above physics', 'supernatural science'. Gradually the word got the idea 'philosophy', 'the study of the mind'. See *Cent. Dict*.

Mettle, I. 7. 73, 'disposition, temper'. *Mettle* is only another spelling of *metal* (Lat. *metallum*); now it is used for the metaphorical senses—'temper, spirit'; cf. 'on his mettle'.

Minion, I. 2. 19, 'favourite', commonly in a bad sense; cf. *3 Henry VI*, II. 2. 84, "Go, rate thy minions, proud insulting boy!" F. *mignon*, 'dainty', which is of Teutonic origin; cf. old Germ. *minne*, 'love', as in *minne-singer*, 'singer of love'. Old writers use *minion* = 'lover'; cf. *The Faerie Queene*, II. 2. 37 ("a mincing mineon").

Modern, IV. 3. 165. Shakespeare always uses *modern* = 'commonplace, trite, ordinary'; that which is 'in the *mode*' soon becomes trite and commonplace. Cf. *As You Like It*,

II. 7. 156, "Full of wise saws and modern instances", i.e. trite illustrations. Constance in *King John*, III. 4. 42, speaks of death as a power "Which scorns a modern invocation", i.e. is deaf to ordinary entreaties.

Moe, v. 3. 35. Middle E. *mo*, from A.S. *mā*, 'more, others', indicated number; *more*, from A.S. *māra*, 'greater', indicated magnitude; now *more* serves both purposes. The root of each is that which we get in the verb *may*. In Elizabethan E. *moe* is frequent; cf. *Much Ado About Nothing*, II. 3. 72, "Sing no more ditties, sing no moe".

Muse, III. 4. 85, 'to wonder'; cf. *King John*, III. 1. 317, "I muse your majesty doth seem so cold". O.F. *muser* is probably the same as Ital. and Lat. *mussare*, 'to mutter, mumble, be in uncertainty'; a word of onomatopœic origin (like *mutter* and *mumble*), imitative of a low sound expressing wonder or meditation.

Napkin, II. 3. 6, 'handkerchief', as always in Shakespeare. F. *nappe*, 'cloth' + diminutive suffix *kin*; cognates *napery*, 'table-linen', *apron* (= *a napron*).

Naught, IV. 3. 220, = *naughty*, which is always used by Shakespeare = 'bad, good for *naught*'; cf. *The Merchant of Venice*, v. 91, "So shines a *good* deed in a *naughty* world". Cf. Proverbs vi. 12, "A naughty person, a wicked man". *Naught* = *ne*, the old negative + *aught*.

Near, II. 3. 123. This is really the old comparative = *neah-r*; the modern *nearer* is a double comparative. The A.S. positive is *nēah*.

Newt, IV. 1. 14. The *n* has come from the indefinite article, a *newt* being = *an ewt*. For the opposite process, due to careless pronunciation, cf. *adder* (*an adder* = *a nadder*), *apron* (*an apron* = *a napron*). *Ewt* is contracted from Middle E. *evete*, 'lizard'.

Nice; O.F. *nice*, Lat. *nescius*, 'ignorant'. *Nice* originally meant 'foolish' (a kindred notion to 'ignorant'), as in Chaucer; then 'foolishly particular, fastidious'—whence its common Shakespearian senses, e.g. 'very precise (IV. 3. 169), punctilious'; 'subtle, sophistical', since fastidiousness implies drawing fine, subtle distinctions; 'coy, prudish'; 'petty, trivial'. The word is notable as having improved in meaning since Shakespeare's time.

Oblivious, V. 3. 43, 'causing forgetfulness'; like *obliviosus* in Horace's line *obliviosi pocula Massici* (*Odes*, II. 7. 21). So Satan, referring to the fiery lake into which he and his rebel angels were hurled in Hell, calls it "the oblivious pool" (*Paradise Lost*, I. 266).

Or ere, IV. 3. 168, 'before'; really *or* and *ere* are the *same* word = A.S. *ǽr*, 'before'. Perhaps *or ere* arose through confusion with another old phrase *or ever*.

Owe, I. 3. 76, I. 4. 10, 'to own, possess'. *Owe* meant originally 'to possess', being closely akin to *own*; then 'to possess another's property', and so 'to be in debt for'. Cf. *King John*, II. 1. 247, 248:

> To pay that duty which you truly owe
> To him that owes it, namely this young prince.

Paddock, I. 1. 9, 'a toad'; Middle E. *padde*, 'a toad'+the diminutive suffix *ock* (as in *bullock, hillock, hammock*). *Pad* was a common word for 'toad'; old writers speak of *pad-stool* and *paddock-stool* for 'toad-stool'. "A *pad* in the straw" was a popular phrase for 'a hidden danger', 'a snake in the grass'— e.g. "Here lyes in dede the padde within the strawe" (proverb). The word is Icelandic (*padda*) in origin.

Passion, III. 4. 57; any strong emotion, feeling, especially great grief; cf. *King Lear*, V. 3. 198, "'Twixt two extremes of passion, joy and grief". Lat. *passio*, 'suffering, feeling', from *pati*, 'to suffer'.

Patch, V. 3. 15, 'a fool, simpleton'. The professional jester or fool attached to a court or nobleman's house was called a *patch* from his *patch*-like, 'motley' dress: hence 'Patch' became a kind of nickname; Wolsey had two jesters so named.

Peak, I. 3. 23, 'to waste away, grow emaciated'; perhaps from the noun *peak* (= anything sharp-pointed) used in reference to the sharpened features of a sick person.

Pent-house, I. 3. 20; corrupted from the earlier form *pentise* (O.F. *apentis*, 'a shed'), from the resemblance of sound between *ise* carelessly pronounced and *house*. Cf. F. *pente*, 'a slope', *pendre*, 'to hang', Lat. *pendere*. So *cutlass* (F. *coutelas*) got corrupted into *curtle-axe* from a similarity of sound which made people think that the weapon was a sort of *axe*. 'Popular etymology', i.e. common and incorrect notions as to the origin of words, influences the form often; cf. *cray-fish*, where *-fish* is a corruption of *-visse* in F. *écrevisse*.

Posset; a hot drink (see II. 2. 6, note), taken just before bedtime. There used to be '*posset*-cups'. We have the verb in the sense 'curdle' in *Hamlet*, I. 5. 68. Probably *posset* is a celtic word; Irish *pusoid*; cf. Welsh *posel*, 'curdled milk'.

Proof. F. *preuve*, Low Lat. *proba*, 'a test', from Lat. *probare*; it was specially used of impenetrable armour, meaning the armour itself, as in I. 2. 54, or its resisting power. All steel used for armour, swords etc. is tested.

Prowess, v. 8. 41; O.F. *proecce*, 'bravery, valour', from *prou*, an old form of *preux*, 'brave', as in *preux chevalier*, 'a valiant knight'.

Quarry, IV. 3. 201, 'a heap of slaughtered game'; a hunting-term. O.F. *cuiree*, the intestines of a slain animal, the part given to the hounds; so called because wrapped in the skin— F. *cuir*, 'a skin, hide', from Lat. *corium*, 'hide'.

Rapt, I. 3. 57, 142, 'transported'; the past participle of an old verb *rap*, 'to seize hurriedly', cognate with Germ. *raffen*, 'to snatch'. The *Cent. Dict.* quotes fron Foxe's *Book of Martyrs* (1522): "Think ye...that they will not pluck from you whatsoever they can rap or reave?" For the figurative sense cf. *Cymbeline*, I. 6. 51, "What...Thus raps you?" i.e. what transports you thus? The form *rapt* comes through confusion with Lat. *raptus*, the p.p. of Lat. *rapere*, 'to seize'.

Ravin, 'prey' (F. *ravine*, Lat. *rapina*). Hence **ravin** (II. 4. 28) used as a verb = 'to devour greedily, as an animal its prey', and **ravined** = 'ravenous' (IV. 1. 24).

Remorse, I. 5. 42, 'pity'; cf. *The Merchant of Venice*, IV. I. 20, "Thou'lt show...mercy and remorse" (said to Shylock). A commoner meaning in Shakespeare than 'compunction, regret' (literally 'biting again', viz. of conscience—Lat. *remordere*). A feeling of pity is akin to a feeling of regret where one's action has caused the state or thing that is pitiful.

Ronyon, I. 3. 6, literally 'a mangy creature'; hence used as a term of great contempt, like the cognate word *roynish*, 'scabby, scurvy' and so 'wretched, low'. Cf. *The Merry Wives of Windsor*, IV. 2. 194, 195, "you hag, you baggage, you polecat, you ronyon!" and *As You Like It*, II. 2. 8, "the roynish clown". O.F. *roigne*, Lat. *robigo*, 'a scab'; cf. mod. F. *rogneux*, 'scurvy'.

Sag, v. 3. 10, 'to droop'; literally 'to sink down from weakness or overweight'. In the literal sense *sag* is now current in England, and a word of everyday use among mechanics and engineers. Figuratively it survives as a Stock-Exchange term to describe a "depressed market"; cf. the following: extract from a financial paper "Immediately the conclusion was jumped to that some serious complication with France had arisen, and everything sagged away", i.e. prices gave way all round. Middle E. *saggen*, from Swedish *sacka*, 'to settle, sink down'; akin to *sink*.

Scotch, III. 2. 13; contracted from *scortch* = *scartch*, a transposed form of *scratch*. The fact that the older uncontracted form was *scortch* may account for the 1st Folio's reading, *scorch'd.* There is no connection with *scutch*, 'to beat like flax', *scutcher*, 'a flail'. Isaac Walton's recipe (*Complete Angler*) for dressing a chub was: "Give him three or four scotches or cuts on the back with your knife, and broil him on charcoal." In masonry *scotching* is a term for dressing stone by chipping it out with a chisel in a particular way. *Cent. Dict.*

Sear, or **sere**; literally 'dry', A.S. *sēar*. Commonly said of flowers or leaves (v. 3. 23), with the sense 'faded', 'withered', as in *Lycidas*, 2, "ivy never sere".

Security, III. 5. 32. Elizabethan writers often use the adjective *secure* = Lat. *securus*, 'careless, free from fear'; especially to imply over-confidence, a false sense of safety. Cf. *Henry V*, Chorus, IV. 17, where "the *confident* French" are described as "Proud of their numbers and secure in soul"; and Fletcher's quibbling lines:

> To secure yourselves from these,
> Be not too secure in ease.

Ben Jonson said, "Men may *securely* sin, but *safely* never".

Seel, III. 2. 46; properly a term from falconry, meaning to close up the eyelids of young hawks, either partially or entirely, by passing a fine thread through them; this was done till they became tractable and patient of the hood. F. *siller* or *ciller*, 'to close up the eyelids'; from F. *cil*, Lat. *cilium*, 'an eyelid'. Elizabethans have the word often in the sense 'to close'; cf. Spenser, describing a wounded deer (*The Faerie Queene*, II. 1. 38):

> Whiles the sad pang approching shee does feele,
> Brayes out her latest breath, and up her eyes doth seele.

Sennet; a term frequent in Elizabethan stage-directions for a set of notes on a trumpet, sounded as a signal, e.g. of entrance (III. 1. 10) or departure; different from a "flourish" (I. 4. 58). Sometimes spelt *signet*, which shows the derivation—O.F. *signet*, Lat. *signum*, 'a sign'.

Sewer, I. 7; a chief servant in a royal or noble household whose duty was to arrange the dishes on the table. "Sewer and seneshal" (steward) is a favourite alliterative combination. Cf. Milton, *Paradise Lost*, IX. 37, 38, describing scenes of chivalry with

> marshall'd feast
> Served up in hall with sewers and seneshals.

The *sewer* had also to act as the king's "taster" and "take the *assay*" (= *essay*, trial, test) of each dish, i.e. taste it for fear of poison before the king ate of it. Note, however, that *sewer* has no etymological connection with F. *essayeur*, 'a taster, trier' (though some confusion arose between the words). The *Cent. Dict.* considers *sewer* short for *assewer*; F. *asseour*, 'one who sets the table', from *asseoir* (Lat. *assidere*), 'to set', or 'sit'.

Shard, or **sherd**, III. 2. 42; A.S. *sceard*, 'a fragment', especially of pottery—cf. *potsherd*; literally 'a cut thing'. A.S. *sceran*, 'to cut, *shear*'; cf. Germ. *scheren*.

Skirr, V. 3. 35, 'to scour'; also written *scur*, which shows its connection with *scurry* and *scour*. It is used in *Henry V*, IV. 7. 64, with the sense to 'hurry off, move away rapidly': "we will . . . make them skirr away".

Sliver, IV. 1. 28, 'to tear off' (a branch); A.S. *slifan*, 'to cleave'. Cf. *sliver* = 'a small broken branch' in *Hamlet*, IV. 7. 174, in the description how "an envious sliver" of the willow tree broke, and Ophelia fell into the stream.

Suggestion, I. 3. 134, 'temptation, evil prompting'. Cf. *suggest* = 'to tempt, incite to do evil', e.g. in *Richard II*, III. 4. 75, 76:

> What Eve, what serpent, hath suggested thee
> To make a second fall of cursed man?

Surcease, I. 7. 4, 'cessation, stop'; properly a legal term = 'the arrest or stoppage of a legal suit'; O.F. *sursis*, from O.F. *surseoir*, 'to pause' = Lat. *supersedere*, 'to forbear'. Note that *surcease* is quite distinct from (though its form may have been affected by) *cease* = F. *cesser*, Lat. *cessare*.

Thane; a title of honour, roughly equivalent to 'Earl', originally an old English word for 'a warrior, knight at a king's court'. Icelandic *þegn*; cognate with Germ. *degen*, 'a warrior', from *gedeihen*, 'to thrive'.

Thrall, III. 6. 13; from Icelandic *þræll*, 'a serf', Danish *træl*. Strictly it meant 'a runner', i.e. on messages, the original root being that seen in Gk. τρέχειν, 'to run'. The notion that *thrall* comes from *thrill*, because the ears of serfs were *thrilled* or *drilled*, i.e. pierced, is wrong.

Toy, II. 3. 76, 'a worthless thing, a trifle'. Cf. *2 Henry IV*, II. 4. 183, "Shall we fall foul for toys?" i.e. quarrel about trifles. So in *Lucrece*, 214, "Who sells eternity to get a toy?" Dutch *tuig*, 'stuff, trash'; akin to Germ. *zeug*, e.g. in *spielzeug*, 'playthings'.

Trains, IV. 3. 113, 'lures, artifices'. The magician in *Comus*, hoping to get a new victim into his power, says (150, 151):

> Now to my charms,
> And to my wily trains!

F. *traîner*, from Latin *trahere*, 'to draw', in Late Lat. 'to betray'—from the metaphor of drawing birds into snares.

In the sense a 'lure' for birds, the word was specially familiar to falconers. If a falcon would not return after her flight, she was brought back by the use of the lure. "This was a sham bird, usually constructed of pigeon's wings weighted, to which was attached food for the hawk, known as a train. Attracted by the semblance of a bird, and by the reality of a meal, the hawk soon descended to the lure" (*The Diary of Master William Silence*, by Mr Justice Madden, p. 198).

Trammel, I. 7. 3. O.F. *tramail*, medieval Lat. *tramacula*, or *trimacula*, 'a three-mesh net', i.e. a net of three layers, different in the sizes of the meshes; from Lat. *tres* (*tri* in compounds) + *macula*, 'a spot', hence 'a mesh like a spot'.

Wassail, I. 7. 64, 'carousing, drinking'. Cf. *Love's Labour's Lost*, V. 2. 318, "wakes and wassails". *Wassail* is the old northern English *wes heil* (A.S. = *wes hāl*), 'be whole' = the imperative of *wesan*, 'to be' + *heil*, cognate with *whole* and *hale*. Originally *wassail* was a salutation used in drinking a man's health; then it came to mean 'a drinking, carousing, revel'. The '*wassail-bowl*' was a great feature of the old Christmas feasting. It is one of Scott's archaic words; cf. *Marmion*, V. 7:

> Old Holy-Rood rang merrily
> That night with wassell, mirth and glee.

Weird, I. 3. 32; properly a noun meaning 'fate, destiny'; A.S. *wyrd*, 'fate', literally 'that which happens', from *weorðan*, 'to become, to take place'; cf. Germ. *werden*. In old writers 'the Weirds' are the Fates. Hence *weird* = 'supernatural, uncanny, mysterious'.

Wreck; in the 1st Folio always spelt *wrack*, the usual form till late in the 17th century, and in some passages of Shakespeare the rhyme requires it. Cf. v. 5. 51, 52. From A.S. *wrecan*, 'to drive', the *wrack* or *wreck* being that which is driven ashore.

Yesty, IV. I. 53, 'foamy, frothy'; a variant form of *yeasty*. Cf. Tennyson, *The Sailor Boy*,

> The sands and yeasty surges mix
> In caves about the dreary bay.

Yeast is from the Aryan root which gives us: (1) Gk. ζέειν, 'to boil', and (2) such Teutonic words as Germ. *gähren*, 'to ferment'.

APPENDIX

A

I. HISTORICAL ASPECTS OF THE PLAY

Dr Furness says:

"Such[1] are the sources from which Shakespeare drew the materials of the tragedy of 'Macbeth', and, of course, for his purpose it mattered little whether it were founded on fact or were the baseless fabric of a dream. Yet, as the editors here and there, during the progress of the tragedy, call attention to various points where historic truth is said to be violated, it may be worth while as briefly as possible to compare the fiction with the fact. What follows is condensed from Chalmers's *Caledonia*, bk iii, ch. vii.

"The rebellion of Macdonwald, from the Western Isles, is mere fable. The old historians may have confounded it either with the rebellion of Gilcomgain, the maormor of Moray, in 1033, or with the rebellious conduct of Torfin, Duncan's cousin. Nor was there during the reign of Duncan any invasion of Fife by Sweno, Norway's king. It was to put down the rebellion of Torfin that Duncan marched northward through the territorial government of Macbeth, and was slain by treasonous malice at Bothgowanan, near Elgin, and many miles from Inverness, in A.D. 1039. Macbeth's father was not Sinel, but Finley,[2] or Finlegh, the maormor, or prince, of Ross, not the thane of Glamis, and was killed about the year 1020, in some encounter with Malcolm II, the grandfather of Duncan. Thus by lineage Macbeth was thane of Ross, and afterwards by marriage the thane of Moray. This same grandfather of Duncan, Malcolm II, also dethroned and moreover slew Lady Macbeth's grandfather; *on both sides of the house, therefore, there was a death to be avenged on the person of Duncan. But of the two, Lady Macbeth's wrongs were far heavier than her husband's, and*

---

[1] I.e. the passages from Holinshed's *Chronicles* which he has quoted and of which we have given the most important in our larger edition.

[2] Professor Hume Brown, whose authority is unsurpassed, writes the name *Finnlaec*.

might well fill her from crown to toe topfull of direst cruelty.[1] Her
name was Lady Gruoch and her first husband was Gilcomgain,
the maormor of Moray, a prince of the highest rank and next to
the royal family; upon him Malcolm's cruelty fastened, and he
was burnt within his castle with fifty of his clan, and his young
wife escaped by flight with her infant son Lulach. She naturally
sought refuge in the neighbouring county of Ross, then governed
by Macbeth, and him she married. About a year after the death
of her first husband, Lady Gruoch's only brother was slain by
the command of that same aged Malcolm II, whose peaceful
death soon after, unprecipitated by poison, flame, or sword, is
not one of the least incredible traditions of that misty time.

"In 1054 the Northumbrians, led by Siward and his son
Osbert, penetrated probably to Dunsinnan, and in that vicinity
Macbeth met them in a furious battle; but Bellona's bridegroom
was defeated, and fled to the North. It was not till two[2] years
afterwards, on the 5th of December, 1056, that he was slain by
Macduff.

"History knows nothing of Banquo, the thane of Lochaber,
nor of Fleance. None of the ancient chronicles, nor Irish annals,
nor even Fordun, recognize these fictitious names. Neither is
a thane of Lochaber known in Scottish history, because the
Scottish kings never had any demesnes within that inaccessible
district.

"Of the fate of Lady Macbeth, apart from the lines of
Shakespeare, history, tradition, and fable are silent."

II. THE SUPERNATURAL IN *MACBETH* AND ELIZABETHAN SUPERSTITION

Speaking of resemblances between *Hamlet* and *Macbeth*
Dr Brandes says:

"The supernatural beings that make their appearance are not
to be taken as mere illusions; they are distinctly conceived as
having a real existence outside the sphere of hallucination. As
in *Hamlet*, the Ghost is not seen by the prince alone, so in
Macbeth it is not only Macbeth himself who sees the Witches;

---

[1] The italics are ours. Cf. Dr Brandes: "There was a blood-feud
between the house of Duncan and the house of Macbeth. . . Both had
the [motive] to a blood-revenge on Duncan."

[2] The Article in the *Dictionary of Biography* gives the date as
15 August 1057.

they even appear with their queen, Hecate, when there is no one to see them except the spectators of the play.

"It must not be forgotten that this whole spirit- and witch-world meant something quite different to Shakespeare's contemporaries from what it means to us. We cannot even be absolutely certain that Shakespeare himself did not believe in the possible existence of such beings. Great poets have seldom been consistent in their incredulity—even Holberg believed that he had seen a ghost. But Shakespeare's own attitude of mind matters less than that of the public for whom he wrote.

"In the beginning of the seventeenth century the English people still believed in a great variety of evil spirits, who disturbed the order of nature, produced storms by land and sea, foreboded calamities and death, disseminated plague and famine. They were for the most part pictured as old, wrinkled women, who brewed all kinds of frightful enormities in hellish cauldrons; and when such beldams were thought to have been detected, the law took vengeance on them with fire and sword. In a sermon preached in 1588, Bishop Jewel appealed to Elizabeth to take strong measures against wizards and witches. Some years later, one Mrs Dyer was accused of witchcraft for no other reason than that toothache had for some nights prevented the Queeen from sleeping. In the small town of St Osees in Essex alone, seventy or eighty witches were burnt. In a book called 'The Discoverie of Witchcraft', published in 1584, Reginald Scott refuted the doctrine of sorcery and magic with wonderful clearness and liberal-mindedness; but his voice was lost in the chorus of the superstitious.... In 1597 James himself produced in his *Dæmonologie* a kind of handbook or textbook of witchcraft in all its developments, and in 1598 he caused no fewer than 600 old women to be burnt. In the Parliament of 1604 a bill against sorcery was brought in by the Government and passed."

The results produced by the introduction of the supernatural in *Macbeth* may be grouped under three headings—plot, character-interest, atmosphere. (1) The supernatural is part of the mechanism of the plot because the influence of the Witches affects Macbeth's actions so much. (2) It serves in III. 4 as a measure of the working of his feelings. (3) It invests the whole theme with mystery and diffuses an atmosphere of awe, through which the tragedy looms more terrible. I think we might venture to compare it with part of Ephesians, vi. 12.

III. DRAMATIC[1] IRONY

One of the most effective of dramatic devices is the use of
"irony". The essential idea of "irony" is double dealing, as
when some speech has a double meaning—the obvious one which
all perceive, and the cryptic which only certain of the hearers
understand. And "irony" of fate or circumstances is a sort
of double dealing by which Destiny substitutes for what we
might expect just the opposite, the unexpected, thing. This
"irony" of the broader kind informs Macbeth's later relations
(IV. I) with the Witches, in that through them revelations are
made from which he anticipates certain results, whereas it
happens that precisely the opposite results accrue to him.

But understood in the more limited sense in which "irony" is
used as a dramatic term, it may be said, roughly, to lie in the
difference between the facts as known to the audience and as
imagined by the characters of the play or by some of them.
Macbeth is remarkable beyond any other of Shakespeare's plays
for the frequency and power of its tragic "irony". Numerous
instances, which it were needless to recapitulate, have been
mentioned in the Notes, and the reader will have observed
others. "The entire atmosphere of *Macbeth*" (it has been well
said), "as of no other tragedy, is oppressive with the sense of
something subtly malignant as well as inexorably revengeful in
the forces that rule the world; of a tragic irony in the ultimate
scheme of things."

But leaving *Macbeth* we will illustrate Shakespearian "irony"
from two or three of the most familiar plays. Thus in *Henry V*,
II. 2. 12–69 the situation is pregnant with "irony" because the
audience know (6, 7) that the conspiracy has been revealed to
Henry, while the conspirators imagine that it is still a secret.
Hence for the audience Henry's bearing, and many of his
remarks, have a significance which is quite lost upon the conspirators themselves, who on their part are unconscious that

---

[1] The term "tragic irony' does not cover the full scope of this
literary artifice, which, as we shall see, is equally used in the romantic
drama for comic purposes, and equally effective as in the classical
tragic drama. Gk. εἰρωνεία, 'dissembling' (Lat. *dissimulatio*). Literally εἴρων = 'one who speaks', but the word came to mean specifically
one who speaks after a particular manner, namely, as a dissembler
who says less than he knows or thinks and affects ignorance, e.g. in
argument—like Socrates. See Mr Moulton's sections on "irony".

their hollow protestations of loyalty are being estimated at their true value. The incident of the pardon (39–60) is introduced— we may remember that it has no parallel in Holinshed's account —entirely for the sake of the "irony". The conspirators urge Henry to be stern, and the audience know how their pleading will recoil upon themselves (79–83). This is "irony" of situation. It often takes the form of attributing to a character a bold, self-confident tone just when he is, as the audience know, on the brink of some catastrophe, as the conspirators are. Thus in *Richard II* the king, in spite of his reverses, gives vent (III. 2. 54–62) to triumphant confidence in his cause just when he is about to know what the audience know already, and feel that he must shortly know, viz. that the Welsh army on which his hope rests (cf. 76, 77) has dispersed. For similar "irony" of situation cf. *Julius Cæsar*, III. 1, where Cæsar is made to use the most exalted language about himself when we know that he is on the very edge of destruction.

Often the "irony" is verbal, the dramatist putting into the mouth of a character remarks which the audience, with their fuller knowledge of the facts, can interpret in two ways, while the speaker himself (or his fellow-characters) is quite unconscious of any secondary point in his words. In a tragedy this verbal irony, which is specially associated with the Sophoclean drama, frequently takes the form of "innocent phrases covering sinister depths of meaning". In comedy it is effectively provocative of mirth. Thus in *Twelfth Night* the humour and interest of the scenes in which Viola is with Olivia and Orsino turn largely upon the fact that they do not know her to be a girl, while the audience do. Shakespeare purposely makes Olivia and Orsino say things which have for the audience a point whereof the speaker is quite unconscious. In the same way many of Viola's remarks (cf. III. 1. 169–72) contain veiled allusions to her sex which the audience perceive at once, whereas Olivia or Orsino sees no allusion at all.

The same effect is gained in *As You Like It* through the same cause, viz. Rosalind's disguise. No more perfect specimen of verbal "irony" could be instanced than the dialogue at the end of the scene (IV. 3) where Rosalind, disguised as a youth, faints at the sight of the blood-stained handkerchief and Oliver lightly chides the "youth" for being so womanly:

"*Oliver.* Be of good cheer, youth: *you a man! you lack a man's heart.*

Rosalind. I do so. I confess it. Ah, sirrah, a body would think this was well counterfeited! I pray you, tell your brother how well I counterfeited. Heigh-ho!

Oliver. This was not counterfeit: there is too great testimony in your complexion, that it was a passion of earnest.

Rosalind. Counterfeit, I assure you.

Oliver. Well then, take a good heart, and *counterfeit to be a man.*

Rosalind. So I do: but, i' faith, I should have been a woman by right."

Often, of course, "irony" of situation and of remark are united. Greek tragedy is full of "irony", especially verbal "irony". Indeed, it compensated to some extent for the lack of freshness in the themes treated. The chief themes of Greek tragedy were drawn from those great cycles of Hellenic myth and story which were common property, so that the audience knew from the outset what would be the course and issue of a play.[1] Verbal "irony", therefore, was made a partial substitute for the absence of the element of surprise and novelty. This is especially the case in the dramas of Sophocles. It is one of the classical features of the most perfect piece of classicism in the English language—Milton's *Samson Agonistes.*

B

I. "If it were done", etc.
Macbeth, I. 7. 1, 2.

The suggestion has been made that we should place a full stop at the end of line 1, remove the colon in line 2, connect *It were done quickly* with what follows, and interpret to this effect:

'If it were done [= done with, ended] when it is done [= executed], then it were well [= a good deed to do]. It were done [= ended] quickly if the murder could arrest the evil consequences', etc.

This method of taking the passage involves a considerable change of punctuation, and seems to me to yield at once an inferior sense and rhythm. In particular it loses the point so characteristic of Macbeth, that to act at all he must act ere his resolution cools, and that for him suspense is a torture. Note

---

[1] Shakespeare dramatising history was to some extent in the same position as Æschylus or Sophocles dramatising well-known legends.

how often we get this thought in the play, e.g. in his own words (II. 1. 61, III. 4. 139, 140, IV. 1. 146–8); how, as a matter of fact, he does suddenly brace himself to the deed (II. 1. 60–4), just as he murders the grooms on a sudden impulse (II. 3).

Again, though the two senses of *done* are clear enough in line 1, yet I do not think that *done* could have any other than its ordinary sense in a familiar phrase like *done quickly*.

II. "An Equivocator"
Macbeth, II. 3. 8

This passage (II. 3. 8–11) is generally recognised as a "direct reference to the doctrine of *equivocation* avowed by Henry Garnet, Superior of the order of Jesuits in England, on his trial for the Gunpowder *Treason*, on the 28th of March, 1606, and to his *perjury* on that occasion, or, as Shakespeare expresses, 'to his swearing in both the scales against either scale'.... The trial, at which King James himself was present incognito, doubtless attracted very general notice"; and the reference here must have been perceived at once by Shakespeare's audience. Malone (the writer just quoted) shows that *equivocation* was a striking feature of the defence. Thus a contemporary letter describes how Garnet "fell into a large discourse defending *equivocation*". The official record of the case proves that one of the judges "desired him *not to equivocate*", and that Garnet, being convicted of inconsistency in his evidence, "cried the lords mercy, and said he had offended, if *equivocation* did not help him". (F.)

Moreover, among the papers of another of the conspirators, Francis Tresham (the betrayer of the plot), was a *Treatise on Equivocation* with corrections by Garnet. It has been noted that many of the places connected with the Gunpowder Plot were in the neighbourhood of Stratford-on-Avon, so that the matter must have had a peculiar interest for Shakespeare. Further, I believe Malone was right in regarding the words *who committed treason enough for God's sake* as an allusion to the motives which Garnet alleged to have moved him to take part in the Gunpowder *Treason*.

Of the principle of "equivocation" Dr Gardiner says:

"According to this doctrine, the immorality of a lie did not consist in the deception practised upon the person who was deceived, but in the difference between the words uttered and the intended meaning of the speaker. If, therefore, the speaker could put any sense, however extravagant, upon the words of which he made use, he might lawfully deceive the hearer, without taking any account of the fact that he would be certain to attach some other and more probable meaning to the words".... The "popular feeling" against this doctrine "found a voice in the words of the Porter in 'Macbeth'"—*History of England* (1603–42); I, 280–2.

III. "The Healing Benediction"
Macbeth, IV. 3. 135–54

The following account is from Brewers' *Dictionary of Phrase and Fable* (1900), p. 707:

"King's Evil; Scrofula; so called from a notion which prevailed from the reign of Edward the Confessor to that of Queen Anne that it could be cured by the royal touch. The Jacobites considered that the power did not descend to William III. and Anne because the 'divine' hereditary right was not fully possessed by them, but the office [i.e. form of prayer for the ceremony] remained in our Prayer-Book till 1719. Prince Charles Edward, when he claimed to be Prince of Wales, touched a female child for the disease in 1745; but the last person touched in England was Dr Johnson, in 1712, when only thirty months old, by Queen Anne. The French kings laid claim to the same divine power even from the time of Anne of Clovis, A.D. 481, and on Easter Sunday, 1686, Louis XIV. touched 1600 persons, using these words: '*Le roy te touche, Dieu te guerisse.*' The practice was introduced by Henry VII. of presenting the person 'touched' with a small gold or silver coin, called a touch-piece. The one presented to Dr Johnson has St George and the Dragon on one side and a ship on the other; the legend of the former is *Soli deo gloria*, and of the latter *Anna D: G. M. BR. F. ET H. Reg.* (= Anne, by the grace of God, of Great Britain, France and Ireland Queen). We are told that Charles II. touched 92,107 persons. The smallest number in one year was 2,983, in 1669; and the largest number was in 1684, when many were trampled to death. (See Macaulay's *History of England*, chap. xiv.) John Brown, a royal surgeon, had to superintend the ceremony."

The "Old Pretender", James III, "touched" children at Lucca, 1721.

"When he first arrived in England James had objected to touch for the king's evil. He had strong doubts as to the existence of the power to cure scrofulous disease, which was supposed to be derived from the Confessor. The Scots ministers whom he had brought with him to England urged him to abandon the practice as superstitious. To his English counsellors it was a debasing of royalty to abandon the practice of his predecessors. With no very good will he consented to do as Elizabeth had done, but he first made a public declaration of his fear lest he should incur the blame of superstition.... In after years he showed less hesitancy, and Shakespeare could flatter[1] him" in *Macbeth*, IV. 3. 150, 141 (*Gardiner*).

The real point, therefore, the true inwardness, of Shakespeare's complimentary reference is that it gave expression to the gratitude of James's English subjects for the concession he had made to English feeling, despite the opposition of his Scots advisers. And no doubt Shakespeare's audience were not slow to show that he had interpreted their sentiments aright.

IV. "He has no children"
Macbeth, IV. 3. 211

"'He' is probably Malcolm, whose talk of comfort at such a moment is thus rebutted and explained. Macbeth lies wholly beyond the pale of such reproach"—*Herford*. This seems to me the right interpretation. Compare *King John*, III. 4. 91, where Constance, after Arthur had been taken from her, refuses all comforts and counsel, and when Pandulph rebukes her for over-indulgence in grief, retorts: "He talks to me *that never had a son*" (and so, like Malcolm here, cannot know what a parent's feelings are).

Some editors, however, refer the words to Macbeth, with one of two possible meanings: (1) "either that Macduff could not, by retaliation, revenge the murder of his children because Macbeth had none himself; or (2) that if Macbeth had any children, a father's feelings...would have prevented him from the deed" (cf. 3 *Henry VI*, v. 5. 63). But as to (1), it seems too soon for Macduff to think of "revenge", in spite of Malcolm's words: for the moment he is lost in dazed grief: and as to (2), one doubts whether Macduff would even credit Macbeth, the detested tyrant, with so much grace as would have kept him, if a father of living children, from the crime.

[1] King James ("whose horror of crowds was notorious") is thought to be meant in the description of the ruler who withdraws himself from his subjects' gaze, *Measure for Measure*, I. 1. 67–72, II. 4. 27–30. He was fond of compliments.

8

C

> Come away, come away,
> Hecate, Hecate, come away!

> Black[1] spirits and white, red spirits and gray,
> Mingle, mingle, mingle, you that mingle may!

These are the first lines respectively of the two Songs referred to in the stage-directions of *Macbeth* (III. 5, IV. 1). The Songs were evidently introduced into the performance of *Macbeth*, and evidently so familiar that a reference to them was considered sufficient by the editors of the 1st Folio. They occur in the version of *Macbeth* made by the 17th-century dramatist Davenant, and were formerly ascribed to him. But in the 18th century a MS. copy of a tragi-comedy, *The Witch*, written by Shakespeare's contemporary (though junior) Thomas Middleton, came to light and was published (1778). *The Witch* contains (*a*) the two Songs, (*b*) a supernatural element of the same general character as the Witches-element in *Macbeth*, and (*c*) certain verbal resemblances to Shakespeare's play in the incantation-scenes.

What, then, is the relation of *The Witch* to *Macbeth*?

The answer commonly accepted is this: that Middleton, who imitates Shakespeare frequently in his other plays, wrote *The Witch* in imitation of *Macbeth* and copied it in parts; that he wrote the two Songs for *The Witch;* that the actors, to increase the supernatural element of the play and admit of more music (two great features of its stage-popularity), introduced the Songs from *The Witch;* and that they were able to do so because Middleton himself wrote for the King's Players (Shakespeare's company) from 1615 to 1624—indeed, the same company performed in both plays at the Blackfriars Theatre. This theory is quite satisfactory.

No one believes that *The Witch* preceded *Macbeth*, i.e. that Shakespeare imitated Middleton, or that the two dramatists wrote *Macbeth* together.

Unfortunately, the presence of these Songs in *Macbeth* gave rise to an unhappy theory that after Shakespeare's withdrawal from the stage *Macbeth* underwent a revision for theatrical purposes by Middleton, and that it contains other portions of Middleton's work than the two Songs.

---

[1] References to the colours of spirits are common in old writers.

The chief portions of *Macbeth* which have been condemned as his interpolations are these:

Act I, Sc. 2 (the Sergeant's scene) and Sc. 3. 1–37 (the Witches' dialogue up to the entrance of Macbeth and Banquo); Act II, Sc. 3, commencement (the Porter's scene); all the Hecate parts (Act III, Sc. 5, Act IV, Sc. 1. 39–47); Act IV, Sc. 3. 135–154 (the "King's Evil" passage); Act V, Sc. 8. 35–75 (the tragedy's close).

The case against and for the authenticity of these parts of *Macbeth* may be roughly summarised thus, under the respective headings 'A' and 'B'.

Act I, Sc. 2.

A. Style un-Shakespearian. It is absurd that a severely wounded soldier should be sent with the news of victory. There is a great discrepancy between the account of Cawdor here and *Macbeth's* question in 1. 3. 72–5.

B. Arguments based on style are uncertain: thus a very eminent critic finds in this "un-Shakespearian" scene a "profusion of Shakespearian touches". The "discrepancy" can be explained (1. 3. 72, note). The Sergeant's state increases greatly the dramatic force of the whole incident: and has a wounded man never brought tidings of battle? The scene is of almost essential importance to the evolution of the piece (see 1. 2. 68, note): are we to assume that Shakespeare's version had no such scene?

Act I, Sc. 3. 1–37.

A. Again un-Shakespearian style.

B. The reason for the condemnation of these lines seems to be the fact that to cut out Scene 2 is to dislocate the whole opening of the tragedy, and make it necessary that the action should pass straight from the first exit of the Witches (1. 1. 12) to the first entrance of Macbeth (1. 3. 38). Without the lines the scene opens very tamely.

Act II, Sc. 3 ("Porter's scene").

A. The note of broad humour jars, and the tone of the passage (as it stands in the 1st Folio) very coarse.

B. The jarring note exemplifies the principle of contrast and relief: compare the Grave-diggers in *Hamlet*. The coarseness, being another phase of evil, helps to create an impression (temporary) of the universality and omnipotence of evil in a world where such a deed as Duncan's murder is possible. (See also p. 114, for other points in favour of the authenticity of the scene, *which is accepted by all modern critics.*)

The Hecate parts we will pass over, for the moment.

Act IV, Sc. 3. 135–54 (the "King's Evil" passage). It is part of the general complimentary purpose of the play. The sole ground for condemning it is the untenable notion that Shakespeare did not allude in his plays to contemporary events.

Act V, Sc. 8. 35–75 (the tragedy's close).

A. There is a confusion in the stage-directions at v. 8. 34 (see note). The description of Lady Macbeth as this "fiend-like queen" disturbs the feeling of sympathy with her which the spectacle of her terrible suffering has roused; and Shakespeare would not "have drawn away the veil which with his fine tact he had drawn over her fate", by telling us that she had committed suicide (v. 8. 70, 71).

B. Confusions in the stage-directions are common. It is not Shakespeare's practice to "draw a veil" over the fate of his criminals. He brings them to a bad end, and tells us so. Nor does he ever excite a sympathy with them so great as to obscure their evil deeds and the justice of their punishment, and he does *not* do this in the case of Lady Macbeth. The description of Macbeth and his wife is absolutely appropriate to Malcolm, the son of their victim. The close of *Macbeth* resembles that of *Hamlet* most markedly.

The whole theory of interpolations, as it affects these portions of *Macbeth*, appears to me to be untenable. It was unknown to the older race of critics and scholars, and seems to me to lead to needless complications.

Act III, Sc. 5, *Act IV, Sc.* 1. 39–47.

A. On the other hand, the theory as it affects the Hecate parts (some forty lines) finds able adherents, on these grounds: that Hecate is a superfluous character; that she represents a mythology entirely separate from that embodied in the "Weird Sisters" and introduces suggestions of an alien fairy-lore (IV. 1. 41–3); that the style of her long speech—smooth, lyrical, graceful—is the very opposite of the style of the Witches' speeches, and the rhythm "iambic", instead of "trochaic".

B. Hecate is *the* goddess of witchcraft in Elizabethan superstition, and a piece like *Macbeth* or *The Witch* would scarcely have been thought complete without her. She acts the traditional part of "the Dame".[1] She may seem superfluous, but she is introduced to fortify the supernatural power when its

---

[1] Cf. Ben Jonson, note to *Masque of Queens*: "Amongst our vulgar witches, the honour of dame (for so I translate it) is given with a kind of pre-eminence to some special one at their meetings."

task of driving Macbeth to his doom becomes more onerous. At first, the Witches have only to suggest the idea of kingship to Macbeth, and so Hecate is held in reserve.

The fact that she represents classical mythology, while the Witches represent northern superstition, and that their union involves a mixture of associations, only illustrates what we see constantly in Elizabethan writers, namely, their carelessness about literary incongruity. The fairy-lore of *A Midsummer-Night's Dream*, for example, is essentially a composite fabric. It blends "the elves of the village with the fays of romance": not a remote parallel, surely, to this mixture of associations in *Macbeth*; and the whole comedy is a medley of the semi-classical and the medieval and romantic. Similarly, there is a distinct element of Elizabethan colouring in Shakespeare's plays founded on Roman history.

As regards the style, naturally Shakespeare would not make the classical goddess speak in the same manner as the grim, barbaric Witches. Finally, the alternation of iambic and trochaic metres is a feature of his supernatural scenes.

Lastly, we may note the current opinion that the 1st Folio's version of *Macbeth* gives us only a compressed stage-version of what Shakespeare wrote. The only definite piece of evidence adduced in support of this idea is the brevity of *Macbeth*. Yet there is a much simpler explanation of this brevity. *Macbeth* has no underplot: with an under-plot of average length the play itself would be normal in length.

HINTS ON METRE

I. Regular Type of Blank Verse

Blank verse[1] consists of unrhymed lines, each of which, if constructed according to the regular type, contains five feet, each foot being composed of two syllables and having a strong stress or accent on the second syllable, so that each line has five stresses, falling respectively on the even syllables, 2, 4, 6, 8, 10. Here is an example from *Macbeth* (I. 3. 38):

So foúl | and faír | a dáy | I háve | not seén.

The rhythm of a line like this is a "rising" rhythm.

Blank verse prior to Marlowe, the great Elizabethan dramatist whose work influenced Shakespeare, was modelled strictly on this type. Further, this early blank verse was what is termed "end-stopt": that is to say, there was almost always *some* pause, however slight, in the sense, and consequently in the rhythm, at the close of each line; while the couplet was normally the limit of the sense. As an example of this "end-stopt", strictly regular verse, take the following extract from the first play written in blank verse, viz. the tragedy called *Gorboduc* (1561):

Why should I live and linger forth my time,
In longer life to double my distress?
O me most woeful wight! whom no mishap
Long ere this day could have bereaved hence:
Mought not these hands by fortune or by fate
Have pierced this breast, and life with iron reft?

If the whole of *Macbeth* were written in verse of this kind the effect, obviously, would be intolerably monotonous. Blank verse before Marlowe *was* intolerably monotonous, and in an especial degree unsuited to the drama, which with its varying

[1] The metre is sometimes called "iambic pentameter verse", but this and other terms of Greek prosody, with its symbols, should be avoided, since classical metres, Greek and Latin, are based on a different principle from English prosody. The basis of classical metre is the "quantity" of syllables, and this is represented by the symbols – (long syllable) and ᴗ (short). The basis of English metre is stress or accent (i.e. the stress laid by the voice on a syllable in pronouncing it); and stress should be represented by the symbols ′ (strong stress) and ` (weak).

situations and moods needs a varied medium of expression more than any other kind of poetry. Marlowe's great service to metre, carried further by Shakespeare, was to introduce variations into the existing type of the blank decasyllabic measure. In fact, analysis of the blank verse of any writer really resolves itself into a study of his modifications of the "end-stopt" regular type.

II. Shakespeare's Variations of the Regular Type

The chief variations found in Shakespeare (some of them often combined in the same line) are these:

1. *Weak stresses.* As we read a passage of blank verse our ear tells us that the stresses or accents are not always[1] of the same weight in all the five feet of each line. Thus in the line

Of nó|ble háv|ing ànd | of róy|al hópe (i. 3. 56)

we feel at once that the stress in the 3rd foot is not equal to that which comes in the other feet. A light stress like this is commonly called a "weak stress". Two weak stresses may occur in the same line, but rarely come together. The foot in which a weak stress is least frequent is the first. It is perhaps with prepositions that a weak stress, in any foot, occurs most often. Here are lines with weak stresses:

Upòn | the síght|less coú|riers òf | the aír (i. 7. 23).

Put rán|cours ìn | the vés|sel òf | my peáce,
Ónly | for thém, | and míne | etér|nal jéw(el)
Gív'n to | the cóm|mon én|emỳ | of mán (iii. 1. 67–9).

Whóle as | the már|ble, foúnd|ed às | the róck,
As broád | and gén|'ral às | the cá|sing aír (iii. 4. 22, 23).

Whát, sir, | not yét | at rést? | The kíng's | a-béd:
He háth | been ìn | unú|sual pleá|sure, ànd
Sent fórth | great lár|gess tò | your óf|ficès (ii. 1. 12–14).

It may not be amiss to remind the young student that in reading a passage of Shakespeare aloud he should be careful to give the weak stresses as weak, i.e. not lay the same emphasis indiscriminately on all the stressed syllables.

---

[1] Dr Abbott estimates that rather less than one line of three has the full number of five strong stresses, and that about two lines out of three have four strong stresses.

2. *Inverted stresses.*[1] The strong stress may fall on the first of the two syllables that form a foot—as the student will have observed in several of the lines quoted above. The following extracts also contain examples:

Vaúlting | ambí|tion, whích | o'erleáps | itsélf (I. 7. 27).

If goód, | whý do | I yiéld | to thát | suggés(tion)? (I. 3. 134).

And yét | dark níght | strángles | the trá|v'lling lámp
(II. 4. 7).

Súch I | accoúnt | thy lóve. | Árt thou | afeárd?" (I. 7. 39).

Cúrses, | not loúd | but deép, | moúth-hon|our, breáth
(V. 3. 27).

How nów, | my lórd! | whý do | you keép | alóne? (III. 2. 8).

I háve | begún | to plánt | thee, ànd | will lá(bour)
To máke | thee fúll | of grów(ing). | Nóble | Bánquo
(I. 4. 28, 29).

Inversion of the stress is most frequent after a pause: hence the foot in which it occurs most often is the first (i.e. after the pause at the end of the preceding line). There may be two inversions in one line, as some of the examples show; but they are seldom consecutive. This shifting of the stress generally *emphasises* a word. It also varies the regular "rising rhythm" of the normal blank verse by a "falling rhythm".

3. *Extra syllables.* Instead of ten syllables a line may contain eleven or even twelve. An extra syllable, unstressed, may occur at any point in the line, and usually comes before a pause: hence it is commonest in the last foot (the end of a line being the commonest place for a pause), and frequent about the middle of a line (where there is often a break in the sense of rhythm). Compare

To-mór|row, ànd | to-mór|row, ànd | to-mór(row)
(V. 5. 19).

Glámis | thou árt, | and Cáw|dor; ànd | shalt bé
What thoú | art próm(is'd): | yét do | I feár | thy ná(ture)
(I. 5. 13, 14).

[1] Cf. Mr Robert Bridges's work, *Milton's Prosody*, pp. 19–21, where Milton's use of inversions is fully analysed and illustrated in a way that helps the study of Shakespeare's inversions.

He's nó|ble, wíse, | judí|cious, ànd | best knóws
The fíts | o' the seá(son). | I dáre | not speák | much
   fúr(ther):
But crú|el áre | the tímes, | when wé | are traí(tors),
And dó | not knów | oursél(ves); | when wé | hold
   rú(mour)   (IV. 2. 16–19).

An extra syllable, unstressed,[1] at the end of a line, as in the
first and last of these examples, is variously called a "double
ending" and a "feminine ending". The use of the "double
ending" becomes increasingly frequent as Shakespeare's blank
verse grows more complex. "Double endings" increase[2] from
4 per cent in *Love's Labour's Lost* to 33 in *The Tempest*, middle
plays such as *Henry V* having a percentage of about 18. The
percentage of "double endings" is therefore one of the chief
of the metrical tests which help us to fix the date of a play. In fact
the use of "double endings" is the commonest of Shakespeare's
variations of the normal blank verse. The extra syllable at the
end of a line not only gives variety by breaking the regular
movement of the ten-syllabled lines, but also, where there is no
pause after it, carries on the sense and rhythm to the next line.

Sometimes two extra syllables occur at the end—less commonly, in the middle—of a line. Compare

My thoúght, | whose múr|der yét | is bút | fantás(tical)
                                     (I. 3. 139).

And táke | my mílk | for gáll, | you múr|d'ring mín(isters)
                                     (I. 5. 46).

Put ón | their ín(struments). | Recéive | what cheér | you
máy   (IV. 3. 234).

That név|er máy | ill óf|fice, òr | fell jeál(ousy)
                          (*Henry V*, V. 2. 391).

Toók it | too eá(gerly): | his sól|diers féll | to spoíl
                          (*Julius Cæsar*, V. 3. 7).

---

[1] An extra syllable that bears or would naturally bear a stress is rare
in Shakespeare. The use of such syllables at the end of a line is a
feature of Fletcher's verse, and the frequent occurrence of them in
Henry VIII is one of the metrical arguments that he wrote a good
deal of that play. Milton has one or two instances in *Comus*; cf. 633,
"Bore a bright golden flower, but not in thís (soíl)".

[2] The metrical statistics in these "Hints' are taken from various
sources.

This licence is specially frequent with proper names; compare

My Lórd | of Wést|morelánd, | and únc|le Éx(eter)
                                        (*Henry V*, II. 2. 70).

My deár | Lord Glós|ter, ànd | my goód | Lord Éx(eter)
                                        (*Henry V*, IV. 3. 9).

The number of lines with two extra syllables increases much in the later plays of Shakespeare. Generally one of the extra syllables admits of some degree of slurring.

4. *Unstopt* (*or Run-on*) *verse.* The blank verse of Shakespeare's early plays shows clearly the influence of the rhymed couplet which he had used so much in his very earliest work. In his early blank verse the rhyme indeed is gone, but the couplet form remains, with its frequent pause of sense, and consequently of rhythm, at the end of the first line, and its still more frequent stop at the end of the second. Lines of this type mark only the first step in the evolution of blank verse: freedom in the expression of sense and varied rhythm are still absent; and freedom and variety come only when the sense "runs on" from one line to another.

If at the end of a line there is any pause in the sense, however slight—such a pause for instance as is marked with a comma—the line is termed "end-stopt". If there is no pause in the sense at the end of the line it is termed "unstopt" or "run-on". There is a progressive increase of "unstopt" verse in the plays. The proportion of "unstopt" to "end-stopt" lines is in *Love's Labour's Lost* only 1 in 18 (approximately); in *The Winter's Tale* it is about 1 in 2. The amount, therefore, of "unstopt" verse in a play is another of the metrical tests by which the period of its composition may, to some extent, be inferred.

The rhythm of a line depends greatly on the sense: where there is any pause in the sense there must be a pause in the rhythm. The great merit of "unstopt" blank verse is that the sense by overflowing[1] into the next line tends to carry the

---

[1] The overflow is helped by the use of "light' and "weak' endings to a line. "Light endings" are monosyllables on which "the voice can to a small extent dwell": such as the parts of the auxiliary verbs, *be, have, will, shall, can, do*; pronouns like *I, we, thou, you, he, she, they, who, which*, etc.; and conjunctions such as *when, where, while*. "Weak endings" are those monosyllables over which the voice passes with practically no stress at all—e.g. the prepositions *at, by, for, from, in, of, on, to, with*; also *and, but, if, nor, or, than, that*: all words which go very closely with what follows and therefore link the end of one line

rhythm with it, and thus the pauses in the rhythm or time of the verse, instead of coming always at the end, come in other parts of the line.

5. *A Syllable slurred.* "Provided there be only one accented syllable, there may be more than two syllables in any foot. 'It is he' is as much a foot as "'tis he'; 'we will serve' as 'we'll serve'; 'it is over' as "'tis o'er'.

"Naturally it is among pronouns and the auxiliary verbs [*and prepositions*] that we must look for unemphatic syllables in the Shakespearian verse. Sometimes the unemphatic nature of the syllable is indicated by a contraction in the spelling. Often, however, syllables may be dropped or slurred in sound, although they are expressed to the sight" (Abbott).

This principle that two unstressed syllables may go in the same foot with one stressed syllable is very important because feet so composed have a rapid, trisyllable effect which tends much to vary the normal line. This trisyllabic rhythm was "a marked feature of the Old English alliterative verse", and is a recognised element of English prosody, especially in the foot called an anapæst ($\cup \cup -$). Examples are:

> As cánnons | o'erchárg'd | with doú|ble crácks; | so théy
> (1. 2. 37).

> That loók | not líke | th' inháb|itánts | o' the eárth (1. 3. 41).

> To the lást | sýlla|ble òf | recór|ded tíme (v. 5. 21).

This freedom is specially characteristic of the later plays. Compare

> Bút that | the séa, | moúnting | to the[1] wél|kin's cheék
> (*The Tempest*, 1. 2. 4).

> And hére | was léft | by the saíl|ors. Thoú, | my sláve
> (*The Tempest*, 1. 2. 270).

with the beginning of the next. The use of these endings belongs to the later plays. "Light endings" are first numerous (21) in *Macbeth* (1606), and "weak endings" (28) in *Antony and Cleopatra* (1608). Some of the early plays have neither "light endings" nor "weak". Some have a very few "light endings". Of "weak endings" no play has more than *two* up till *Antony and Cleopatra*. The proportion of these endings—"light" and "weak"—is therefore another of the metrical tests applied to the later plays (Ingram).

[1] Sometimes in such cases the Folio prints *th'*, showing that the word was meant to be slurred (Abbott).

Hím that | you térm'd, sir, | 'The goód | old lórd, |
  Gonzá|lo'   (*The Tempest*, v. 1. 15).

I' the lást | night's stórm | I súch | a fél|low sáw
                              (*King Lear*, IV. 1. 34).

6. *Omissions*. After a pause or interruption there is sometimes an omission (*a*) of an unstressed syllable (oftenest in the
first foot), or (*b*) of a stress, or (*c*) even of a whole foot.

"It is obvious" (says Abbott) "that a syllable or foot may be
supplied by a gesture, as beckoning, a movement of the head
to listen, or of the hand to demand attention": or the blank may
be accounted for by an interruption, such as the entrance of
another character, or by a marked pause or break in the sense.
Compare

(*a*) Whó | comes hére? | The wór|thy tháne | of Róss
                              (I. 2. 45).

Má|ny yeárs | of háp|py dáys | befál (*Richard II*, I. 1. 20).

Thén | the whí|ning schoól|boy wìth | his sát|chel
                              (*As You Like It*, II. 7. 145).

(*b*) And fálls | on th' óth|er. [*Enter Lady M.*] | How nów!|
  what néws? (I. 7. 28).

Flátter|ers! [*Turns to Brutus*] | Now, Brú|tus, thánk |
  yoursélf   (*Julius Cæsar*, V. 1. 45).

Messá|la! [*Messala turns and salutes*] | Whát says | my
  gén|eràl?   (*Julius Cæsar*, V. 1. 70).

(*c*) He's tá'en. | [*Shout*] | And, hárk! | they shoút | for
  jóy   (*Julius Cæsar*, V. 3. 32).

7. *Lines of irregular length*. Shakespeare uses lines of three
feet often; less frequently, lines of two feet, especially to break
the course of some passionate speech; lines of four feet; half-
lines occasionally; brief questions, answers and exclamations,
which metrically need not count; and rarely lines with six
strong stresses, i.e. Alexandrines[1] (the sonorous type of verse
which ends each stanza in *The Faerie Queene*).

As a rule, the use of a short line corresponds with something

---

[1] So called either from Alexandre Paris, an old French poet, or
from the *Roman d'Alexandre*, a 12th century poem about Alexander
the Great, written in rhymed lines of six feet, in couplets. It is the
metre of French tragedy (e.g. of the tragedies of Racine and Corneille).

in the sense, e.g. a break (as at the end of a speech), agitation, conversational effect of question and answer, strong emphasis. Thus "the irregular lines in the excited narrative of the battle (I. 2. 20, 41, 51) are perhaps explained by the haste and excitement of the speaker"; while in I. 5. 59 we feel that Lady Macbeth "pauses to watch the effect of her words" (Abbott). At the close of a speech a short line gives perhaps greater emphasis, and certainly variety.

There are not a few lines which look somewhat like Alexandrines ("apparent Alexandrines", as Abbott calls them) but which on examination are found not to have six unmistakable stresses. Thus in each of the following seemingly long lines of *Macbeth* one syllable or more can be slurred or elided or treated as extra-metrical.

> (*a*) Of thè | impé|rial théme. | I thánk | you, gén(tl'men)[1]
> (I. 3. 129).

> (*b*) But théy | did sáy | their práy|ers, ànd | addréss'd
> (them) (II. 2. 25).

> (*c*) In oúr | last cón(f'rence), | páss'd in | probá|tion wi'
> yoú,
> Hów you | were bórne | in hánd, | how cróss'd, | the
> ín(struments) (III. 1. 80, 81).

> (*d*) I'll cóme | t' you anón. | We áre | resól|v'd, my lord
> (III. 1. 139).

> (*e*) With thém | they thínk | on? Thíngs | withoút | all
> ré(medy) (III. 2. 11).

An unstressed vowel like the middle *e* in *remedy* or *enemy* (III. 1. 105) may be slurred.

> (*f*) Meéting | were báre | withoút (it). |
> Sweét re|mémbran(cer)! (III. 4. 37).

> (*g*) Is góne | to práy | the hó|ly kíng, | upon his (= *on's*)
> aíd (III. 6. 30).

Here *upon* = *'on*, like *against* = *'gainst*; so we find *into* and *unto* = *'to*.

---

[1] In this and similar cases the symbol ' is intended to show that a vowel is ignored in the scansion, though heard more or less in pronunciation. There is no means of marking the different degrees of slurring: thus, *conf'rence* represents with fair accuracy the pronunciation which must be given in line (*c*), whereas *rem'dy* in line (*e*) or *en'my* (III. 1. 105) would over-emphasise the slurring sound required there.

(*h*) And àn | etér|nal cúrse | fáll on you! | Let me knów

(IV. 1. 105).

(*i*) Be líke | our wárrant|ed quár(rel)! | Whý are | you
sí(lent)?   (IV. 3. 132).

An unstressed vowel is often lost in a preceding *r* sound; so
we find *barren* = a monosyllable (*barr'n*).

(*j*) All mór|tal cónse|quences háve | pronoúnc'd | me thús

(V. 3. 5).

The *s* of the plural and possessive cases of nouns of which the
singular ends in *s*, *se*, *ss*, *ce* and *ge* is often not sounded, being
absorbed into the preceding *s* sound (Abbott). Cf. II. 4. 14.

(*k*) "The núm|bers òf | our hóst | and máke | discó(v'ry)"

(V. 4. 6).

Again, some seemingly six-foot lines are really "trimeter
couplets": that is, "couplets of two verses of three accents each
...often thus printed as two separate short verses in the Folio.
...Shakespeare seems to have used this metre mostly for rapid
dialogue and retort, and in comic and the lighter kind of
serious poetry" (Abbott). Generally some notion of division is
suggested. Examples of these couplets in *Macbeth* are: I. 3. 65;
II. 2. 30 (where each half has an extra syllable); and IV. 1. 89
(divided between two speakers, as is often the case with the
trimeter couplet).

These, then, are the chief modes by which Shakespeare
diversifies the structure of regular blank verse. Their general
result has been well summed up thus:

They make the effect of Shakespeare's maturer blank verse
rather rhythmical than rigidly metrical:

I.e. more a matter of stresses distributed with endless variety
than of syllables calculated and accented according to a normal
standard. Every student should grasp these variations thoroughly,
particularly the first five, and observe the illustrations of them
that occur in any play (especially the later plays) that he may be
studying.

And he must, of course, remember that scansion depends
much on the way in which a writer abbreviates or lengthens
sounds, as the metre requires.

Abbreviation comprises all the cases in which a syllable does not count metrically—whether it be elided,[1] contracted, or slurred.[2] Many abbreviations belong to everyday speech, others to poetical usage.

Of lengthening sounds the most important example is the scansion of a monosyllable as two syllables.[3]

For full details the student must refer to the standard authority, viz. Dr Abbott's *Shakespearian Grammar*, pp. 344–87.

III. Accent

The accentuation of some words differs in Elizabethan and in modern English. The influence of the Latin words[4] from which they came still affected a good many words when Shakespeare wrote.

Also,[5] there is an important class of dissyllabic words—adjectives and participles—like 'obscure', 'extreme', 'complete', 'forlorn', in which the accent is variable in Shakespeare and Milton. Normally accented on the second syllable, they throw the accent on to the previous syllable when they are followed immediately by a stressed syllable, e.g. a monosyllable like *grave*. Cf.

Obscúre and lowly swain, King Henry's blood
(2 Henry VI, IV. 1. 50);

and

A little little grave, an óbscure grave
(Richard II, III. 3. 154).

Is yond despís'd and ruinous man my lord
(Timon of Athens, IV. 3. 465);

and

The pangs of déspis'd love, the law's delay
(Hamlet, III. 1. 72).

---

[1] Cf. the common elision of *the* before a vowel, e.g. in I. 5. 42, "Stóp up | *th*' accéss...", and 45, "*Th*' efféct | and ít"; I. 7. 10, "To plágue | *th*' invén|tor...", and II, "Comménds | *th*' ingré|dients...".

[2] Cf. the footnote on p. 191.

[3] Abbott gives the following instances in *Macbeth*: hail (I. 2. 5); feel (I. 5. 55); wrought (II. 1. 19); sleep (II. 1. 51); here (II. 3. 104); worst (III. 1. 103); cold (IV. 1. 6); fire (IV. 1. 21); sight (IV. 1. 122); fare (IV. 3. 106); and weird in several places—a scansion to which the Folio's reading wayward clearly points. A following pause in some of these cases helps the prolongation of the vowel-sounds.

[4] See Abbott, pp. 388–92.

[5] Schmidt, *Shakespeare Lexicon*, pp. 1413–15; Bridges, pp. 52–61.

Cf. Milton, *Comus*, 273,

> Not any boast of skill, but éxtreme shift,

and 421,

> She that has that is clad in cómplete stéel.

IV. Shakespeare's use of Rhyme

In his early plays Shakespeare uses the rhymed couplet[1] very largely; but gradually the amount of rhyme declines, so that the proportion of rhymed couplets in a piece is one of the surest indications of the period to which it belongs.

> Is there much rhyme? the play is early.
> Is there little rhyme? the play is late.

"In *Love's Labour's Lost* there are about two rhymed lines to every one of blank verse. In *The Comedy of Errors* there are 380 rhymed lines to 1150 unrhymed. In *The Tempest* two rhymed lines occur; in *The Winter's Tale* not one" (Dowden).

In applying the rhyme test we must exclude the cases where there is a special reason for the use of rhyme—as in the Witches-scenes of *Macbeth*. Thus the rhyme of the Masque in Act IV of *The Tempest* has no bearing whatsoever on the date of the play, because Masques were usually written in rhymed measures. Similarly all songs such as we get in *As You Like It*, *The Tempest*, and *The Winter's Tale* must, of course, be excluded.

Let us consider for a moment the reasons which led Shakespeare to adopt blank verse and gradually abandon rhyme.

As a medium of dramatic expression blank verse, of the varied Shakespearian type, has these points of superiority over rhyme:

1. *Naturalness*. Rhyme is artificial. It reminds us, therefore, —perhaps I should say, never lets us forget—that the play *is* a play, fiction and not reality, because in real life people do not converse in rhyme. Especially in moments of great emotion does rhyme destroy the illusion of reality: we cannot conceive of Lear raving at Goneril in rhymed couplets. Blank verse on the other hand has something of the naturalness of conversation, and naturalness is a very great help towards making fiction appear like truth.

2. *Freedom*. The necessity of rhyming imposes restraint upon a writer such as blank verse obviously does not involve, and often forces him to invert the order of words or even to use

---

[1] I.e. of five feet in each line; cf. 1. 5. 67–70.

a less suitable word. The rhythm too of the rhymed couplet tends strongly to confine the sense within the limits of the couplet, whereas in the blank verse of a skilful writer the sense "runs on" easily from line to line. In fact, in the rhymed couplet the verse is apt to dominate the sense; while in blank verse the sense finds unfettered expression. And so blank verse has not only something of the naturalness but also something of the freedom of conversation.

3. *Variety.* In a paragraph of rhymed couplets the pauses in the sense and therefore in the rhythm are monotonous. We constantly have a pause at the end of the first line and almost always a pause at the end of the second. With the uniformity of a passage composed in this form contrast the varied rhythms of such blank verse as that of *The Tempest*, where the pauses are distributed with ever-changing diversity of cadence.

Again, the rhyme of a long narrative poem when read, or of a short lyric when recited, has a pleasing effect; but in a long spell of spoken verse I think that the sound of rhyme, though at first agreeable to it, gradually tires the ear.

What rhyme we do get in Shakespeare's later plays is mainly at the end of a scene, when it serves to indicate the conclusion, and (less commonly) at the close of a long speech, when it forms a kind of climax. As to the former use (cf. i. 7. 81, 82) Dr Abbott says: "Rhyme was often used as an effective termination at the end of the scene. When the scenery[1] was not changed, or the arrangements were so defective that the change was not easily perceptible, it was, perhaps, additionally desirable to mark that a scene was finished."

And just as rhyme often marks the close of a scene so it sometimes marks the close of a chapter in a man's career, and suggests farewell. A striking example of this use of rhyme occurs in *As You Like It*, ii. 3. 67–76, where old Adam and Orlando, about to set forth on their expedition, severally bid farewell to their former life. Similarly in *Richard II*, ii. 2. 142–9, the rhyme expresses the feeling of the King's favourites that their period of prosperity is over and they are parting for ever; while in v. 5. 109–19, it emphasises the tragedy of the close of Richard's life. Again, in *King Lear* (a comparatively late play, 1605–6)

[1] There was no movable scenery; the only outward indication of the locality intended was some stage 'property'—e.g. "a bed to signify a bed-chamber; a table with pens upon it to signify a counting-house; or a board bearing in large letters the name of the place" —*Dowden.*

the banished Kent is made to use rhyme in his leave-taking
(I. 1. 183–90).

One other noticeable purpose of rhyme is found in plays as
late as *Othello* (about 1604) and *Lear*, viz. to express moralising
reflections on life and give them a sententious, epigrammatic
effect. Dowden instances *Othello*, I. 3. 202–19, and II. 1. 149–61.
This use of rhyme is natural because proverbial wisdom so often
takes a rhymed form. Maxims stick better in the memory when
they are rhymed.

V. Shakespeare's use[1] of Prose

The proportion of prose to verse, unrhymed and rhymed, in
Macbeth is very small. That this should be so will not surprise
us if we consider (*a*) the main purposes for which Shakespeare
uses prose in his plays, (*b*) the peculiarly tragic character of the
play.

The chief use to which Shakespeare puts prose is as a colloquial medium of expression. He introduces it where he wishes
"to lower the dramatic pitch". A good illustration of this use
is part of the talk between Lady Macduff and her little boy
(IV. 2), where the prose gives a simple, domestic colouring which
contrasts pathetically with the tragic surroundings. Another
example—indeed, the only other instance in *Macbeth*—is the
scene with the Doctor and the Gentlewoman (V. 1). The alterna-
tions of verse and prose in each scene are not arbitrary. It is,
indeed, always instructive to note how in parts where a conversational, not tragic or poetical, effect is desired, verse gives
place to prose, and *vice versâ*; and how characters which are
viewed in a wholly tragic or poetical light normally use verse
alone.

Thus—to take some illustrations from one of the most popular of the plays, viz. *Henry V*—Henry is made to use prose in
talking familiarly to his soldiers (III. 6. 102–20), but verse
directly afterwards in the formal interview with the French
herald (III. 6. 122–81). Prose again is the medium when the
French nobles are chatting together in a light bantering style
(III. 7. 1–134) and laughing at the English, but verse in their
last words together at the moment of riding off to the battle-
field (IV. 2), and in the hour of defeat (IV. 5). Perhaps the most

---

[1] Strictly, it does not come under the heading "metre"; but it is
convenient to treat the subject here. See Abbott, p. 429.

striking transition in *Henry V* from prose to verse occurs at
IV. I. 247, where the reason for the change is self-evident. And
the wooing-scene (V. 2) must be remembered. The alernations
of verse and prose in a play are often very suggestive, and the
reason in each case should be carefully weighed in the light of
the context.

Prose is commonly assigned to characters of humble position,
e.g. servants and soldiers (such as Bates, Court, Williams in
Henry V). It is the normal medium in scenes of "low life"; cf.
the Falstaff-scenes in *Henry IV*.

Another conspicuous use of prose in Shakespeare is for comic
parts and the speech of comic characters like the Clowns of the
Comedies, e.g. Touchstone in *As You Like It*, who never drops
into blank verse.

In *Henry V* the Hostess, Bardolph, Nym and the Boy speak
wholly in prose as being at once humorous (three of them un-
intentionally) and of humble status. The same criticism applies
to the Porter's-scene in *Macbeth* (II. 3. 1–25).

Other minor uses of prose by Shakespeare are for letters
(I. 5), proclamations, documents, etc., and occasionally (as
though even blank verse were too artificial) for the expression
of extreme emotion and mental derangement (cf. *King Lear*,
III. 4). So in the sleep-walking scene (V. 1) the prose-form of
Lady Macbeth's part expresses the "great perturbation in
nature" from which she is suffering and gives the appropriate
effect of broken, disjointed utterance such as might be expected
from a somnambulist.

Shakespeare's use of prose increases as the character of his
plays grows more varied and complex. Thus, *Richard II*
(1593–4), written five or six years before *Henry V* (1599), has
no prose. The amount of prose in a play therefore is, as a rule,
an indication of its date, like the amount of rhyme, though not
so conclusive an indication. But the general character of *Macbeth* makes it an exception to the rule. The scheme of the tragedy
did not admit the colloquial and comic, save for those contrasts
which to be effective must be infrequent.

I. INDEX OF WORDS
AND PHRASES

This List applies to the **Notes** *only; words of which longer explanations are given will be found in the* **Glossary***. The references are to the pages.*

Abbreviations:

adj. = adjective.   intr. = intransitive.   n. = noun.

syll. = syllable or syllables.   trans. = transitive.   vb = verb.

II. GENERAL INDEX
TO NOTES